‖ PUSHING ‖

TIME AWAY

ALSO BY PETER SINGER

Animal Factories
(with Jim Mason)
Animal Liberation
A Darwinian Left
Democracy and Disobedience
Ethics into Action:
Henry Spira and the Animal Rights Movement
The Expanding Circle
Hegel
How Are We to Live?
Marx
One World: Ethics and Globalization
Practical Ethics
The Reproduction Revolution
(with Deane Wells)
Rethinking Life and Death
Should the Baby Live?
(with Helga Kuhse)
Unsanctifying Human Life
(edited by Helga Kuhse)
Writings on an Ethical Life

Books edited by Peter Singer

Animal Rights and Human Obligations
Applied Ethics
A Companion to Ethics
A Companion to Bioethics
Embryo Experimentation
Ethics
The Great Ape Project: Equality Beyond Humanity
In Defense of Animals
Test-Tube Babies

‖ PUSHING ‖
TIME AWAY

My Grandfather and the
Tragedy of Jewish Vienna

Peter Singer

ecco

An Imprint of HarperCollins*Publishers*

Photographs of Otto Soyka and The Akademisches Gymnasium courtesy of Bildarchiv d. ÖNB, Wien (the Picture Archive of the Austrian National Library, Vienna).

Photograph of Freud's waiting room courtesy of Gerald Zugmann. © Gerald Zugmann.

HarperCollins books may be purchased for educational, business, or sales promotional use. For information, please write: Special Markets Department, HarperCollins Publishers Inc., 10 East 53rd Street, New York, NY 10022.

FIRST EDITION

Designed by Cassandra J. Pappas

Printed on acid-free paper

Library of Congress Cataloging-in-Publication Data
Singer, Peter.
    Pushing time away : my grandfather and the tragedy of Jewish Vienna / Peter Singer.
        p. cm.
    ISBN 0-06-050131-6
    1. Oppenheim, D. E. (David Ernst), 1881–1943. 2. Jews—Austria—Vienna—Biography. 3. Psychoanalysts—Austria—Vienna—Biography. 4. Holocaust, Jewish (1939–1945)—Austria—Vienna. 5. Vienna (Austria)—Biography. I. Title.
    DS135.A93.O657 2003
    943.6'13004924'0092—dc21
    [B]   2002029715

03 04 05 06 07 BVG/RRD 10 9 8 7 6 5 4 3 2 1

Contents

Acknowledgments

This book draws on the work of Dr. Adolf Gaisbauer, who, in collaboration with my aunt, Doris Liffman, published an edited selection of the letters that her parents (and my grandparents) wrote to their children in Australia between 1938 and 1941. Dr. Gaisbauer prefaced the letters with a biographical sketch of my grandfather, which in turn drew on Doris's Master of Arts thesis on her father's life and times. I am most grateful to Dr. Gaisbauer for generously sharing his materials with me. I am also very thankful to Doris, as well as to Michael Liffman, her son, for allowing me free access to the wealth of materials in her possession. Other family members also contributed. My sister, Joan Dwyer, shared with me her memories of our grandmother and helped me to locate family photographs and documents. The curiosity of my daughter Esther about the contents of an old case in my mother's home led to the discovery of the letter from Amalie that is quoted extensively in Chapter 33. My grandparents' nieces and nephew, Gerda Buchler, Alice Ritter, and George Kunstadt, told me all that they remembered and gave me copies of letters and photographs in their possession. Thanks to Elisabeth Markstein, I was able to speak to her mother, Hilde Koplenig, who remembered well meeting my grandmother on her return from Theresienstadt. Nava Kahana, the daughter of Max Rudolfer, and her daughter, Smadar Shavit, found an informative letter from my grandmother. David Stern put me in touch with his father, Kurt Stern, who not only knew my grandparents but could recall visiting the home of my great-grandparents.

Many of my grandfather's former students told me about their experiences of him as a teacher; they include Livia Karwath, Walter Friedmann, Ellen Kemeny, and Frank Klepner. In Vienna I spoke to my mother's close friend Eva Berger (formerly Hitschmann) and to the remarkable Albert Massiczek. Romana Jakubowicz generously made me welcome in my grandparents' apartment, where she now lives. Thanks to Google.com and a little luck, I was able to make contact with Liz Tarlau Weingarten and Jill Tarlau, who told me what they knew of my grandmother's friend and their grandmother, Lise Tarlau.

I owe an enormous debt to Hermann Vetter and Wendelin Fischer, who between them read more than a hundred letters in my grandfather's indecipherable (to me, anyway) handwriting and e-mailed me the transcripts. Hermann Vetter was especially untiring in this work and was also extremely helpful in answering many questions I had about the content of the letters. Agata Sagan's belief in the value of this project was encouraging at times when I wondered if it was worth doing, and she found information on some of the most obscure references in my grandfather's letters. Hyun Höchsmann commented on a draft and helped me to find some of the German literary sources to which my grandfather referred. Helga Kuhse and Udo Schüklenk gave me valuable comments at an early stage of the project. In the Austrian court records, Marianne Schulze found for me documents about my family that I did not even know existed—and thanks to Dymia Schulze for starting that search. John Oldham allowed me to see the manuscript that my grandfather wrote with Sigmund Freud. Clemens Ruthner and Reinhard Urbach provided me with information about the life of Otto Soyka and comments on my grandfather's early letters. Bernhard Handlbauer answered my queries about the records of the founding of the Society for Individual Psychology.

The support and advice of Kathy Robbins, of the Robbins Office, has been splendid. Dan Halpern and Julia Serebrinsky of Ecco have made a wonderful publisher/editor combination. Kathy and Julia bullied me into paring down a much longer typescript, a painful task that has, I grudgingly concede, resulted in a better book. Adam Goldberger's copyediting cleaned up many infelicities and inconsistent spellings.

I began work on this book while still at Monash University, in Australia, and thanks are due to Professor Marian Quartly, then dean of arts, for allowing me to take leave without pay to complete a first draft. Since coming to Princeton University, my work has benefited from the outstanding research resources available here, and from helpful comments at two Princeton University seminars. I am grateful to Josh Ober of the classics department for organizing a seminar at which some of my grandfather's letters on the classical ideas of eros were discussed and I received many helpful suggestions. Bob Kaster, of the same department, kindly assisted with the translation of a Latin quotation. For comments on a paper that raised the philosophical issue with which this book ends, about the possibility of benefiting someone after he or she is dead, I thank the faculty of the University Center for Human Values and the Center's 2001–2 Rockefeller Fellows. Kim Girman, my staff assistant at Princeton, was always willing to help with every task I gave her. Finally I thank Renata, my wife, for her love and companionship during the long period that it took to bring this project to fruition.

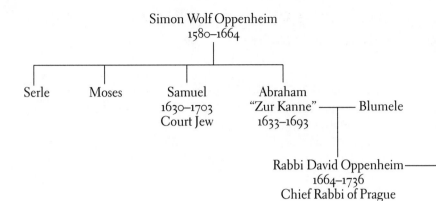

Simon Wolf Oppenheim
1580–1664

Serle   Moses   Samuel
1630–1703
Court Jew

Abraham
"Zur Kanne" —— Blumele
1633–1693

Rabbi David Oppenheim ——
1664–1736
Chief Rabbi of Prague

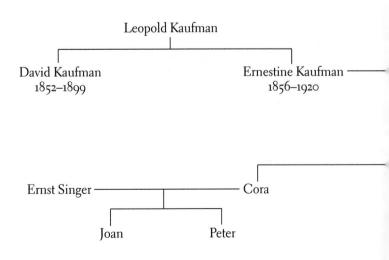

Leopold Kaufman

David Kaufman
1852–1899

Ernestine Kaufman ——
1856–1920

Ernst Singer —— Cora

Joan   Peter

David Oppenheim's Family Tree

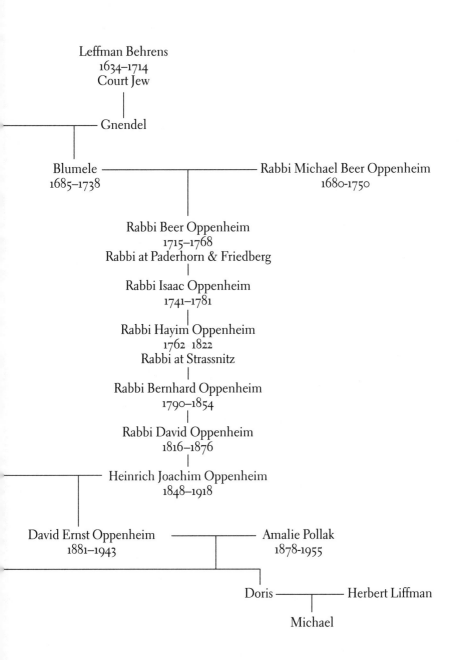

Leffman Behrens
1634–1714
Court Jew

Gnendel

Blumele ———————————————— Rabbi Michael Beer Oppenheim
1685–1738   1680-1750

Rabbi Beer Oppenheim
1715–1768
Rabbi at Paderhorn & Friedberg

Rabbi Isaac Oppenheim
1741–1781

Rabbi Hayim Oppenheim
1762 1822
Rabbi at Strassnitz

Rabbi Bernhard Oppenheim
1790–1854

Rabbi David Oppenheim
1816–1876

Heinrich Joachim Oppenheim
1848–1918

David Ernst Oppenheim ———————— Amalie Pollak
1881–1943   1878-1955

Doris ———————— Herbert Liffman

Michael

"What binds us, pushes time away."

—*David Oppenheim to Amalie Pollak,*
March 24, 1905

||| **PART I** |||

Prologue

1

Vienna, Now and Then

January 1997

A FREEZING FOG HANGS over Vienna, softening the light of the street-lamps. There is snow on the ground, and the bare branches of the trees are tipped with frost. I am walking down Porzellangasse, a broad street in Vienna's Ninth District. It is 7:00 P.M. The street is quiet, for most people prefer not to drive in this weather, the roads are too slick. The street is lined with buildings four or five stories high. They have changed little since the days before the First World War, when Vienna was one of the great cities of the world, the capital of the Austro-Hungarian Empire, and that empire was a major power, surpassed only by Russia in the extent of the European territory over which it ruled. Its lands spread northeast as far as what is now Ukraine, east over today's Czech and Slovak Republics, and southeast through Hungary, Slovenia, Croatia, and Bosnia to the fateful city of Sarajevo.

All of my grandparents lived in this city then. I knew only my mother's mother, Amalie Oppenheim, the sole survivor of the tragedy that overwhelmed Vienna's Jews after the Nazi annexation of Austria. But tonight, pushing away the time that has passed since that calamity, I will begin to get to know one other grandparent. In a backpack I am carrying a stack of papers—they must weigh about fifteen pounds—by and about my mother's father, David Oppenheim.

Included in this treasure trove of family history are more than a hundred letters my grandparents wrote to my parents, Kora and Ernst Singer, and to my mother's sister, then Doris Oppenheim, after they left for Australia in 1938. I have just collected them from Dr. Adolf Gaisbauer, director of the Library of the State Archives of Austria, who last year published some of them in a book called *David Ernst Oppenheim: Von Eurem Treuen Vater David*. The subtitle means "from your faithful father David" and is the way in which my grandfather closed his letters. Although I had long known of the existence of the letters, which Doris and my mother had carefully preserved, I had never read them. I can read German, but my grandfather's handwriting was difficult to decipher, and its legibility was not helped by the fact that the letters were often written on both sides of very thin paper. When my mother and Doris had, many years ago, read one or two letters to me, I had been busy with my work as a philosopher and bioethicist, writing and teaching about the ethics of our treatment of animals, and life-and-death decisions in the care of infants born with severe disabilities. I did not ask them to read me the other letters.

I learned more about my grandparents ten years ago, when Doris retired from her career as a social worker and wrote a master's thesis about her father. I returned it with a scribbled note:

Doris,
    I read this with great interest. Congratulations on making your father live again. Now I'd like one day to read his works myself, to see what parallels (if any) there are with my own views, despite our rather different fields, and intellectual backgrounds.

One sentence from Doris's summary of an essay my grandfather wrote on the Roman philosopher Seneca struck a particular chord with me. She described how her father distinguishes between the "genuine philosopher," who aims to integrate his teaching and his life, and the "theoretical professor," who is concerned only with his professional standing and personal reputation. This distinction resonated with me. I certainly hoped that I was a genuine philosopher, in this sense, and for the first time I wondered how much I had in common with this grandfather I had never known.

Nevertheless, my work in ethics continued to take priority over delving further into my grandparents' life. So last year, when I read the selections from the letters in Dr. Gaisbauer's book, I was reading them for the first time. They reached across nearly sixty years, and opened up a world that was closely linked with mine and yet utterly different from it. My parents were educated people, my father a businessman and my mother a doctor, but neither of them was a serious scholar, and they did not spend much time thinking about the big questions—about understanding human nature, or how we ought to live. My career had seemed, to some, a surprising turn—my cousin Michael Liffman, Doris's son, once told me that of all the people he had known at university, I was the only one who had followed a path that he could not have predicted. By that he meant, I think, that he had expected me to go into my father's business, or perhaps to practice law, like my sister. Instead, I had taken up philosophy. David Oppenheim, I now learned, wrote about fundamental values, and what it is to be human. Was my own life echoing that of a grandparent I had never known? That thought began to take hold of me, and would not let go. I had to find out whether, despite the different times and places in which we lived, there was something that bound us together.

———

AT THE END of Porzellangasse, I cross Berggasse, just a few doors from number 19, where Sigmund Freud had his home and his consulting rooms. Earlier in the day, seeking traces of my grandfather, I had visited Freud's rooms, now a museum. Here the famed "Wednesday Group," more formally known as the Vienna Psychoanalytical Society, met. My grandfather became a member of the group in January 1910, and attended its meetings for nearly two years. On April 20, 1910—his twenty-ninth birthday—he gave a presentation entitled "Suicide in Childhood" to a group of sixteen people, including Freud and most of the regular members of the society. His paper was a great success, stimulating so lively a conversation that the group voted to publish a pamphlet including David's talk and the ensuing discussion. Quite a birthday present for a young high school teacher! As I left Freud's rooms, I imagined my grandfather walking down those same steps in a state of elation. As a talented young scholar with whom Freud was eager to collaborate, he appeared to have a bright future ahead of him. Yet within eighteen months my grandfather had parted from Freud, following instead the first of the great heretics of psychoanalysis, Alfred Adler. In opposition to Freud's insistence on unconscious sexual desire as the key to understanding human behavior, Adler developed the idea of the inferiority complex, and saw the drive to gain power, as compensation for a sense of inferiority, as more significant. Why, I wondered, did David take the decision to side with Adler, knowing that this must mean the end of all further contact with Freud?

Another man also celebrated his birthday in Vienna on that April 20, 1910. His prospects were not so good. He was living in a shelter set up by the municipal government to provide beds for single men at a token cost, on the fringes of the city. Having twice failed the entrance test to Vienna's Academy of Fine Arts, he was making a meager living painting postcards in watercolors. A friend sold them for a few pennies in taverns and cafés. Here, on the day my grandfather had his twenty-ninth birthday, this second-rate painter turned twenty-one. While my grandfather was trying, through his work with Freud and then Adler, to understand the springs of human nature, the would-be artist had his own shrewd insights into the yearnings of millions of Germans and Austrians. His fiercely nationalist and anti-Semitic aims were diametrically at odds with my grandfather's hopes for the spread of a universal recognition of our common humanity. But in 1910 the improbable intersection of the lives of Adolf Hitler and David Oppenheim lay many years ahead.

———

I AM STAYING in a small hotel on the far side of the city from Berggasse. I could take the underground, but I am in the mood for walking. I soon come to the Ringstrasse, the broad tree-lined boulevard that, following the lines of the ramparts of old Vienna, encircles the First District, the historical heart of the city. If I were to follow the Ringstrasse to the right, I would pass some of the grandest buildings of late-nineteenth-century Vienna: the Renaissance-inspired university, where my grandfather studied; the town hall, in an extravagant Flemish Gothic style; and the classic Graeco-Roman parliament building. Instead of following the Ringstrasse, however, I cross it and take a more direct line through the center of the city, along narrow streets lined with the palaces of noble families of the eighteenth and nineteenth centuries. The shops are closing. I come to Michaelerplatz, one of Vienna's most beautiful small squares. In summer it would be busy with tourists, but on this winter evening it is quiet and lovely. Easy to imagine that it looked just like this when my grandfather lived here. In front of me stands the Hofburg, the great palace of the Hapsburgs, who ruled Austria from 1282 until 1918 and for most of that period also had the title of Holy Roman Emperor, thus claiming a glorious if dubious continuity with the line established by the real Roman emperor Augustus. There is a grandeur in the architecture that reminds me that this was a seat of power. From here, at various times, the Hapsburgs ruled over much of Europe, including Germany, the Netherlands, Spain, and parts of Italy, as well as what later became the Austro-Hungarian Empire.

Some of the palaces making up the Hofburg go back to medieval times, others date from the eighteenth century, and the latest additions were still being built when my grandfather was alive. I pass under an arch with an inscription saying that Franz Josef I completed the building begun by his predecessors. When my grandfather came to study at the University of Vienna, the "Old Kaiser" had already been on the throne for half a century. Austria's ignominious defeat at the hands of the Prussians early in his reign was a blessing in disguise, for it led the empire to build a new future as the dominant power in the Danube basin and the Balkans. It included among its subjects not only Austrians and Hungarians, but Poles, Czechs, Romanians, Slovenians, Italians, Croats, and other nationalities. The new constitution of 1867 made Franz Josef emperor of Austria and king of Hungary. Everything in the empire became "Kaiserlich und Königlich"—"Imperial and Royal"—or for short, "K.u.K." The new constitution established separate parliaments in Austria and Hungary, and for the first time it extended full equality before the law to all citizens, including Jews. From the eastern provinces, where pogroms were still to be feared, Jews flocked to civilized, sophisticated Vienna. When my grandfather moved here he was joining 150,000 other Jews, making up nearly a tenth of the city's population. The growing Jewish population boosted Vienna's cultural, intellectual, musical, and artistic life to new heights, providing it with musicians like Gustav Mahler and Arnold Schoenberg, writers such as Arthur Schnitzler and Karl Kraus, the theater director Max Reinhardt, and of course Sigmund Freud and Alfred Adler. The existence of a large Jewish middle class helped to create the critical mass of an educated public sufficiently numerous to support the theater, opera, and concerts, and to buy books and discuss them over coffee and cake in the city's many elegant coffeehouses. It was the yeast in a cultural mix that made Vienna one of the most exciting cities in the world.

I walk through the courtyards of the imperial palace, and emerge in a vast open space: the Heldenplatz, or Heroes Square. To the southeast it is flanked by the curving wing of the New Hofburg, built in the last flush of imperial grandeur. In the middle of the square are gigantic equestrian statues of two of Austria's military heroes, Prince Eugene of Savoy, who crushed the Turks in 1697, and Archduke Karl, victor, albeit very temporarily, over Napoleon in 1809. The square is snow-covered and empty apart from a couple of civil servants on their way home. In my head, though, is a photograph of this square at another time, packed with people, tens of thousands of them, filling the entire square and swarming over the statues to get a better view. It is March 1938. A few days earlier, German tanks had rolled across the border. Now the people had come to cheer Adolf Hitler's triumphal entry into the city and hear him announce the incorporation of Austria into the Third Reich.

On the other side of the Heldenplatz I again cross the Ring, and emerge onto Mariahilferstrasse, a busy street lined with brightly lit department stores, trendy clothing boutiques, and the inevitable McDonald's. For a few blocks, I am a long way from the Vienna of Freud or the Nazis. Then my hotel takes me back to an earlier era. It is at the end of the department-store strip, in an old building with high ceilings. There is no elevator, and after walking up three flights of stairs, I am glad to get to my room and to take my grandfather's papers off my back.

I SORT the papers into several stacks. The largest consists of the letters written to my parents and my aunt. Almost as large is the stack of published writings—photocopies of sections of my grandfather's book, and of his many published articles. I put them to one side and pick up a document in my grandfather's handwriting, an official application to the University of Vienna for admission to the final examination for the degree of doctor of philosophy. The date is May 4, 1904. In my grandfather's handwriting, small but legible, he sets out his course of studies up to that point, beginning with his birth on April 20, 1881, in Brünn—now Brno—the capital of what was then the province of Moravia, now part of the Czech Republic. There he attended high school, after which he went to the University of Vienna to study classics. Over four and a half years he took courses on Greek and Latin grammar, Homer, Plato and Aristotle, the Greek lyric poet Pindar, Cicero's orations and letters, the satires of Juvenal, the elegies of the Latin poet Tibullus, and the histories of Livy and Sallust. To round out his classical education he studied Greek and Roman culture, including the Greek temples, antique art, monuments and dress, mythology, coins, the buildings of the Acropolis, Roman cosmology, the Roman Forum, Pompeii, Roman law, and theater productions in Greek and Roman times. Along the way, he found time for occasional seminars on the history of German literature, on philosophy in medieval and modern times, on Nietzsche, on European folktales, and on high school teaching and reform, as well as taking a basic English course and a course on "Foundations of Psychology."

I continue to scan through the documents and find one typed in English. Headed "My Scientific Work," it is five pages long, and looks like a draft because it has added handwritten corrections to the English. Even with the corrections, the English is awkward, showing a good vocabulary and knowledge of the grammar of the language, but no grasp of its nuances and idiom. My grandfather wrote this summary of his scholarly work in 1941, when Jews from Vienna were beginning to be deported to Poland. In the faint hope of improving his prospects of being able to obtain an immigration visa, he sent it to his sister in America, asking her to circulate it among academic circles there. As the 1904 application to sit his final exam portrays a young man setting out on his life of inquiry, so this document, written under much grimmer circumstances, marks the close of that life. Nevertheless, the opening sentences confirm that, despite the differences in our education and in the fields in which we work, my grandfather and I are interested in similar, timeless issues:

> As a teacher of the classic languages in a Vienna secondary school I was bound by profession to interest my pupils in classic antiquity. . . . However in spite of cultivating a field belonging to history it was not the view of an historian that led me to my particular work, but rather that of a humanist, in the original meaning of the word. For retrospections of ages and peoples long past—though I was charmed by them—did not by far seem to me so vital as a thorough insight into what hardly ever changes, the essence of humanity. For this very reason, I preferred to make this knowledge the very aim of my classic pursuits.

WHEN I BEGAN to study philosophy at university, my interest in ethics often led me beyond the bounds of philosophy to broader psychological questions about human nature. Is there a conflict between acting ethically and acting in accordance with self-interest? If so, how can human beings act ethically? Why do people do what they know to be wrong? To what extent is our ethics the outcome of our biological nature, rather than our culture? These are questions that David Oppenheim would have been familiar with, for they underlie many of the ancient Greek texts that he knew well, and they link up with the theories of psychology that he discussed with Freud and Adler. As I read my grandfather's outline of his work, I realize that I still don't know what my grandfather thought about these questions. Perhaps the texts in front of me will tell me.

Thinking about my own work raises another question: What am I doing in Vienna with my grandfather's papers? Why am I planning to put much larger issues aside to study the life and work of a minor, forgotten scholar who died half a century ago? Because he was my grandfather? Why should I be so concerned about my ancestors? What difference does the fact that this man was *my* grandfather really make?

The Viennese Jewish writer Stefan Zweig, whose life span coincides exactly with that of David Oppenheim, wrote:

> Against my will I have witnessed the most terrible defeat of reason and the wildest triumph of brutality in the chronicle of the ages. Never—and I say this without pride, but rather with shame—has any generation experienced such a moral retrogression from such a spiritual height as our generation has.

There lies part of the fascination that my grandfather's life holds for me. He came of age at the end of a century of peace and progress. European civilization was at its peak. Europe ruled the world because it was more enlightened than any other civilization before it—or so it seemed. For the educated classes in Vienna, life was good. It was not difficult to earn an income sufficient for a comfortable apartment with a live-in maid, evenings at Vienna's famous opera or theater, time to sit and chat over an excellent slice of cake at a coffeehouse, and in summer, a vacation by one of Austria's many lakes set amid tranquil forests and alpine peaks.

By the time my grandfather reached his sixtieth birthday, this world was in ruins. Europe was, for the second time in his life, in the midst of a devastating war, and all the humane values and enlightened reasoning of his youth had been defeated by visceral emotion and brute force. The tragedy of this moral collapse is compelling in itself, but that is not the only reason I feel the need to confront it. When the Nazis came to Austria many Jews, my parents among them, immediately began seeking another country to which they could go. My grandparents did not. There is a terrible, tragic irony in the fact that my grandfather spent his whole life trying to understand his fellow human beings, yet seems to have failed to take sufficiently seriously the threat that overwhelmed Vienna's Jewish community and ultimately led to the loss of his own life. Did my grandfather perhaps have too much confidence in human reason and the humanist values to which he had dedicated his life? Did this render him unable to conceive that they could be so completely trodden underfoot as to allow barbarism once again to hold sway across Europe? These questions lead to a disquieting thought. Since my own life, no less than that of my grandfather, is premised on the possibility of reason and universal ethical values playing a significant role in the world, could I be sharing my grandfather's delusion?

There is one other factor that urges me to read my grandfather's writings, something related to the fact that it wasn't just illness or accident that deprived me of the opportunity to grow up with my grandparents around me. It is because to read him is to undo, in some infinitely small but still quite palpable way, a wrong done by the Holocaust. We all know that six million Jews died, but that is a mind-numbing statistic. I have a chance to portray one of them as an individual. But if I am to do it, I must do it soon. The handful of people still alive who knew my grandfather are getting old. My grandfather's thoughts and work will be brought back to life as fully as possible by me, now, or not at all.

IT'S GETTING late. I want to get some sleep, but first I need fresh air. The room has a tall casement window set in a white-painted wooden frame, curved at the top, divided down the middle and held together with a brass handle. I turn the handle and the doors swing toward me, but I have forgotten about the double glazing. There is another window, with a similar handle. That opens too, and now a blast of cold air hits me. I look out at the deserted streets. These buildings were here when the Nazis came to Vienna. Fifty-five years ago my grandparents were living in an apartment a few kilometers away, dismissed from their employment, forced to take other families into their apartment, made to wear the yellow star whenever they went out, not allowed to use public transport, or even to walk in a park, learning of friends and relatives being deported to "the East" and not knowing their fate. That is when they wrote the letters I now have in this hotel room. Fifty-five years seems a relatively small amount of time that I must push away, if I am to get to know my grandfather. Less than one lifetime. Yet there is such a gulf between their times and mine. Has the world changed so much?

Looking at the streetlights, I can see snow falling gently. It tells me that I am a long way from home. In Australian cities it never snows.

2

In My Aunt's Flat

July 18, 1998

MY INTENTION to get to work on the pile of papers I brought back from Vienna fell victim to more urgent tasks. Now that at last I have time to read them, I recall that Doris had, in her thesis, quoted from letters that my grandfather had written to my grandmother before they were married. But these letters are not in the papers I have. Where are they? Doris, who sadly has begun showing signs of dementia, has moved into a home for elderly people. When I ask her about the letters she is vague, but happy for me to look for them. Michael, her son, gives me the keys to her flat, and one wintry Saturday morning, I go looking for my grandfather's letters to his bride-to-be.

COLD AND MUSTY though it is, the empty flat is still very much the home of European refugees. Pictures of old Vienna hang on the walls, the bookshelves have uniformly bound sets of the works of Goethe, Schiller, and other German writers. Right by the entrance door is a large Oppenheim family tree, tracing Doris's ancestors—and mine—back to the sixteenth century.

I walk down the passage to the small study that Doris used as a bedroom for her grandchildren when they visited. Folders are heaped on every flat surface in the room. Inside the first one are gas bills. The next contains postcards from friends on vacation. But soon I find a folder containing a small envelope with a faded pink stamp portraying Franz Josef I. On the envelope is written, in black ink in my grandfather's spidery handwriting:

An Fräulein Dr Amalie Pollak,
Wien
II Malzgasse 5

I turn the envelope over, and on the back I read: "Abs: Dr D. Oppenheim IX Pramerg. 6." The postmark is clearly legible: "Wien, 1.6.05." Both the date and the use of my grandmother's maiden name show that this is one of the letters I am looking for, written by my grandfather to my grandmother before they were married. The address shows that Amalie Pollak lived in Vienna's Second District, only a few blocks from where my grandparents were later to make their home.

In a filing cabinet, I find more of my grandfather's papers, and a few more letters, all from David to Amalie. I check the desk drawers. Just old bills and bank statements there. Across the back of the room, behind a sofa, are built-in floor-to-ceiling cupboards. The bottom section is stuffed with coats, scarves, hats, and other items of clothing. There is a separate door to the top section. I reach up to open it, and find myself in a scene from a Three Stooges movie: a book falls on my head. As I bend down to pick it up, folders of papers cascade over me. When I get them, a lamp shade follows, then a handbag, some large brown envelopes, a plastic bag containing something heavy, and more folders. I wait, my arm protecting my head, until I am confident that the avalanche is over, and then I take a look at what is now around my feet. Some of the folders contain more old bills—how long does my aunt think she needs to keep a phone bill?—but the large brown envelopes are made of a different kind of paper, the kind I now recognize as coming from Austria before the war. In one of these I find a passport. "Republik Österreich" it says on the front, for it was issued in 1929; but a large red "J" for *Jude* ("Jew") was added on October 19, 1938, showing that the passport was still used after the Republic of Austria had ceased to exist. "Dr David Ernst Oppenheim" is described as having a face that is "oval," "brown" hair, and "gray-green" eyes. A good-looking man stares out at me from his passport photo. His hair is brushed back from his forehead.

He has a mustache that points out horizontally on both sides, and a short, neat beard, confined to the area of his face directly below his mouth. I flip through the pages used for stamps from border control officials. There are a few showing entry to and exit from Czechoslovakia in the summers of 1936 and 1937—to visit relatives, presumably. Then on the next page is a series of stamps added after the Nazi takeover of Austria. The first one says "Wien 17.IX.38," and next to it is written "Freigrenze 10km September 1938." A ten-kilometer limit on freedom to travel. Similar stamps appear for October, November, and December. The remaining pages are blank.

I put down the passport and pick up the plastic bag that fell on my head, the kind you get at supermarket checkouts. More old bills? No, it is full of the same little envelopes in which my grandfather wrote to my grandmother—there must be at least a hundred here! I sit down and open some. Each envelope contains a letter, some only two pages, some six or eight, in the same tiny, barely legible script. The postmarks are all from 1904, 1905, and 1906. Astounded that so much has been preserved, I wonder what the letters will tell me.

A few things did not fall out of the cupboard. I reach in and take out an overfilled light brown cardboard folder, on which is scrawled in German, with a red pencil, "Materials on Knowledge of Humanity in the Old and New Testaments." Inside is a bundle of sheets with penciled notes, some in German and some in Greek. I can make out references to Luke, Mark, Matthew, and other books of the Bible, but I can't read much of it. Underneath the folder is a stack of large used envelopes. Across one envelope my grandfather has written "Ritual Nudity" and a reference to a passage in Ovid. Inside it are dozens of sheets of notepaper, all with references to classical works or extracts copied out by hand from them. The envelopes, all previously used, have postmarks from the 1920s. Many also have "Ritual Nudity" written on them—there is more material on that topic than on anything else—but others have different topics, such as "Seneca, problem of value" or "Shakespeare, basic questions of human nature." Inside another envelope I find a dozen or so slips from the National Library of Austria, showing details of books borrowed by D. Oppenheim on various dates in 1926 and 1927. There is even an old Vienna tram ticket, with references to passages in texts on the back.

I had not expected so much to have survived the death of the man who created them, and the loss of his home. In anticipation of deportation, he must have given them to someone for safekeeping. Whoever that was must have kept them safe, so that they survived the Allied bombardment of Vienna at the end of the Second World War. Then they must have been given to my grandmother when, against the odds, she returned to Vienna.

I think about my grandmother returning to the city she had loved, now fouled by what her fellow citizens had done. Her beloved husband was dead, and her many relatives—she had nine siblings, most of them married with children and in some cases grandchildren—were either dead or scattered all over the world. Did she, in packing her things to go to her daughters in Australia, look through these papers to see what they contained? Or did she just take everything that was left of her husband's work, because she could not bear the thought of going through it? And why did I have only one side of the correspondence of their courtship? Had she thrown out her own letters when she left Vienna, because she wanted to preserve only what her husband had written? I might never be able to answer these questions, but I could at least find out what was in the letters I now had.

||| **PART II** |||

David and Amalie

3

"A Relationship of the Heart"

THOUGH MY MOTHER and aunt had often told me stories about their parents, I had never been told how they met or became close. The letters I had found in Doris's apartment gave me, once I found someone who could help me read David's near-impossible script, a startling answer. The correspondence began in the summer of 1904, when David was twenty-three and Amalie three years older. They were both students at the University of Vienna—he was studying classics, and she math and physics—and they both came from highly educated Moravian Jewish families. David was lodging with an aunt, but Amalie lived with her mother in Vienna, her father having died nine years earlier. Her mother had given birth to fourteen children, of whom two had died in infancy, and two in childhood. Amalie was the second youngest of the ten surviving children, but by this time she was the only one still unmarried and living at home. During this particular summer, though, Amalie was staying with a relative or friend in Mödling, then a small town just outside the city. Amalie was one of a handful of women at the university, for Austrian universities were only opened to female students in 1897. Amalie herself had not, at first, intended to go to university, doing so only after a visit by a deputation seeking to encourage well-qualified women to study there. The visitors told her that with the results she had received during high school, she would be letting her sex down if she did not continue her education. She enrolled in 1899 and was the thirty-ninth woman to graduate from the University of Vienna.

The first letter was mystifying. It seemed that Amalie had offered to mediate in some situation relating to "a boy," but David had thought it best not to take up her offer, for fear that the entry of a third person would cause the boy to shy off. There is a reference to Eros, the Greek god of love, and an offer, if all goes well, to send Amalie "the letters that I wrote when mad." What could that mean?

In the second letter, written a month later, David tells Amalie that on returning home after a three-week trip to Italy, he found "the letters that my cousin demanded of Victor," and that he was sending them to Amalie, together with two letters he had himself written. Victor was evidently the boy referred to in the first letter. To help Amalie understand the letters, David included some explanatory notes. If they were helpful to Amalie, they were nothing short of astounding to me:

> The entire correspondence extends over 4 years, 1900–1904. The first letter of any significance that I wrote to Victor is, unfortunately, missing. It was a monstrous piece of writing, in the style of a final year high school student and a freshman. In it I told him the story of how we had become acquainted two years previously in Olmütz,* and the impression that he had made on me. I gave him clear signs that led him to understand, as I believed, that I was in love with him and I invited him to come to me in Kojetein:† He came for one afternoon, but with what result you will learn from no. 2, which is from the following Easter, the famous "Amfortas letter." The question that Parsifal-Victor was to direct to poor Amfortas was of course, how I really stood in regard to him, whereupon I would then have explained to him the miracle of the Grail, that is the socratic-platonic Eros. Unfortunately it did not come to this sublime consecration, although I really did speak to the boy in Olmütz and made every effort to make his head spin just as much as mine was spinning.

My head was spinning too. My grandfather had been in love with a "boy" called Victor! What did he mean by the "socratic-platonic Eros" and why was this "the miracle of the Grail"? Neither my mother nor my aunt had ever mentioned anything like this. How old was "the boy"? From a

* A town in Moravia, not far from Brünn.
† Now Kojeten, the Moravian town where David's mother's parents lived.

later reference I discovered that Victor finished high school in the summer of 1902, so he was probably around sixteen at the time David was wooing him. That summer David again invited Victor to Kojetein, but Victor declined. After that there are further references to other letters, and to a "farewell letter" from Victor, and a final letter from David, with which he sent a short book on how to live one's life, by the Stoic philosopher Epictetus. "With this letter," David writes, "the story is really at an end."

If David's relationship with Victor was over by the time David wrote to Amalie, why, I wondered, was he writing to her about it, and even sending her the correspondence he had had with Victor? The last paragraph gave at least a partial answer to that question:

> I hope, dear Miss Pollak, that you are now in a position to see clearly into this dark matter, and also, through your fine psychological judgment, to make things clear to me. You can show the letters to whomever you trust, as I trust you. I am sure that I have intended to do nothing wrong, but it would be better that not too many know about it.

David was looking to Amalie to "make things clear" to him. But I still didn't know why he had chosen her—a woman he did not know very well, as I could tell from the formal style in which he addressed her—for this purpose. In a later letter, David provides the reason. He says that he got to know Amalie "fleetingly" when he was a high school student in Brünn. She made such an impression on him that he formed "an audacious plan, to get so close to you that I could tell you about the secrets of my heart, which of course to me were completely identical with a problem in the cultural history of Greece." David's motivation for wanting to get to know Amalie, in other words, was his attraction toward those of his own sex. This was at the same time "a problem in the cultural history of Greece," because David's familiarity with Greek texts gave him a window onto a highly civilized culture that had an attitude to same-sex relationships very different from both the Jewish and the Christian cultures in which he found himself.

In this specific form of appreciation of the classics, David was by no means unique. Oscar Wilde had pointed out in his trial that "the love that dare not speak its name" is also the love that "Plato made the very basis of his philosophy." In Oxford the poet-scholar A. E. Housman made the same connection, as Tom Stoppard has shown in his play *The Invention of Love*.

E. M. Forster's long-suppressed novel *Maurice*, set in Edwardian Cambridge, tells of a student who, in love with his uncomprehending male classmate, urges him to read Plato's *Symposium* over the summer vacation in the hope that he will better understand the possibilities for their relationship. That is very like David's desire for an opportunity to explain to Victor the "socratic-platonic Eros."

Years passed before David could carry out his plan to get closer to Amalie. At the end of his third year at university he returned early to Brünn because he knew that she was there, probably staying with her sister and brother-in-law. He met her at the synagogue but was "extraordinarily silent." Looking back, now that his plan has succeeded, he is amused at the recollection of his "stunned-fish behavior" at that time. David then explains that the reason he singled out Amalie so early as the one to whom he wanted to reveal the secrets of his heart was that he "had the instinctively sure feeling that you would understand and your understanding would enable me to clear things up myself." Though the feeling was instinctive, when he discussed it with a cousin he justified it by reference to "the high level of your intellectual talents." Amalie's reputation as a brilliant student must have been known widely enough to reach David. But now David thinks that he was responding to something else, to a "new form of the feminine" that Amalie represents for him. Though she has, through her education, "absorbed much from the culture of men," she is still very much a woman, and this means that she possesses what he views as the "specific excellence" of a woman, namely "calm self-certainty," "freshness of perception," and the gift of "understanding human feelings through sharing them."

David's portrait of my grandmother fits with the way others saw her later. Doris, comparing her mother and father, found Amalie "more self-controlled, perhaps more energetic, more logical, but calmer." My sister Joan, who is six years older than I and so was able to talk to my grandmother in ways that I, nine years old when she died, could not, remembers Amalie, fifty years after David's letter was written, as still a sensitive, calm, wise, and very understanding person.

———

IN SEPTEMBER 1904 David went home to spend the Jewish festivals of Rosh Hashanah, the Jewish New Year, and Yom Kippur, the Day of Atonement, with his family in Brünn. Writing from Brünn on September 20,

David told Amalie that her letter had "cheered me up on a frosty Yom Kippur afternoon." As if in exchange for Amalie's comments on Victor's letters, David sent her an attempt at a psychological analysis of letters that Amalie had received from someone called Martina. Martina, it seemed, was interested in studying the classics, for Amalie had asked David about which of his professors' lectures he could recommend. After discussing some of his professors and urging Martina to study "the foundational science of psychology," David closes by telling Amalie that he saw Victor at the synagogue in Brünn, and Victor then came to visit him. So David and Victor came face-to-face again, after an interval of almost two years. David describes his feelings by saying: "I have not become indifferent to the boy, but I am also not in love with him anymore." He wants to "take advantage of the position" to seek to confirm, by Victor's own statements, a theory that Amalie has suggested, which David refers to as "your excellent anxiety theory." All David promises himself from this fleeting renewal of his relationship with Victor is, he tells Amalie, "scientific benefit."

In November David writes to Amalie that some events of "unusual significance" have taken place in his life, "which is otherwise so quiet":

> Last Friday Soyka, my friend who is as highly gifted as he is unfortunate, visited me, and again delivered a comprehensive confession. It is of course again a tale of the heart, of the old type, but with mighty new power. He loves the son of a well-known Vienna socialist leader, with the kind of passionate torment that only a person of consequence can feel. What he has already told me of this matter is important and would be worth your while to hear. But this time the matter goes still further. Without my friend's knowledge and wish, I myself have entered the drama as a bit player. I turned to the boy, in writing, had him last Sunday in my house, and had a discussion with him that I believe I will always be able to count among my most remarkable experiences. I feel a deep need to tell you of these things, which move me so powerfully. Therefore I permit myself to request to be allowed to visit you on Sunday afternoon, if this can occur without disturbing your duties of care in regard to your esteemed mother.

So David had at least one friend who shared his sexual preferences. Otto Soyka was Viennese, Jewish, similar in age to David, and about to launch a literary career by writing an article on Oscar Wilde for *Die Fackel*, the much admired and much hated satirical magazine edited by Karl Kraus. Soyka went on to write a daring book attacking sanctions against "unnatural" sexual behavior, including sodomy, fetishism, and even—where it did not involve cruelty—bestiality. He also wrote ten novels, mostly thrillers, crime fiction, science fiction, and fantasy, often focused on the influence a person can have over others.

That Soyka should have chosen the case of Oscar Wilde for his first contribution to Kraus's magazine indicates the resonance that Wilde's trial for homosexuality still had. In German-speaking Europe, a movement for more open and tolerant attitudes to homosexuality was getting under way. In the year after Wilde's conviction in 1895, 320 works on homosexuality were published in Germany alone. In 1897 Dr. Magnus Hirschfeld, already the author of a small study of homosexuality entitled *Sappho and Socrates*, founded his "Scientific Humanitarian Committee" to advance the campaign for reform. In 1905 the committee discussed a proposal to advance its course by having one thousand people declare to the police that they were homosexuals and demand that charges be pressed. Though the plan was never carried out, to David and Soyka in these first years of the new century, love between people of the same sex might have seemed to be on the verge of coming out of the closet.

Two weeks after writing to Amalie about Soyka, David again suggests a Sunday walk, saying that he would like to continue the conversation that they had on the previous walk about matters relating to eros, or sexual desire. Like Socrates in Plato's *Symposium*, he tells Amalie, he considers this area "to be my real domain," but he would like to learn more from Amalie. He calls her his "wise Diotima," after the woman from whom, according to Plato, Socrates learned the true nature of eros.

The conversations David and Amalie had on their Sunday walks around Vienna would have been unusual for their period. Though liberating ideas were afoot, in most respectable circles sex was not something one discussed with women. Stefan Zweig reveals just how little young women "of good family" knew about such matters when he recalls one of his aunts storming home to her parents on the night of her marriage, telling them that her new husband was a madman and a beast. Her evidence for this conclusion was that he had attempted to undress her!

David's letters to Amalie are not, however, only about the nature of eros. At the end of November, David and Amalie went together to a lecture by a Wilhelm Ostwald, a German scientist with an interest in philosophy, on "the energetic conception of happiness." Afterward David wrote Amalie a long letter in which he defends himself against the charge—which Amalie appears to have made because of his criticism of the lecture—that he has a general dislike of science. The issue would have been an important one between them because Amalie had studied math and physics. David tells her that he is not against the natural sciences, "but only against the unjustified extension of their concepts and methods into the area of the humanities." He then laments the fact that his specialization in the humanities has given him no time to pursue his interests in science, and acknowledges that this is a "serious deficiency" in his intellectual life. He would particularly like to study biology because it is the foundation of the study of his chief concern, "the life of the psyche." But mathematics is not for him, because "in no way can I move permanently in abstractions. . . . I am really a historian, and love the concrete, the vivid, the living." Even in philosophy, he says, he dislikes "pure conceptual philosophy" and "will probably never really get into the study of Kant's writings."

David's next letter is long and intensely personal. His feelings about himself are "at a very low point" and in this mood he is ready to "betray a secret." The secret is that not only is he inadequate in mathematics, as he wrote in the previous letter, but even in his own field of classical philology, or the study of ancient texts, "I really have no proper right to call myself a philologist." David then tells Amalie that although he has a reputation at the university of being almost the equal of his teacher, the renowned Professor Arnim, in understanding Greek texts, this reputation is undeserved. Though he has "a certain facility" in the translation and interpretation of Greek texts, even after five years of university study he lacks "the living knowledge of the language" and so is not capable of reconstructing Greek texts that have been damaged and have words missing. He tells Amalie that he might have been more competent if he had made his field history or German literature, but "you already know, as I have told you, how deeply grounded my relationship to the classical age is, and that it is a relationship of the heart in the truest sense of the word." He fears, therefore, that he has chosen a field in which he cannot do work of real value. Should this prove to be true, he adds, "then that will signify a catastrophe for me from which I will hardly know how to recover. . . . I have identified myself with the classical scholar in me, and if that falls, what should then remain?"

Telling Amalie of this episode leads David to reflect on an important decision that he will shortly have to make. Earlier he had thought that the only worthwhile task that he could set himself was to pursue research in the classics, with the ultimate goal of trying to understand what it is to be human. But now his doubts about his own abilities with ancient Greek have led him to realize that the world needs not only university professors, but also proficient high school teachers. "Could I be that?" he asks himself. "A timid, almost anxious person like me is scarcely suited to hold a troop of rascals in check."

4

"Let There Be Truth Between Us"

ON DECEMBER 19 David wrote to Amalie telling her that he would leave for Brünn on Friday afternoon. Could they meet before that? From the next letter it is evident that they did meet, and they had a conversation about David's friend Soyka that left David filled with "turbulent unrest." While "a merciful fate" has kept David from the "wrong turnings" into which Soyka has been driven, David also experiences the tension that has led Soyka to his problems. This is, David explains, the unforgiving conflict between nature and culture, between the "barbaric force" of natural desire, which "demands satisfaction in sensual pleasure," and the "innumerable, infinitely fine and tender mental needs" that any relatively high-minded young man has.

Does the fact that David has been spared Soyka's "wrong turnings" mean that David's relationship with Victor, as well as any other homosexual relationships he might have had, did not lead to physical intimacy, whereas Soyka's did? Freud wrote that "restrictions of sexual aim—to the point of its being limited to simple outpourings of emotion—are commoner among [homosexual] than among heterosexual lovers." Though this seems unlikely to be true today, it might have been true of homosexuals at the time and place Freud wrote this—Vienna in the first years of the twentieth century—and it might also have been true of David. But if it was true of David, it was not without a struggle. David continues by confessing to Amalie that, like Soyka, he doesn't know how to reconcile his intellectual and ethical life with his "dominant natural desire." He writes of "wounds" that bleed, that are hidden from the world and are (in an early reference to unconscious sexual feelings, which Freud had begun to explore in *The Interpretation of Dreams*, published four years earlier) "at times hidden also from those who bear them." These wounds "hurt like no others" and reach "to the seat of life." Then David wonders if his confession has gone too far:

> I have again let you see a lot deeper, or rather very, very deep, into my inner nature. For what still remains will signify little in comparison with the revelations that I have made to you today, at first in conversation and then in this letter. Now I almost fear that through an excess of candor I have lowered myself in your regard. But "Let there be truth between us."

As the new year, 1905, begins, David starts his letters with "Valued Friend" instead of the more formal "Dear Miss Pollak" with which the earlier letters began. David and Amalie continue to meet and converse about "the two-sided Eros." When David sees Amalie together with her friend Martina, he quotes a line from *Faust*: "This beauty, how she dazzles, dazzles me, poor one, completely," and continues: "I hope that this will not now make you jealous." Even if a joke, this is the first sign that the relationship between David and Amalie may be the kind in which jealousy can arise.

In the winter of 1905, David and Amalie begin reading together in Greek a dialogue called *Erotes*. This work, which has been translated into English under the title *Affairs of the Heart*, was once attributed to the Greek writer Lucian but was subsequently judged to be by another, unknown author, who is therefore referred to by scholars as "Pseudo-Lucian." The centerpiece of the dialogue is a debate between two young men about the merits of loving boys as compared to loving women. The defender of the love of women argues that his is the natural inclination, serving the purpose of procreation, and that it is degrading to use a member of one's own sex as a mere tool of one's lust. But his opponent turns this argument on its head, arguing that the love of boys is indeed cultural, rather than natural, but it is precisely this that shows those who practice it to have risen above mere nature. The narrator then adjudicates between the two debaters, concluding that love of women is for all, and brings the highest true happiness, if the right partner is chosen, but the love of boys is only for philosophers.

The experience of reading this work with Amalie brings David "high intellectual pleasure." He is startled by her ability to read the Greek, which he says is at a level that he could achieve only by five years of specialist study, and he is also delighted by her ability to enter into the author's thoughts. The reading leads David and Amalie "to a renewed examination of the old problems" of the differences between homosexual and heterosexual attachments, and the tension between nature and culture. David tells Amalie that if one takes into account the idea that humans can thrive, in the long run, only if there is harmony between nature and culture, then one will have to favor love between men and women. But he adds a plea for bisexuality:

> I would nevertheless not like to dispense with something that is somewhat alienated from nature, the refined romantic love of the beauty of one's own sex. He who has taken both forms of love into his heart will thereby seem to me, through the richness of feeling, to be the more highly developed, cultivated human being.

In January Amalie meets David's friend Soyka. Like David, she is able to sense "the power of his personality," but she also find that he quite consciously breaches limits that, to her, are inviolable. David agrees that despite "great things" that bring him and Soyka together, it is just those limits that pull them apart, because David is not willing "to grant to the individual all the rights against society that Soyka demands for himself." David's conservative nature is evident here. Whatever the "rights against society that Soyka demands for himself" were, it seems certain that today they would be seen as properly within the realm of individual choice. Amalie tells David that he stands in relation to Soyka as Victor stands to him. David accepts that this is possible, although he cannot believe that he could make as powerful an impression on anyone else as Soyka makes on him. If David stood to Soyka as Victor stood to him, perhaps he was half in love with Soyka and half fearful of being overwhelmed by him.

At this point the relationship between David and Amalie encounters its first problems. A minor one arises from David's savage criticism of an essay by an unnamed friend of Amalie's. In a letter written on January 31, David says that even before he left Amalie the previous Sunday he had the feeling that he had done something stupid, but only when he received a letter from her did he realize what a bad mistake he had made. Another letter written just two days later indicates that already they had met again and discussed David's letter. But in that conversation David revealed that he had shown Amalie's letter to his cousin, and this obviously upset Amalie. David, writing afterward, declares himself "painfully alive to the thought that I have done something that you could regard, even in the most remote way, as a desecration of yourself." In mitigation he tells her that he had not thought he was doing anything wrong, because he himself would not mind his views and feelings being known to others, as long as he is sure that he will not be misunderstood. When he sent Amalie his correspondence with Victor he gave her freedom to show the letters to whoever she thought would understand them, and he assumed that she had the same attitude. She should bear in mind, when judging this error, that "I have been a lot, perhaps all too much, by myself, mixed a little with companions of my age, but not at all with women." This may explain his lack of understanding, for which he seeks her forgiveness. Their relationship is at a dangerous point in his view, for the subject of their discussions has become what they have or have not said to each other. In his relationship with Victor, he says, "I painfully discovered that a relationship that lives on self-examination, decays."

Amalie must have forgiven David, and in accordance with his wise counsel that a relationship that feeds upon itself decays, the next letter moves on to a different topic. David sent Amalie a photograph showing a classical Greek statue, head and shoulders only, in profile, looking slightly away. On the bottom David has written: "Your socratic friend invites you, Diotima, to look at these works of art, ensouled with the breath of Eros." The statue in the photograph is of Aphrodite, the goddess of erotic love, in fact a copy of the celebrated Aphrodite of Knidos by the Greek sculptor Praxiteles. David is sending it to Amalie because the debate between the lover of women and the lover of boys is supposed to have been spurred by a discussion of this statue. After expressing the hope that the photograph will give Amalie an idea of the "dazzling beauty" that equally impressed the lover of women and the lover of boys, David goes on to make a comment that adds another twist to the relationship between him and my grandmother:

> That you too will be impressed by it I do not expect, since your ideal of beauty, as I could see on Thursday evening, far from being mere stone, is

walking across the world in rosy freshness and health. But if the goddess appeals to you just half as well as Martina, then she can probably already be satisfied. And I wish very much that you could satisfy the capricious Cypris, for she is jealous, and could easily revenge herself—in the end, even on Martina, surely the blackest revenge for you.

"Cypris" here is another term for Aphrodite. So David was suggesting that the beautiful Martina embodies Amalie's idea of beauty, and joking that this could lead to the goddess's becoming jealous and revenging herself on Martina, which would also be the blackest revenge for Amalie. For the first time it occurred to me to ask: Was this beautiful young woman more to Amalie than a pupil, relative, or friend? That my grandfather had been in love with a young man came as a complete surprise to me but was not difficult to accept. I had not contemplated the possibility, however, that both my grandparents had been attracted to their own sex. Had I been blind to the obvious? A week later, David refers to a meeting Amalie will have with Martina and writes: "May the beloved appear with the girdle of Aphrodite, so as to delight your heart with heightened gracefulness." If Martina was "the beloved" who, with the help of the goddess of erotic love, could delight Amalie's heart, I had to accept that not only David, but also Amalie, had a personal interest in homosexual love. This shared interest must have been important to David's decision to seek out Amalie to share the secrets of his heart—and hence to the marriage that grew out of this common interest in love for one's own sex.

5

The Engagement

ON THE FIRST DAY of March 1905, David pauses to take stock of his life. It is, he tells Amalie, a time when, more than any other moment in the twenty-four years he has been alive, his life is flowing "in mighty, rolling, roaring waves." Although in earlier years he took his studies very seriously, now that he is facing the university exams that will determine his future, he is living as if the exams were "froth and fragrance." He has run a zigzag course so far, but now he is determined to make a binding decision about his life. For his career, he is weighing "the goalless rambling of being without a profession" against "the solidity of an official position"—that is, the choice he mentioned earlier between attempting to continue his scholarly work after he graduates, and becoming a schoolteacher. But that is not the only decision on his mind. He goes on to mention another choice: between "inexorable celibacy versus freely chosen *gamos*." *Gamos*—which David writes in Greek letters—is Greek for marriage. Only marriage, he tells Amalie, can resolve the conflict they have previously discussed, between his physical and spiritual needs, and bring him inner calm. But that is not all. He has recently been fortunate to find a number of people who understand him well, and this has led him to a better appreciation of the value of such a relationship. It is, he thinks, indispensable to the best kind of life, and for that reason should not be left to chance. He then adds:

To have a person whose profession, so to speak, is to understand me, an educated and knowledgeable observer of my character . . . this thought is very important to me at present, and its fulfillment probably points in the direction of *gamos*.

David's description of the "person whose profession, so to speak, it is to understand me, an educated and knowledgeable observer of my character" fits unmistakably with the way in which he described Amalie in previous letters. He must have known this, and known that she, reading the letter, would also know it. He does not ask her directly if she is willing to be this person, but he closes the letter with a more oblique request:

These are the thoughts that now move me powerfully. Just because of that I have to tell you of them, and I would like to hear from you what you think about it. The friendly benevolence with which you favor me, together with the precise knowledge of my nature that I have myself endeavored to bring about in you, will give your judgment the highest significance for my decision.

> Best wishes from your always true friend
> David Oppenheim

This is a proposal of marriage, though an extraordinarily delicate, tentative, and abstract one. It contains no declaration of love, and the word "you" appears only in the invitation to Amalie to say what she thought about his general idea. That "you" is still the formal German *Sie*, not the intimate *Du* that close friends—and lovers—use. David's proposal is barely more than a hint waiting to be taken up, a hint that could be ignored without disturbing the friendship that already existed between the writer and the recipient.

How would Amalie reply to such a strange proposal? What kind of marriage was David envisaging? How would a marriage between people attracted to their own sex resolve the conflict between physical and mental needs? I hoped to learn more from David's next letter, but it was again about Victor, who was visiting Vienna. Victor has not come to see David, but the fact that Victor's distance is not painful to him is "the desired proof of the independence that I have achieved in regard to the boy." For this he thanks Amalie, for having "so completely satisfied my need for complete community of the soul." Had Amalie, in response to David's proposal, said that she wanted proof that David was no longer attached to Victor?

In his next letter David thanks Amalie for her "kind letter" but says nothing about its contents. From the tone, however, it appears that nothing dramatic has happened between them. Amalie is about to graduate, and David says that he will see her at her graduation. Perhaps she is delaying her response until this milestone is behind her.

On the day after Amalie's graduation, David writes that his relationship with Victor is heading for "gentle dissolution" and he does not want to hasten that by any sudden intervention. All that concerns him is "to finish up the thing in an inwardly clean way." Then, saying that he has "done all that is in my power," he begs Amalie not to take offense at anything in the history of his relations with Victor. Though highly significant, that relationship is but a "pale shadow" of the "beautiful reality of my relationship to you, dear friend."

At this point the pace of events picks up. Victor does come to visit David, but only to say hello, for he is about to leave Vienna. David walks with him to his next destination, but they find that they have little to say to each other. "With that, the whole story of Victor should be finished," David writes, and he again thanks Amalie for her "wonderful, subtle understanding" in this matter. Up to now there has been no evidence of a response from Amalie to David's hint that he would like to discuss the possibility of marriage, but now, suddenly, something happens. "Beloved!" has replaced "Valued Friend" at the head of David's next letter to Amalie, dated March 17. In high-flown prose, he writes that the "miraculous work" of the "great all-ruling goddess"—he means Aphrodite—"has become manifest on us ourselves." He tells Amalie that deep within himself he cannot stop smiling at the fact that people take him to be his old self, while unbeknownst to them, he is "secretly engaged." With the relationship with Victor settled, Amalie must have accepted David's veiled proposal of marriage.

David and Amalie meet the next day, and afterward he writes to her of their meeting:

> Now something for which I dreamed during years of fruitless longing, for which I hoped, but never found, with Victor, is being miraculously realized. Now, with a beloved being, I can be raised on the wings of love into

the eternal realm of thought. The longing that the divine Plato poured into my heart will be fulfilled, but differently from the way he described it, and I expected it. Not the love of boys, which yet has left such ineradicable traces in my life, but the love of women, which you, beloved, first taught me to know, has taken Plato's sacred love out of the world of beautiful dreams, and transformed it into flesh-and-blood reality. . . .

And now, beloved, I send you a good-night kiss, that by the time you receive this letter will have been transformed into a good-morning kiss, but I hope will have lost none of its sweetness.

This and the previous letter have the authentic tone of a young man in love. What is unusual about David's love letter, however, is that love has led him not to an ecstasy of physical pleasure, but into "the eternal realm of thought." In this he is a faithful follower of Plato, for the metaphor is drawn from the *Phaedrus*. "Love is a certain madness," Socrates says there—and in the very first letter to Amalie, David referred to his letters to Victor as "the letters that I wrote when mad"—but for Socrates it is a special form of madness, "a divine release of the soul from the yoke of custom and convention" that can serve as an inspiration for the philosopher seeking to know truth. One who "has loved boys with philosophy" may through his appreciation of the beauty of his beloved be "furnished with wings" and fly up to the gods in the realm of true beauty—or as David says, be "raised on the wings of love into the eternal realm of thought."

———

ACCORDING TO a story my mother used to tell, when David's mother learned that he was planning to marry Amalie, she said to him: "Why do you want to marry her? You are young, rich, and handsome, and she is old, poor, and ugly!" I always wondered if the story was true. The age difference—Amalie was the older by three years—was easy to establish. The relative wealth of the families was more difficult to ascertain, but what I knew supported the view that Amalie's family was, relative to David's, "poor." Amalie's mother, Minna Pollak, was a widow living in Vienna's Second District, a lower-middle-class neighborhood. The Ninth District, where David stayed with his aunt, was more affluent, and in Brünn his family home was centrally located on one of the city's better streets with a pleasant view over a park. As secretary of the Jewish community organization in that city, David's father, Joachim Oppenheim, received the modest salary of 3,600 kronen. Over the forty years that he held this post, he was repeatedly offered increases, and repeatedly refused them. When he retired, the community association granted him a pension of 6,000 kronen; he said he wanted to continue on 3,600, and had to be persuaded to split the difference, and accept 4,800. Though he might well have lived modestly—his daughter certainly thought of him as incredibly stingy—his indifference to salary increases could be a sign that he had other assets sufficient to meet the family's needs.

On the question of David and Amalie's physical appearance, there is more direct evidence. I have three photographs of Amalie from around this time, each produced by a different studio in Vienna. Two of them must have been taken on the same day, probably her day of graduation, for her clothes and hair are identical. In one of them Amalie sits in a chair, her elbow resting on a French Empire–style table. Her other hand is on her lap, holding some pages with writing on them, probably her thesis. In the background there is a Grecian column—or is it only a trompe l'oeil? Her hair is up, tied on top of her head, and she wears a formal black lacy dress with long sleeves. Her face is turned toward the camera, and her strong dark eyes look directly at the viewer. Her complexion is flawless, her figure, as far as I can tell given the dress she is wearing, is good, and I have no difficulty in finding her quite beautiful. In the other photograph taken on that day she is standing, in half profile, and although she still looks attractive, a highly critical gaze might find her nose just a little too large. The third photograph might have been taken a year or two earlier. Her hair is simply brushed back, her eyes look a little downcast, her expression has a touch of sadness about it. The portrait bears a striking resemblance to one of my mother, taken at about the same age, and I have always thought of my mother as a good-looking woman.

Two photographs of David from this period have survived. In one, taken by a studio in Brünn, his hair is quite short and stands up from his strong forehead. His deep-set eyes seem to be looking into the distance, or maybe he is lost in thought. His nose, the recognizable ancestor of my own, has a rounded bulb at the end. He has a mustache, and a short beard around his chin. The rest of his face looks more as if it has a few days' growth on it, rather than a full-grown beard. His full, rounded cheeks give his face a soft appearance. He wears a double-breasted jacket and a bow tie that has dropped a little from the collar of his white shirt. In another, passport-size photograph, he is standing in the main courtyard of the University of Vienna, again wearing a bow tie, this time light colored and with what seem to be polka dots on it. In contrast to the previous photograph, his face looks longer and leaner, but he has the same deep-set eyes and serious expression. Though both portraits show a sensitive, scholarly young man with a certain appeal, I cannot see that David surpasses Amalie in physical beauty. Yet both my mother and my aunt agree that David was considered particularly good-looking, while Amalie was not. They remember him as "almost blond" with blue eyes—although, as we have seen, his passport says his eyes are "gray-green" and his hair "brown." There is a family story that he was once chosen to play Jesus in a school play, and the point of the story is not that this showed him to be Semitic in appearance, as Jesus would have been, but rather that he conformed to the blond, blue-eyed Germanic image of Jesus. Amalie, on the other hand, looked distinctively Jewish and was so dark that there was speculation about the family having descended from Sephardic Jews, from Spain or North Africa. The unfavorable judgment of Amalie's beauty, as compared to David's, may therefore reflect the dominance of a "Nordic" stereotype of beauty, even among Jews.

Within a week of the secret engagement, David visited his parents to tell them of it. In a letter written from Brünn he tells Amalie that his parents have said that they will not "put any obstacles in the way of the development of our relationship and its possible future conclusion by marriage." He hopes that Amalie will be able to achieve the same with her mother, because then "all external obstacles" will have been overcome. Nevertheless,

> . . . my parents, in consideration of the difference in age, doubt the constancy of my feelings, and therefore regret that I have, through my declaration, bound you, and me, for an indeterminate time.

So Ernestine, David's mother, did raise the fact that Amalie was three years older than David, and saw it as an objection to the match. She might have been influenced by the thought that David was taking a bride who, despite (or because of?) her undoubted intellectual qualities, had been "left on the shelf"—for twenty-six was then a late age for a woman to marry. David himself admits as much in a subsequent letter, when he likens Amalie to "a late plucked, sweet little apple, forgotten or rather not reached by the apple-pickers." Now, however, to his parents' objection about the difference in their ages, David sees "only one possible refutation," namely "that we maintain our sentiments in respect of one another despite the passing years." He tells Amalie that he considers it "a requirement of the love of truth, in which we are surely united" that if his feelings toward her change in any way, he would let her know, "infinitely painful" as that would be for both of them. But even if he would cease to love her "as a woman," then they could still "as friends, be together for life." For the foundation of their relationship "is not sensuously aesthetic, but spiritually ethical: the highest mutual esteem . . . we are not welded to one another, but hold one another firmly, as a magnet and iron hold each other in accordance with their own nature, and as long as, and not longer than, the magnet remains a magnet and the iron remains iron."

The next day David writes to Amalie again, but whereas the previous letter went to her usual Vienna address, this one is sent to the town of her birth, Holleschau, and addressed to her at the residence of Bernhard Ehrlich, the husband of her oldest sister, Louise. Although the journey from Vienna to Holleschau would have taken Amalie through Brünn, she evidently did not visit David's family, but left the delicate discussions to him. He writes that the firmness of his resolve to marry her, and his joy at the prospect of doing so, is favorably influencing his parents. Then he adds a comment that indicates how much his parents knew of his life, and how surprising the news of his engagement to Amalie must have been to them: "And so it is to be hoped that by the time they have got over their astonishment at the novelty of it all—I refer only to Victor—they will have a better understanding of my peculiar nature and the needs that grow out of it." He assures Amalie that his parents "are both truly of a noble nature, and are aware that I, in any case, am acting from thoroughly pure motives."

Discussions in the Oppenheim household continue for some days. Their cause is advanced, David tells Amalie, by the fact that he read some of her letters out loud to his parents, who admired "their perfection of form and the maturity of their thoughts." He has succeeded in conveying to them "the thing that is for me the foundation of my relationship with you, the clear insight into the worth of your character," and they can also see that David's choice is indeed a person of worthy character. His father, at least, no longer presses the objection that Amalie is older than David, for he understands that "what binds us pushes time away." Moreover, his parents approve "the first decisive step that will lead me in the direction of our common goal, the decision for a profession as a high school teacher instead of exclusive devotion to a university career." Finally, after five days of discussions, David tells Amalie that he has now won his parents' acceptance of his "right to carry on my relationship with you as it was previously, and guided by the thought of marriage as its ultimate conclusion."

If these letters confirm the old family story about David's mother saying that Amalie was "old," did Ernestine also say that she was ugly and poor? This is nowhere stated in the letters, but she might still have said it, and the principle David frequently proclaims to Amalie — "Let there be truth between us" — could have bent sufficiently for David not to repeat it. On the point about Amalie's appearance, there is one further piece of evidence. In a subsequent letter David tells Amalie that he has been reading *Lucile*, a novel by the prolific German writer Paul Heyse, in which the heroine, a woman of great character and intellect but ugly appearance, wins the man she loves away from his beautiful but shallow wife. In reading it, he says, he soon realized that it applied to him — not, he hastens to tell Amalie, because she seems ugly to him — but "to stick to the truth, I could also not describe you as a cameo beauty." That may already be as far as a young man should go in sticking to the truth when writing to his fiancée. If David could write this, no doubt Ernestine could have said far worse.

6

Brno

December 7, 1998

THE TRAIN FROM Vienna to Brno, as Brünn is now known, takes about two hours. The route crosses the Austrian lowlands—no dramatic alpine scenery here, only open fields, snow-covered now, and gentle wooded hills. David traveled along this track when he left his hometown to go to university in Vienna, when he returned to spend Jewish holidays or Christmas with his parents, and when he went to tell his parents of his engagement to Amalie. Moravia was then part of the Austro-Hungarian Empire. After the First World War he needed a passport to visit his mother, who now lived in Czechoslovakia. Today Moravia makes up, with Bohemia, the Czech Republic, and if that country succeeds in its application to become part of the European Union, it may again be possible to travel from Vienna to Brno without showing a passport. Since the wheel has not quite turned full circle, I still need to show mine. When the Czech officials stamp it, I recognize the name of the border crossing: "Břeclav" appears several times in my grandfather's passport.

From the return addresses that David conscientiously put on the back of his letters when he was writing from Brünn, I know that his parents lived at 25 Jesuitengasse, "the street of the Jesuits"—an ironic address for the secretary of the Jewish community. It was not in the city's Jewish district, but between that and the center of the city. Jesuitská, as the street is now called, is a short walk through the center of the town from the main railway station. Together with Renata, my wife, and our daughter Marion, I walk down it, past the Church of Our Lady, a Baroque church used by the Jesuits from which the street got its name. When we get to where number 25 should have been, however, we are standing in front of an exhibition hall. A plaque tells us that it was built in 1928. My grandfather's childhood home no longer exists.

David's childhood in Brünn was not happy. While staying with his parents there over the Jewish New Year holiday in September 1905, he tells Amalie that he does not like the city, probably because of "the absence of really happy childhood memories linked to this place." He only hints at the reason for this: "at the deepest foundations of the sadness of our home there are forces at work which would wrestle even your splendid strength to the point of exhaustion." About these "forces" David says that he has never spoken to anyone, not even to Amalie. Nor will he put them in a letter, for who, he asks rhetorically, would be willing to put on paper "a judgment about the bond of marriage to which he himself owes his origin, and reveals the deficiencies that burden his creators?"

Amalie then came to stay with him and his parents for a few days, and David was able to, as he put it in a subsequent letter, "draw away the deceptive veil" that hid his "painful secret." He feels calmer now that Amalie also knows "this saddest side of my life," but exactly what the problem was in his parents' relationship remains mysterious. That there was for a time a breach between David and his parents is apparent from a letter David wrote when he was in Brünn to tell his parents about their engagement. He then wrote to his fiancée that his mother had recognized that Amalie's influence "has led me back to the house of my parents." In another letter, David tells Amalie that in contrast to his strong ties with his chosen friends, his feelings for his family are "relatively limited."

═══

BRNO RETAINS the air of an Austro-Hungarian provincial capital. The thirteenth-century former town hall still stands, along with other fine buildings that my grandfather would have known. Still standing too is the German-language high school that David attended, a Classical building complete with caryatids, now housing the Academy of Music and Dramatic Art. The atmosphere of Austria-Hungary in this period was well described by David's contemporary, Stefan Zweig:

> Our currency, the Austrian crown, circulated in bright gold pieces, an assurance of its immutability. Everyone knew how much he possessed or what he was entitled to, what was permitted and what forbidden. Everything had its norm, its definite weight and measure. He who had a fortune could accurately compute his annual interest. An official or an officer, for example, could confidently look up in the calendar the year when he would be advanced in grade, or when he would be pensioned. Each family had its fixed budget, and knew how much could be spent for rent and food, for holidays and entertainment; and what is more, invariably a small sum was carefully laid aside for sickness and the doctor's bills, for the unexpected. . . . In this vast empire everything stood firmly and immovably in its appointed place, and at its head was the aged emperor; and were he to die, one knew (or believed) another would come to take his place, and nothing would change in the well-regulated order. No one thought of wars, of revolutions, or revolts. All that was radical, all violence, seemed impossible in an age of reason.

Today, this conjures up an almost inconceivable sense of predictability (or unimaginable naïveté?). At the city's tourist office I ask about the Great Synagogue, built in 1855, where David met Amalie during his third year at university and was too tongue-tied to say anything to her, and where a few years later he saw Victor. I am told that it was burned down in 1939, under the Nazi "protectorate." Of the thriving Jewish community that lived here when Zweig and my grandfather were boys, there are hardly any traces. There is still a Jewish community organization, located in a run-down office building outside the central part of the city. When my great-grandfather was its secretary, there were twelve thousand Jews in the city; now there are only a few hundred.

We get directions to the Jewish cemetery. It has survived six years of Nazi rule, the Second World War, the destruction of the Jewish community, and forty years of Communism, astonishingly unscathed. Joachim and Ernestine Oppenheim both died in this city, and presumably are buried here; but there are thousands of graves, and no one around to ask where their grave might be. We crunch through the snow, checking separate rows, hoping to find it before our toes freeze. Renata calls out. I hurry over and read:

Dr Joachim Heinrich
Oppenheim
Secretary of the Israelite Denominational Community, Brünn
born 10 April 1848 died 7 August 1918
You loved righteousness and you hated wickedness

Mrs Ernestine Oppenheim
born 31. 12. 1856 died 11 May 1920
Love is as strong as death

I imagine the scene when David and Amalie came here to bid farewell to each of David's parents—leafier, greener, no snow in August or May, but otherwise very like it is today. The high brick walls of the cemetery keep out the rest of the world. Perhaps a few more graves have been added, but not many, for the community that filled it has gone, their remains scattered in many places, but not here.

I look at the dates and calculate that when David was born his father was thirty-three and his mother, twenty-four. When she had her first child, Cornelia, she was only twenty-one. I have a photo of David with his older sister, a studio portrait taken in Brünn when he was five or six years old. He sits on a three-legged stool, wearing a kind of pleated dress with a large floppy bow at the neck. It seems an extraordinary outfit to put on a boy, but from photos of my father and his brothers I know that young boys commonly wore dresses, at least when they were getting their photos taken. Cornelia, older by only three years but looking much more grown-up, is standing next to him, her right arm reaching across her body to take her little brother's right hand. She wears a tight-fitting jacket unbuttoned over her dress, with a white lace collar at her neck. They both have rounded, slightly plump faces, and they gaze seriously—or is David's look one of boredom?—into the camera. The illness and death of Cornelia, at the age of sixteen, must have been the most traumatic event of my grandfather's youth. She had diabetes, a disease for which, until insulin became available in 1922, there was no effective treatment. An ancient account of diabetes describes it as "a dreadful affliction" in which the patient suffers from "nausea, restlessness and a burning thirst, and in a short time, they expire." At the time Cornelia died, that would still have been an accurate description of the course of the illness.

7

The Religious Problem

IN APRIL 1905 David's father, Joachim Oppenheim, took the train to Vienna to visit Amalie's mother, Minna Pollak. From surviving photographs I can picture Joachim and Minna at the time of their meeting. Joachim is a fine-looking gentleman of his period, with a graying, neatly cropped beard and mustache. He wears a jacket with a crisp white shirt, and a small dark tie. His head is bare, and there is nothing distinctively Jewish about his appearance. Minna is much easier to recognize as a Jewish woman. She wears a lace-fringed bonnet. More telling, though, is her hair, or rather what at first glance appears to be her hair. On closer inspection it turns out to be a wig. Jewish law requires married women to cut off their hair, but does not say they should not wear a wig, and most do. Minna was following the law. Joachim, in not wearing a skullcap or yarmulke, was not.

Joachim personifies the modern loss of religious belief. He came from a line of rabbis that includes the illustrious scholar Rabbi David Oppenheim, born in 1664, and at the time of his death in 1736 chief rabbi of Prague and of Bohemia. His grave is still pointed out to visitors to the old Jewish cemetery in Prague, and his collection of more than five thousand Hebrew books and manuscripts is now in the Bodleian Library in Oxford. For the next seven generations, there was always a Rabbi Oppenheim, and Joachim too trained to become a rabbi, and served briefly in that role in the fashionable Bohemian spa town of Karlsbad. His rabbinical career ended when, at the age of twenty-three, he decided that he could no longer believe in what he was doing. He ceased to keep the traditional Jewish dietary rules and favored an enlightened, secular form of Judaism. He took up a post as secretary of the Jewish community organization in Brünn—a body authorized by the imperial government to collect a tax from every Jew in the city, and to be responsible for the affairs of the Jewish community in the provincial capital.

In putting into English the words on Joachim's tombstone I translated quite literally the name for this body as "Israelite Denominational Community." The name reflects the desire of Austro-Hungarian Jews to be regarded as just another religious group within the empire. "Israelite" is, like "Mosaic," also used in official documents at the time, a euphemism to avoid the derogatory overtones of "Jew." Second, describing Jews as a "denomination" is a way of saying that, like Catholics or Protestants, what Jews have in common is their religious belief. The age-old, still unresolved problem of Jewish identity lies in the fact that this is palpably false, because many people who consider themselves Jewish—and are held by anti-Semites to be Jews—are not religious believers at all. This was true of my grandfather, and might even have been true of Joachim himself.

Amalie, on the other hand, was the daughter of the rabbi of Holleschau, where she grew up and where her father served for twenty-three years before being called to join the court of Jewish law in Vienna. In his photograph Marcus Pollak—who died of a heart attack a decade before Amalie's engagement to David—looks exactly like a nineteenth-century rabbi should, with a full beard, a heavy black jacket, and a large skullcap dominating his head. Minna Pollak was a very suitable wife for an Orthodox rabbi, for she was the daughter of Isak Lew Freistadt, a cofounder of the Schiffschul, one of Vienna's largest Orthodox synagogues, set up to combat the dramatic swing among Viennese Jews toward more liberal forms of Judaism. That Marcus and Minna followed Orthodox Jewish law is suggested not only by Marcus's skullcap and Minna's wig, but by the fact that they had fourteen children. Joachim and Ernestine had three, but David's younger sister, Hannchen, was conceived only after the death of Cornelia.

On April 27, 1905, David wrote to Amalie that he had hoped that his father's visit would achieve "the overcoming of the last of the external obstacles to our relationship." Instead of having this happy outcome, however, the visit gave rise to a new difficulty. "The religious problem," David says, "had to come up between us, and, now that it has come up, we must discuss it right to the end, but I would rather have chosen the circumstances my-self, and then chosen differently." The nature of the problem was obvious: Amalie ate only kosher food and observed the Sabbath. David did not go to synagogue and regarded the rules by which Orthodox Jews lived as a lot of superstitious nonsense. How would their common household function?

After David's father's visit had stirred up the problem, David and Amalie sat down to "negotiations" on it. David was troubled by something about these discussions. To convey to Amalie his feeling that somehow they had only touched the surface of the problem, he used an elaborate analogy. He and Amalie had seemed to him, he writes, like diplomats, formally dressed, solemnly conducting difficult negotiations in an elegant conference room. But all the while, in a basement in the same building, a wild party is going on, almost an orgy, in which people are giving themselves over entirely to their primitive instincts. From time to time the racket from the party in-trudes into the conference room. The diplomats notice it, wince nervously, but say nothing, and proceed with their negotiations. Just so, David says, while he and Amalie conducted their negotiations with "a historically edu-cated understanding," he was aware that "beneath the threshold of con-sciousness, the demons were howling." These are the same demons that led the heathens to persecute the Christians, the Christians to massacre the Jews, and the Protestants and Catholics to fight the Thirty Years War. David's point is that no matter how calmly and rationally he and Amalie may discuss their religious differences, history shows how difficult it is for reason to assert its hold over the irrational elements that are "at the deepest core of human beings."

Despite David's forebodings, the "negotiations" were successful. They agreed that Amalie would remain kosher and that they would celebrate the Sabbath and Jewish festivals such as Passover, Jewish New Year, and the Day of Atonement—though "celebrate" here did not mean keep according to strictly Orthodox Jewish law. One of Amalie's nieces, who lived nearby and whose father had died when she was quite young, often came with her mother and sister to the Oppenheims' for Sabbath dinner. She recalls that while David walked around with a book in his hand, whatever he hap-pened to be reading at the time, Amalie took over the traditionally male role, covering her head and saying the prayers. My mother recalled that at Passover they had matzo, the traditional unleavened bread, and they played the usual game in which a piece of matzo is hidden and the children have to find it. But then, alongside that, she said, they ate ham. (Doris disagrees on this point: "Father said, we don't have to eat *treyfe* [nonkosher food] there.") The family did not celebrate Christmas, but my mother was allowed to spend Christmas Eve with the Catholic family of her best school friend, Eva Hitschmann.

Amalie accepted that David would continue to eat nonkosher food, and any children they had would not be compelled to be kosher. That is how my mother and aunt recall their family life. They had, as Jewish dietary law requires, two completely separate sets of plates: one for dishes containing meat, and another for dishes containing dairy products. They also had another two sets to be used only for Passover, on which no bread could be placed. And then, for David and the children, there was yet another set, for *treyfe* food like ham. David ate whatever he liked, and the children did the same. Amalie observed the religious holy days. She fasted on the Day of Atonement, and afterward went to the synagogue. David, my mother, and Doris did not go to the service, but they met her there afterward with a bunch of violets. David viewed religion, whether classical, Jewish, or Christian, as a fascinating human phenomenon; but he was a scholar and observer of it, not a participant.

Doris later characterized her parents' arrangement as one based on complete tolerance, in which "each could do as he or she wished." But that simple formula did not solve all religious difficulties. The hardest question was: If they had a son, would he be circumcised? An uncircumcised boy cannot have a bar mitzvah, the ceremony that makes him an adult member of the Jewish community; but David, as an enlightened, secular thinker, regarded circumcision as an unnecessary mutilation, and refused to have it inflicted on any son of his. Amalie yielded, but so reluctantly that each time she became pregnant she prayed that she would not have a son. After her first two children were girls she decided that since God had granted her prayer twice, she would not test him any further. They had no more children.

One aspect of Judaism on which David and Amalie did agree was their rejection of Zionism. In February 1906 Amalie wrote to David that Lise Tarlau, a close friend of hers, had become a Zionist. David happened to come across one of Lise's essays in the leading Austrian Jewish weekly, and wrote to Amalie that it was remarkable how "the oath to the party catchword so completely robs such a fine, tender mind of all charm, so that nothing distinguishes it anymore from that of the other 'comrades.' " He asked Amalie if she agreed with his view, saying that if she did, it would not be the first time that the two of them got cross over Zionism.

I found the essay to which David was referring. Lise Tarlau praises the Jews of the East for having retained their own distinctive cultural identity and their own language, Yiddish. In contrast, the educated, Western Jews have "lived as parasites on the creative possibilities of the dreams of beauty of other peoples." These Western Jews felt themselves to be "in the seventh heaven of culture" if they managed "to sing the songs of others so well that no one can notice the difference, so that it can be described as 'authentically German.' " No wonder David hated this essay! It was an attack on much that was at the core of his being. He was a passionate devotee of "the dreams of beauty of other peoples," not only of the Greeks and Romans, but of the great works of German literature too. He would undoubtedly have thought that the Jewish people had produced no statues to compare with those of Praxiteles, no writers to rank alongside Shakespeare or Goethe. So he was precisely one of those educated, cultivated Western Jews whom Lise derides as slavish followers of other peoples; and he was proud to speak the language of Goethe, and not the Yiddish of the shtetl. In any case, philosophically he was a universalist, a man with a cosmopolitan soul. How could he identify with the Jewish nationalism, Zionism?

Amalie's position as a religious Jew was different, but probably equally unsympathetic. Rabbi Moritz Güdemann, chief rabbi of Vienna, said: "A Jewry equipped with cannons and bayonets would exchange the role of David with Goliath and be in itself a travesty." The Orthodox Jews associated with her grandfather's Schiffschul saw Zionists as godless Jews who were turning the ancient religion into a political movement.

In their rejection of Zionism, David and Amalie were typical of Viennese Jews. Although Theodor Herzl, Zionism's founder, was Viennese, he was a prophet rejected by his own people. No wonder, for he was telling them to leave their beloved Vienna, with its opera and coffeehouses, for a life of toil under the hot sun of a harsh desert land. Vienna was a place where, by the beginning of the twentieth century, Jews could feel at home. It was different from Germany, where the Protestant ethos had fostered the rise of industry and kept Jews out of the most important positions. In Catholic Austria-Hungary, it was Jews who built the steel mills and railroads, established the leading banks, owned the fashionable stores, edited the leading newspapers, founded hospitals, and dominated the medical profession. The surgeon general of the army and the personal physician to the emperor were Jewish. Jews formed and sustained Vienna's greatest musical, theatrical, and literary achievements, sat in the imperial and provincial parliaments, and even made up 8 percent of the dual monarchy's military officers—thus making Austria-Hungary the first modern nation with a proportion of Jewish military officers greater than the proportion of Jews in the population. The historian Hans Tietze wrote: "Without the Jews, Vienna would not be what it is, and the Jews without Vienna would lose the brightest era of their existence during recent centuries."

Then, just when the Jews of Vienna were at last able to enjoy the fruits of assimilation into Austrian life and culture, Herzl came along and told them that they were not loyal Austrians at all, but a separate nation—just what the anti-Semites wanted to hear, of course, and you could be sure they would make good use of it. From Paris, Baron Rothschild said that Zionism turned Jews into objects of suspicion in the lands in which they lived. Herzl's ideas were best ignored, and that is just what most Viennese Jews did. In 1896, when Herzl published his famous Zionist tract, *The Jewish State*, he was literary editor of the *Neue Freie Presse*, Vienna's leading liberal newspaper. Herzl's sudden espousal of Zionism shocked Moritz Benedikt, the newspaper's Jewish publisher and editor in chief, a man who so successfully pursued the path of assimilation that the emperor appointed him to the upper house of the imperial parliament. Benedikt refused Herzl's request that the newspaper give space to the Zionist issue. When Herzl died in 1904, the paper published a long eulogy giving a detailed account of his work as a journalist and editor without mentioning Zionism, except for a single sentence stating: "The deceased devoted much time and energy to the Zionist cause." After Herzl's death, there was no Viennese Jew ready to step into his position as a leader of the Zionist movement, and the headquarters of the Zionists soon moved to Berlin.

The fear that Zionism would play into the hands of Austrian anti-Semites was not groundless. The popular mayor, Karl Lueger, had campaigned for office as an anti-Semite. The adulation displayed by his supporters had shown Herzl how deeply these feelings were rooted in the hearts of many Viennese. (It had also taught the young, near-destitute Hitler how a successful politician could play on the hatred of the Jews.) Four times the city council, dominated by Lueger's Christian Social Party, elected Lueger as mayor, and four times Emperor Franz Josef refused to ratify the choice. On the fifth occasion the emperor called Lueger in for a long private audience, and then agreed to the election. Perhaps a deal was struck; no one really knows. But once elected, Lueger's bark proved much worse than his bite. When criticized for socializing with Jews, he remarked, "I decide who is a Jew," a comment that was seen as typically Viennese in its dilution of ideology with pragmatism and human feelings.

Nevertheless, by present-day standards, Jews had to put up with an astonishing level of abusive, anti-Semitic rhetoric in public life. Lueger's popular lieutenant, Ernst Schneider, once made a speech in which he proposed, presumably because he thought it would amuse his audience, that the Austrian government should offer a cash prize to any good Christian who killed a Jew. The anti-Semitism came, however, not only from Lueger and his followers, strongly supported by the Roman Catholic Church, but even from the Socialists, who in their attacks on capitalism did not hesitate to play on anti-Semitic prejudices. For example, in commenting on the Dreyfus affair in France, the leading Social Democrat newspaper, the *Arbeiter-Zeitung*, or *Workers' News*, praised Emile Zola's defense of the Jewish army captain wrongly convicted of espionage, but added: "Behind Zola's courageous and high-minded attack march the whole dubious band of Jewish parasites who greedily hope for their personal whitewash, and from it, opportunities for new misdeeds." Considering that this newspaper was edited by two leading Social Democrats of Jewish origin, it is easy to see that anti-Semitic clichés were everywhere. But for individual Jews such as David, this might not have meant much. Stefan Zweig wrote: "I personally must confess that neither in school nor at the University, nor in the world of literature, have I ever experienced the slightest suppression or indignity as a Jew."

Zweig must have been fortunate, for the University of Vienna was no safe haven from anti-Semitism. Around the time when he and my grandfather were there, Jewish students were harassed and sometimes beaten up by members of nationalist Austro-German student organizations. The attitudes of these groups to Jews can be seen from the practice of dueling. Within the student organizations, any slight to another student's honor was likely to lead to a duel with sabers. The object of the duel was to inflict a cut on the opponent's face, which would later result in a dueling scar. Until the late nineteenth century, Jewish students did not know how to fence.

Then, either because of their desire to integrate with non-Jews, or from motives of self-defense, they took it up, and eventually became so proficient at it that by the time David entered university, according to the Viennese correspondent of the London *Times*, "The Jews were in a fair way to becoming the best swordsmen of the University." The student organizations then denied them the right to challenge. This decision was justified by a formal resolution that asserted: "Every son of a Jewish mother, in whose veins Jewish blood circulates, is by reason of birth, without honor. . . . He cannot distinguish between filth and cleanliness. Since no Jew can be insulted, he therefore cannot ask for satisfaction." Nevertheless, a Jew could be, and sometimes was, assaulted by a mob of non-Jewish students. In 1913, a few years after David's time at the university, Freud's son Martin was stabbed and seriously wounded in one of these brawls.

David might have been just as lucky as Zweig in his university life. (During his military service, however, as we shall see, he did not altogether escape insults based on the fact that he was a Jew.) Still, somewhere in his consciousness there must have been a sense of unease: Could a Jew feel really "at home" in a country as anti-Semitic as Austria? Arthur Schnitzler, himself a successful assimilated Jew, explored that question in his novel *The Road to the Open*, first published in 1908. One of the novel's Jewish characters, trying to explain to a Christian friend what it is like to be a Jew in Austria, asks him to imagine living as if one always has to find one's way about in an enemy country, ready for all the dangers and ambushes that lurk there. When an assimilated Jew says that he would never allow himself to be baptized, even if that made it possible to escape anti-Semitic bigotry, a Zionist asks: "But supposing the medieval stake were to be lit again?" The assimilated Jew says that in that case he would accept the Zionist's advice. "Oh," the Christian interjects, "those times will certainly not come again."

8

The Erotic Factor

AFTER DAVID RETURNS to Vienna the young couple, now openly engaged, see each other almost every day, and as a result the letters become less frequent. Among them, however, is one written near the end of April 1905 that begins with a recapitulation of difficulties that David and Amalie have had in their relationship. Most of these have already been mentioned, but there is one that is completely new: ". . . when we were already determined to belong to each other for life, then out of your relationship to your Lise, the counterpart to my Victor story, a factor suddenly emerged fit to build barriers between us."

"Lise" was Lise Tarlau, the author of the Zionist essay that David had disliked so much. Though only twenty-four, she had behaved scandalously by running off with a pianist. Brought back by her father, she was now married to a prosperous merchant. She was also an accomplished poet and writer. Her father, Joseph Bloch, was one of Vienna's most celebrated Jewish leaders, a rabbi in the largely working-class district of Floridsdorf, for a time the most prominent Jewish member of the Austrian parliament, an untiring opponent of anti-Semitism, and the founder of the leading Austrian Jewish weekly, in which his daughter's essay had appeared. If Amalie's relationship with Lise was the counterpart to David's relationship with Victor, and was a potential barrier between David and Amalie, then Amalie must have had some kind of romantic attachment to her—in addition to the attraction she appears to have felt for Martina. But if Martina was no

barrier to the relationship between David and Amalie, why should Lise
have been?

There is no further mention of Lise in the letters until, three months
later, David responds to a letter from Amalie telling him that Lise has sent
her a congratulatory letter on her engagement. But another letter, written
in November, shows that the news of Amalie's engagement to David did
not mean the end of the relationship between Amalie and Lise:

> Above all I want to say a word in response to your information about your
> Lise. Her jealousy is as understandable as it is psychologically interest-
> ing. She obviously feels the erotic factor in your relationship, and is now
> quite thoroughly jealous of the rival who seems to take a fair part of your
> inclination from her.

The next reference to Lise is the one already referred to, in February
1906, which discusses her conversion to Zionism. Then, in May 1906,
while David is away from Amalie doing his military service, Lise becomes
the subject of a long discussion, over three letters, that displays the interest
in human sexuality that was to lead David to Freud. The first of these letters
shows that Lise has written directly to David, though in a tone, he says, that
"still echoes softly of jealous resentment against the shameless robber of
her lover." But Amalie has also told David about conversations that she had
with Lise, and David says that the information she has provided "touches
on the deepest questions of my Eros-research. . . . For a verdict about love
within one sex, it is of the greatest importance how being loved is per-
ceived." But David has not been able to investigate this, because he lacks
the data. With respect to his own experience with Victor, "while really bad
misunderstandings ensured that Victor remained unsullied, he faced my
love with uncomprehending awkwardness." In contrast, Amalie's relationship with Lise is more open and carried on with greater self-understanding:
"You however can speak freely with Lise about your love . . . she finds it
quite natural, she strives to be loved by you, and is surprised only when you
give your love to a man." David finds it remarkable that "a fine lady of culture like Lise" chooses not to limit "the effect of her erotic allure, the light
and core of her being," to men, where it serves a reproductive purpose, but
makes herself attractive to "as many people as possible" and is thereby better able "to enjoy her own personality."

This leads David to ask Amalie for a fuller account of what Lise has told her. He speculates that whereas men appeal to men because of the similarity between the female body and the bodies of young men, women appeal to each other more directly, "because in a cultural world dominated by men, they are 'the beautiful sex.' " This explains, he thinks, "why women among themselves display so incomparably many more erotic relationships than do men."

The letter includes an explicit statement of what brought David and Amalie together:

> You say that, of that which first brought us together, you told Lise only that which concerns you alone. That is obviously the love that you felt for her. But how could you make it possible for her to understand that you became closer to me through that, if you did not also tell her that my erotic nature has developed in a parallel manner to yours?

At first Amalie rejects David's request for more details of her conversation with Lise. He repeats the request, asking her to "use your pen to tell me of your conversation with Lise and create a valuable piece for my and your study folder of human documents." To add weight to the request, he tells Amalie how, at twenty-five, he sees his life's task:

> For me there is really only one great secret, the secret of the human soul. To bring it to light, as far as my limited powers allow, is the work of my life. Ceaseless observation of my own soul, and untiring research into those of others, whether they lived thousands of years ago, or are my closest contemporaries, are the means that I use for this. My business is a holy one, and holy things, so an old sage teaches, may be shown only to holy people. But I regard as holy a weak human being who strives for a lofty goal.

David's quest for knowledge again overrides all the usual niceties, and his pleading is not in vain. On May 26, 1906, he writes that Amalie's "fine study" of Lise's nature serves as a basis for refuting the theory of sexuality put forward by Otto Weininger, a Viennese Jewish author who, at the age of twenty-three, published a book called *Sex and Character*. Just one year older than my grandfather, Weininger also studied at the University of Vienna and was attracted to his own sex. In *Sex and Character* he argues that all human beings include both male and female elements in their biological nature. Men who have a large female element, and women who have a large male element, are liable to be homosexual. Men may be biologically male but psychologically female, whereas all women are psychologically female. This claim serves as the basis for a sweeping attack on women as a whole. Women do not have free will, for they are possessed by their sexual organs, which seek union with the male. They are mothers or sluts, loving either the product of union with the male or the act of union itself. All of them share the "really and exclusively feminine" characteristic of matchmaking. The slut's desire for sex is only a special case of the general feminine desire "that sexual unions shall take place; the wish that as much of it as possible shall occur, in all cases, places and times." Since women live "unconsciously," not understanding their drives, they are naturally untruthful, and have no standards of right and wrong. They are simply not part of the ethical realm. They have no ego, no individuality, no character, and no soul.

Weininger attributes all that is wrong with the modern age to the feminine principle. Man must choose between the masculine and the feminine, and Weininger sees it as every man's duty to renounce the feminine. That is the only path to the highest human type, the genius, the human being furthest removed from the feminine. A man cannot love a woman without either knowing of her unworthiness, or deceiving himself about it. In the former case he will be unhappy, and in the latter he is immoral. That his suggestion would, if generally followed, lead to the extinction of the human race is a point that Weininger grants, but which he says "is of no interest whatever to reason," for "he who would perpetuate humanity would only perpetuate the problem and the guilt."

Another aspect of Weininger's bizarre theory was particularly potent in appealing to some readers. The Jew, he wrote, is so "saturated with femininity" that "the most manly Jew is more feminine than the least manly Aryan." Like the woman, the Jew has no ethical standards, and no soul. Like the woman, he represents a danger for all mankind.

Sex and Character received poor reviews and seemed destined for well-deserved oblivion until, in October 1903, Weininger went to the house in which Beethoven had died, pulled out a pistol, and shot himself. His dramatic death captured the public imagination. Here was a man who lived—

and died—what he wrote. As a Jew he was essentially feminine, and thus part of the negative force that stands in the way of all true greatness. So he had drawn the logical conclusion and removed himself from the world—in a place sacred to the memory of greatness. Two weeks after Weininger's death the Swedish playwright August Strindberg wrote in a Vienna newspaper that *Sex and Character* was "awe-inspiring" and had "probably solved the most difficult of all problems." The book began to attract attention, and was taken seriously by many thinkers, among them Ludwig Wittgenstein, another young Viennese man of Jewish origin with an attraction to his own sex. Of all the books Wittgenstein read during adolescence, Weininger's had the greatest and most lasting impact on his outlook.

David had met Weininger, and that, together with what he had heard about *Sex and Character*, was enough to arouse his strong antipathy. Weininger, he told Amalie, had selected from the whole range of feminine natures that which best fits his subjective negative value judgment of "the feminine," and then declared this to be what is essential to woman's nature. "It is the same method," David continues, "by which the race theorist constructs 'the German,' or 'the Jewish,' and Weininger too is a race theorist, and indeed anti-Semitic, despite being a Semite himself." Amalie's pen portrait of Lise helped David to refute Weininger because Lise was a "complete woman, no man masked as an anatomical-physiological woman" and yet was loved by women—who therefore were not seeking union with the male. "If women do not envy each other's greatest treasure, their womanly charms," David wrote, "then they will love one another for it. . . . That is my interpretation. It is surely more humane, and, I hope, truer than the Weiningerian mythology."

9

That New, Troublesome Highway

WHAT SORT OF a relationship could there be between a man and a woman who were each attracted to their own sex? From the letters it was clear why they became close friends; but on what basis did they *marry*? Was the marriage first intended merely as an intellectual companionship that would put a respectable face on David's and Amalie's lives, while allowing them to continue to pursue their own inclinations to be with members of their own sex? That was my initial thought as I read the letter in which David wishes Amalie "much pleasure" from her meeting with Martina, and hopes that the latter may "appear with the girdle of Aphrodite, so as to delight your heart with heightened gracefulness." This is not the language of a man who wants Amalie's erotic desire for himself. My interpretation seemed supported by David's rhapsody about being "raised on the wings of love" to "the eternal realm of thought." This strongly suggests an attraction that is intellectual, not physical.

As I read on, however, this interpretation of the relationship crumbled under the mounting evidence of something more than close friendship and intellectual synergy between David and Amalie. When visiting his parents to tell them of his engagement, David assures Amalie that his "intellectual perception of your womanly nature . . . will have—or actually already has—its certainly indispensable sensual correlate." This not entirely convincing declaration of physical desire is followed two weeks later by a more significant expression of passion. This letter uses another new salutation, "Dearest Melittion," which eventually becomes David's usual way of starting his letters to Amalie. David explains it the first time he uses it, saying that it is a "hellenized" version of her name, Amalie, which comes from the Greek word for honey, and he will call her that because

> does not sweet honey flow from your lips? True, by that I, the godless heathen, am not thinking at all of your enjoyable wise talk and poetic words, but on the contrary—however, I shall remain silent. . . . These things are better done than written about.

In July 1905 David is even more explicit, exclaiming how "unforgettably beautifully" Amalie has allowed him to enjoy the community of minds that he had hoped, in vain, to have with Victor, but in addition "you, darling girl . . . also let me taste the earthly blessing of the game of love, which I did not even dare to request from the masculine Eros."

I had been assuming that since the letters showed both David and Amalie to be homosexual, they were unlikely to be sexually interested in each other. I found a clue to my mistake in David Halperin's *One Hundred Years of Homosexuality, and Other Essays on Greek Love*. The "hundred years of homosexuality" to which the book's title refers is not a long-ago century in the heyday of Athens, but the century that separates me from David's letters. Halperin uses the love life of ancient Greece to argue that the concepts I was applying to my grandparents' sexuality are part of a cultural construct that sprang into existence only in the late nineteenth century, when the word *homosexual* first entered European languages through Krafft-Ebing's best-selling *Psychopathia Sexualis*. In ancient Greece an older man might have a kind of mentor relationship with a boy—generally one who had not yet developed a beard. The older man acted as a counselor and educator to the boy, and helped him to make the right social contacts by inviting him to dinners with friends. The man might also admire the beauty of the boy's body, and find him erotically arousing. If so, sexual contact could be part of the relationship, but it was not essential to it. If it did occur, the boy might masturbate the man, or the man might move his penis between the boy's legs until he reached orgasm. Anal penetration was something no respectable Greek man would do to his protégé, for it was looked upon as humiliating for a future free citizen. None of this made either the man or the boy a "homosexual." The man was probably married and had a sexual relationship with his wife. He might also have sex with prostitutes, or his slaves, of either sex. All of this would have been normal and socially acceptable. He would be very unlikely to have sexual relationships with men of his own age or older, and if he did, this would have exposed him to contempt and ridicule.

If this customary sexual contact between the older man and the boy does not allow us to typecast the older man as a homosexual, this is even more true of the boy. He was not expected to be erotically aroused by the older man, but to surrender to his advances because he admired the older man, was fond of him, and felt grateful for what he had done for him. This kind of relationship is not unique to ancient Greece. In the nineteenth century, ethnic Pashtuns serving in the British army in India sang odes telling of their longing for young boys. In Afghanistan such relationships were tolerated until the 1990s, when the Taliban's Ministry for the Suppression of Vice and the Promotion of Virtue suppressed them. In post-Taliban Afghanistan, the practice has revived. As with the ancient Greeks, boys are considered suitable objects of an older man's desires only up to the point at which their beards begin to grow—a fact recognized in a post-Taliban government edict barring "beardless boys" from police stations and military bases. Ahmed Fareed, a nineteen-year-old man, told a *New York Times* reporter how, when he was twelve, he was seduced by an older man. But in sharp contrast to the American men who around the same time were speaking out about being abused by Roman Catholic priests—some of whom evidently had a Greek, rather than Christian, view of what it is to be a boy's mentor—Fareed did not claim that he had been damaged by the relationship. In fact, he smilingly told the reporter, he was now looking for a young boy himself.

Amalie and David once had a disagreement over the merits of some contemporary poetry written by one of her friends. He explained his inability to appreciate it by saying: "I have a classical soul." If we use that sentence as a key to David's sexuality, many things fall into place. When David refers to Victor as *der Junge*, "the boy"—a term that conjured up alarming visions of child seduction—he was translating *pais*, the Greek term that was used for "child," for "young person," and for the junior partner in a homosexual relationship, regardless of actual age. That David wanted Victor as his *pais* is quite explicitly stated in the covering letter he sent Amalie with the correspondence he had had with Victor. David wanted Victor to ask him "how I really stood in regard to him," and if Victor had asked that, David "would then have explained to him the miracle of the Grail, that is the socratic-platonic Eros." But Victor never asked, and David missed his opportunity to explain what he was seeking, leaving Victor confused about David's intentions.

What would David have explained, if he had had the chance? I imagine him saying that he admires Victor's youthful beauty and finds it erotically appealing; but he is not expecting any physical consummation, nor that Victor will feel sexual desire for him. Instead, David would like Victor to regard him as his special friend and mentor, someone a little older, and more learned, someone who can assist him in the crucial years when he completes his studies and chooses a profession. David would have pointed out that—as he put it when writing about Victor to Amalie—"to find a person who understands you is of decisive significance," and that he, David, did possess the capacity to understand Victor. Perhaps he would have quoted from Plato's *Phaedrus*, to the effect that although the beloved may at first repel the lover, when once he has allowed himself to associate with the lover, he finds, in "the god-inspired friend," a kind of friendship that surpasses that of all his friends and relatives together. All of that would have been entirely within the bounds of what the Greeks regarded as correct pederasty, and it is also consistent with what we know of David's relationship with Victor. David's conception of sexuality probably was, like that of the Greeks, more fluid than ours, able to encompass attraction to both sexes without categorizing a person as either homosexual or heterosexual.

If there is a clear precedent in ancient Greece for the kind of relationship David sought to have with Victor, relationships between women, like Amalie's with Martina and Lise, are not so prominent in the classical texts. The most famous example is that of Sappho, the Greek poet of love between women who gave the name of her island, Lesbos, to female homosexuality. One of her poetic fragments suggests that a relationship between a woman and a girl is a transitional stage, a kind of sexual awakening before the girl is married. In the fragment the narrator, presumably Sappho herself, bids the girl not to be sad at the prospect of leaving her. She tells her to remember the happy times they have shared, and wishes her well. But women were not generally expected to take delight in younger girls, in the way that men were with boys, and the key role of the older man, in being a mentor to the boy, assisting in his education, and helping him to make the right social contacts, would have been seen as unnecessary for a girl, or as something that, to the limited extent it was desirable, her husband would do for her. If Amalie consciously drew on the male Greek model for her own relationships, it would have been in a spirit of self-conscious liberation from the conventions, both ancient and modern, of the inferior status of women.

———

WHEN DAVID AND AMALIE'S relationship takes its decisive turn in March 1905, he sends her a postcard addressing her as "Diotima" and referring to himself as "your Socratic friend." In Plato's *Symposium* a group of men, Socrates among them, are gathered at a symposium, basically a party for drinking and talking. The conversation is about the nature of eros, a term that in Greek can refer to any strong desire, but usually means sexual love. After listening to the views of others on the nature of eros, Socrates says that he too once held such views, but abandoned them after his beliefs were refuted by a prophetess, "Diotima, who was wise in this and many other things." Thus Socrates brings a woman's voice to an all-male gathering, and gives a woman's view of the nature of eros—one that Socrates accepts as correct.

In calling Amalie his Diotima, David is telling her that she is wise and knowledgeable, and that he hopes to learn from her the mysteries of eros that one cannot expect to learn from a man. But that is not all. Diotima's account of the nature of eros is a woman's view in one very specific way. She had asked Socrates what it is that is desired by the person who loves something beautiful. Socrates had answered: "To have it." Diotima was not satisfied with this answer, and told him that eros does not aim at possessing the beautiful. Instead, eros seeks birth and procreation in the beautiful. Even the sexual desire of a male for a male is, according to Diotima, a procreative desire, not literally but nevertheless a desire to produce something, and in particular to produce something beautiful or good, to mold the boy into a beautiful and good man. In Diotima's view sexual desire aims ultimately at something intellectual, the creation of a more virtuous and beautiful soul in the beloved. That view has been twisted into the popular idea that a "platonic" relationship is one without sexual contact—a misunderstanding of what Plato, through Diotima, was saying. In sharp contrast to later Christian ascetics who tried desperately to keep their mind on higher things, Diotima's understanding of eros accepts sexual desire, and does not oppose its physical gratification. She does, however, see the desire for the other's body as just one part of eros, and as a step toward something more important.

Diotima's view of eros fit well with the hopes that David and Amalie had of their union. As David wrote on April 27, 1905:

> . . . we are on a path that lies far, miles away, from that which "lovers" tread. That is straight, paved flat and smooth, and therefore even the blind god of love can lead the way down it. We however stride down that new, troublesome highway, of which my cousin wrote to us, which we ourselves must first pave, by working together, and which just for that reason will be entirely ours, and entirely ours together.

What was the new road that David and Amalie were working together to pave? To answer that question we should begin with David's veiled proposal expressing his interest in forming a lifelong union with a person "whose profession, so to speak, is to understand me." That is followed by a letter in which David tells Amalie that the foundation of his relationship with her is "the clear insight into the worth of your character." This is certainly a cooler evaluation of the beloved than one would expect from conventional lovers, but it needs to be read together with David's thoughts after reading *Lucile*, the novel that he felt applied to his own situation. From this letter I have already quoted the sentence in which David tells Amalie that she is no "cameo beauty." He continues:

> It was really a worrying experience to see how this noble man first became a close friend of the "ugly" Lucile, and then he began to love her with all his passionate desire, which he could not forget even in the arms of his splendidly beautiful wife. Here one can learn that for a truly finely sensitive man, who does not seek in the union with his wife the most fleeting sensual intoxication, the erotic ideal is to be found not in an aesthetic standard idea of beauty, but in the form of a distinctive character.

David would have seen himself as just such a "finely sensitive man." He was telling Amalie that though her appearance did not arouse his desire, his appreciation of her character was having that effect.

Central to David's love for Amalie is the clear sense throughout the letters that he regards her as his intellectual equal, if not superior. Indeed she probably was his superior. He was a very good student, but she was nominated by the University of Vienna to graduate "under the auspices of the Emperor," the highest possible honor the university could bestow. Candidates graduating in this manner received a diamond ring engraved with the emperor's initials. But no woman had ever previously been nominated for such an honor, and the emperor refused to bestow the award upon a person of her sex. David wrote Amalie a consoling letter about the inability of those who guide the ship of state to see ahead. Hence another aspect of the new road that David and Amalie were trying to pave was equality between the sexes. "We want to remain," David writes, "self-sufficient personalities even in the union. Precisely by means of the union we seek to achieve the highest possible unfolding of our most individual self."

The idea that a woman should preserve her independence in marriage was, in 1905, most unusual. Nor is it easy, even today, to remain fully independent with respect to one's career, and yet committed to a relationship with another, equally independent person. David's plan to marry Amalie shaped his future, leading him to become a schoolteacher rather than take up an academic career, which would have meant years as a *Privatdozent*, a university lecturer without a chair, waiting until he might be eligible for such an appointment. Such a post offers an existence so economically precarious that it is difficult to set up one's own household. Nevertheless, David was only twenty-four, and if he had not been in a hurry to marry, he could have become a *Dozent* and hoped that a chair would eventually come his way. He refers to this, after the decision has been made, as a time "when I believed I had to choose between . . . my academic career and my girl." He then goes on to say: "Now I know, of course, that there was really no choice at all, that a simple feeling of cleanliness forbade entering into this academic swamp. Croaking, blown-up frog-spirits like Chatterhand [a nickname for one of his professors] find themselves in their element there." But in a later letter, David admits that there is an element of sour grapes in this comment, and entertains the thought that after working diligently as a schoolteacher for twenty years, it would be nice to spend the rest of his years "in a comfortable academic throne." Subsequently David declined a stipend that would have enabled him to undertake a research trip to Greece. His reason for turning this down was that it would have delayed by a year his appointment to a teaching position. His professor was baffled by the decision, and it is easy to imagine how much a trip to his beloved Greece, and a chance to do research there, would have meant to David at this stage of his life. The prospect of life with Amalie must have meant still more.

Amalie had her own hard choice to make. In September 1905, when David was about to begin a year of military service in Brünn, Amalie had plans to spend the year studying in Berlin. The attraction of Berlin for a brilliant young student of mathematics and physics is obvious. Max Planck was then professor of physics at the University of Berlin. Five years earlier he had founded quantum theory with the discovery of "Planck's constant," for which he was later to win the Nobel Prize. Now he was the first prominent scientist to recognize the importance of Einstein's special theory of relativity, published in that very year, 1905. Later Einstein himself was to go to Berlin. What my grandmother's career might have been if she had carried out her Berlin plans is a matter of speculation, but the possibilities are shown by the career of Lise Meitner, one of the handful of women doing physics at the University of Vienna when Amalie was there, and someone she must have known personally. Meitner, who was born in the same year as Amalie, obtained her doctorate in physics from the University of Vienna in 1906, and did go to Berlin to study under Max Planck. Like Amalie, she planned to go for only a year. She ended up staying for thirty years and becoming head of a section of the Kaiser Wilhelm Institute for Chemistry. In 1938 the Nazis forced her to leave (though a Protestant, she was of Jewish—indeed like Amalie, Moravian Jewish—descent). Working with Otto Hahn, she played a major role in the discovery of nuclear fission and made several other important discoveries, becoming the first woman to receive the prestigious Fermi Award (though many thought she should have shared the Nobel that was given to Hahn). This was the career Amalie might have had. One of David's letters makes it clear why she did not. When he cannot get leave from his military service to go to Vienna over Christmas, he writes to Amalie asking her to come to Brünn, and says: "I also want to remind you that in the autumn you gave up Berlin, in order to be able to hurry to me, whenever it was right to do so." It was to remain close to David that Amalie gave up her prospects of a dazzling scientific career. (To complete the symmetry of these two gifted women science graduates of the University of Vienna, Meitner might have given up what Amalie gained. She never married, and her biographer found no evidence that she was ever involved in a romantic relationship.)

The "new, troublesome highway" that David and Amalie had to pave and then follow might have been their conception of a marriage between equal, independent beings. But there was something else that was novel in their relationship, something that still today is a rocky road rather than a paved highway. Though the letters show that David and Amalie's relationship developed to include "the earthly blessing of the game of love," they also provide evidence that they continued to respect each other's independence not only in respect of intellectual or professional matters, but also in the realm of love. In October 1905, when they have been engaged for more than six months and David is doing his military service, he writes:

> . . . what you write about Martina really was of great interest to me. Your relationship with this magnificent girl is realizing, in its constant development, the dream of love that I dreamed, for such a long time, and with such longing, and so in vain.

For his part, David does not appear to form any new relationship to replace that which he had with Victor, though in one letter he jokes about falling in love with the "unattainably distant" captain of his regiment.

If David and Amalie's relationship left each of them open to same-sex romances, this would indeed justify his statement that they were taking a road very different from that which conventional lovers tread. But I think it was also different from what such a relationship might be like today, in that the extramarital romances seem not to have involved sexual contact. I draw that conclusion in part from what David wrote about his relationship with Victor, and the discussion between David and Amalie of Otto Soyka's conduct, but also from what David says to Amalie about the marriage of his uncle, David Kaufmann, a professor of biblical studies in Budapest, and a scholar whom he greatly admired. In August 1905 Amalie sent David an obituary of his late aunt, Inna Kaufmann, David Kaufmann's wife. In response David tells Amalie that his uncle, who died before his aunt, did not make full use of his great talents. He raises the question of whether if he had been married to a different woman, he might have fulfilled his potential. Shortly after David Kaufmann married Inna, David has heard, he met a very talented young woman, and they were very much interested in each other. They corresponded a lot, but nothing happened between them. Inna is said to have offered to set David free, but by that time the young woman had decided to marry someone else. David then comments that this story shows that fact is richer than fiction. People who get their knowledge from novels believe that everything begins with the act that is legally recognized as "infidelity." Then David adds a comment about Sappho, saying that those same novel readers cannot imagine how she could love her girls passionately without desiring physical intimacy with them. He adds:

> Granted, we know better about all that. We also understand what to others must be the most incomprehensible of all, how this same Sappho, who loved her girls with manly ardor, could nevertheless strike up a jubilant wedding song when the time came to accompany one of her darlings to the bridal chamber.

Here there is a gap between myself and my grandfather that my imagination cannot bridge. I am one of those "others" David is talking about. I can imagine that Sappho could love her girls "with manly ardor" without any sexual contact taking place between them; but I cannot imagine Sappho not *desiring* such contact, at least not once she has passed beyond a naive innocence about such possibilities. And I do, as my grandfather suggests such people will, find it most incomprehensible of all that Sappho could be genuinely jubilant about the marriage of someone she loved so passionately. Since David and Amalie could understand this, and might have felt the same way about each other, there is something in their relationship that remains mysterious to me.

10

Marriage

DAVID AND AMALIE were married on December 26, 1906. Neither a certificate of marriage nor any letters from the months before or after that date have survived. The sole item I have from the wedding is a piece of white card, about the size of a modern greeting card. The front has a decorative gold border, surmounted by a wreath. Inside the border, hand-lettered in black ink, is:

> *To his dear*
> *friends*
> *Amalie and David*
> *on*
> *26 December 1906*
> *Berthold*

This must be David's cousin Berthold Jellinek, who had told David and Amalie that they were going down a "new, troublesome highway" that they had to pave together. On the back of the card he has written:

> *Before my eyes today you travel, as if*
> *From your distant realms and from distant paths*
> *Down to the solid place of everyday life,*
> *To stride through the venerable old gateway,*

To endow with new nobility, and special sacredness
The well-trodden way.

I know nothing else about the wedding except that the newlyweds went to Venice for their honeymoon and stayed at the Hotel Danielli. Then, as now, one of Venice's most famous hotels, the Danielli occupies a palace built by the doge, Venice's head of government, at the end of the four-teenth century, when the city-state was at the height of its power and prosperity.

11

Venetian Reflections

November 26, 1998

IN THE JOINT CAUSE of historical research and the celebration of our thirtieth wedding anniversary, Renata and I are in Venice. We walk through the lavishly decorated Venetian Gothic foyer of the Hotel Danielli, its ceiling supported by marble columns. Amid this splendor it is easy to push time away, and imagine my newlywed grandparents passing through this foyer, and up the grand staircase that led them to their room, and their nuptial bed.

David had been to Venice before, but Amalie apparently had not. In 1905 David sent her two small pictures that he had bought in Venice the previous year. One was of the much-photographed Bridge of Sighs, which links the fanciful pink-and-white-checked facade of the Doges' Palace to the grim prison of the Bargello. The other was of the Church of San Giorgio, which he described as "Palladio's high temple," for it is one of the masterpieces of the sixteenth-century architect Andrea Palladio. On leaving the Danielli through its Gothic main doorway, we look straight across the water at San Giorgio, glowing in the wintry afternoon sun reflected off the pale green-blue water. Palladio's perfectly proportioned columns and architraves, based on the architectural principles of classical antiquity, appealed to my grandfather's "classical soul."

My grandparents would have walked, as we walk, down the quay from the Danielli, past the Bargello and the Bridge of Sighs, and then along-side the Doges' Palace. Where the Grand Canal widens and enters the la-goon, the gondoliers moor, and encourage the tourists into their delicate craft. What an experience this city of water, light, and ancient buildings must have been for Amalie! She would have known Venice only from black-and-white photographs, and from paintings, especially those by Canaletto in the Imperial and Royal Museum of Art History, in Vienna. Now she could see it all for herself. It is still a breathtaking experience, surely the most beautiful city in the world. For David, though not so new, Venice must have been full of wonders at every turn. It was evocative, not only of a long-distant past, but also of his favorite German writer, Goethe, who wrote his *Venetian Epigrams*—short verses about life, love, and the transience of both—here. David had told Amalie that one day they would read them together, on the spot where they were written, so it is easy to imagine him, at the start of this momentous stage of his life, seeing the gon-dolas on the Grand Canal and recalling Goethe's lines:

> *This gondola I liken to a gently swinging cradle,*
> *And the small box on it seems a spacious coffin.*
> *Rightly so! Between the cradle and the coffin we sway and float*
> *On the Grand Canal, without a care, through life.*

From the edge of the Grand Canal, the Piazza San Marco beckons. In the last three centuries, only Napoleon has dared to tamper with one of the finest squares in Europe, so my grandparents saw it much as it is now. Still following in their imagined footsteps, we visit San Marco to see its glorious mosaics and jeweled golden screens. They could not have failed to admire the four magnificent bronze horses, ancient works made by an unknown artist in antiquity. When David and Amalie were there, the originals were outside, over the entrance to the cathedral. Now, to prevent deterioration due to polluted air, the horses outside are copies, but the originals are still on view inside. Perhaps afterward they strolled across the square, as we did, to drink a leisurely cup of coffee at the Café Florian, marvel at the paradox-ical way in which they had come together, and wonder about the future they would share.

What is the best basis for a good marriage? A thirtieth anniversary seemed a good time for reflection on that issue. If I try to raise this topic with friends, many of them refuse to contemplate anything except love. Nor are they willing to analyze this notion of love. "Could you imagine," I ask them, "loving one person while finding another more attractive sexually?" They squirm uncomfortably and usually don't give a straight answer. Sometimes it seems as if they are fearful that acknowledging that their partner is not, for them, the most physically attractive person in the world would endanger the marriage. How widespread, I wonder, is the attitude represented by the advice a friend gives to Richard Tull, the central character in Martin Amis's novel *The Information*: "Marry your sexual obsession. Marry the one who made you hardest. Marry *her*." Is that more in keeping with the way people contemplating marriage think today than: "Marry the one whose intellect and character you most admire"?

If sexual attractiveness is so central to people's idea of the person they want to marry, this is a relatively new, and culturally specific, idea. David's classical training always gave him a broader view. He would, for example, have been familiar with Xenophon's *Oeconomicus*, in which the well-respected Ischomachos tells Socrates that soon after he was married, he asked his wife: "Tell me, woman, have you thought yet why it was that I took you and your parents gave you to me?" And he adds: "That it was not for want of someone else to spend the night with—this is obvious, I know, to you too." Ischomachos then answers his own question: he chose his wife "as the best partner for the household and children." David's initial letter about marriage shows that he too was not simply seeking "someone to spend the night with," but a partner who would, through her knowledge of his character, be a source of good counsel and support.

When my grandparents married, arranged marriages were still common in many Jewish (and some non-Jewish) communities in Eastern Europe, including parts of Austria-Hungary. Even among the more modern Jews of Moravia, if Amalie and David had lived one or two generations earlier they would probably have had little choice about whom they were to marry. Matchmakers brought the young couple together, with a chaperon of course, and they spoke only a few words to each other before they were married. Before marriage there was often neither love nor an appreciation of the worth of the other's character. With luck, one or both of those would come afterward. Though my grandparents chose each other, their relationship shared something with the tradition of arranged marriages: the idea that romantic love is not the key to a good marriage. Whether this was because romantic love for a member of the opposite sex did not come naturally to David and Amalie, or because of a more philosophical view of the nature of love, I do not know. What is clear is that my grandfather married a woman to whom he had come for advice and understanding. He had admired her before he knew her well, but even after they had decided to marry, he did not think her beautiful. Instead, his "clear insight into the worth of [Amalie's] character" formed the basis for his decision to spend his life with her, and the passion came later. It turned out to be "an exemplary marriage. A wonderful marriage." That is how Hilde Koplenig, whose father was David's first cousin, described it. Everyone else who knew them agreed.

Can I say the same of my own marriage? Not exemplary, perhaps, but wonderful in its own way. It began quite differently from that of my grandparents. Renata and I were in bed together before we had time to gain much insight into the worth of each other's character. But that is a superficial difference, an indication of how much more casual we were about sex in the 1960s than in the 1900s. Sex did not indicate a long-term commitment, and in forming a serious relationship with Renata, my attitude was not so different from that of my grandfather. There were other women I found no less sexually attractive, but Renata, like Amalie for David, was someone whose character and wisdom I admired, with whom I felt I could have a lifelong conversation that would not become dull, and with whom I could see myself traveling together down "life's troublesome highway."

So "marry the one who makes you hardest" wasn't the basis for either my grandparents' marriage or my own. Of course, a good marriage needs love, and that goes far beyond admiration of intellect and character, or a sense that someone will make a good companion. Nevertheless, as David was saying when he told Amalie about *Lucile,* if admiration of intellect and character comes first, love can follow, and passion too. It doesn't work the other way around. Will the one who makes you hardest today still be the one who makes you hardest ten, twenty, or thirty years later? I can't imagine being married to one woman for ten years—let alone thirty—and *not* sometimes finding other women more sexually exciting. So if you go into the marriage on the basis that *this* woman is the one who attracts you most, what happens when that is no longer true? Do you end the marriage? Is that why so many people of my age are now onto their second or third marriages? That may not be a bad thing, but it is a different ideal of marriage. If what binds a couple together is their passion for each other's body, then it is not possible for them to say, as David said to Amalie: "What binds us pushes time away."

||| PART III |||

In Freud's Circle

12

An Invitation from Freud

IN THE WINTER OF 1906–7, David's quest for the secret of the human soul took him, on Saturday evenings, to the psychiatric section of Vienna's General Hospital. There he joined seven other people, sitting in an almost empty lecture theater, listening to Sigmund Freud give a series of lectures entitled "Introduction to Psychoanalysis." Today it seems extraordinary that Freud should draw so small an audience, especially since he was already a controversial figure. A year earlier he had published *Three Essays on the Theory of Sexuality*—a book that, in the words of his biographer Ernest Jones, "brought down on him more odium than any other of his writings." The odium had not, however, brought him a large following. His pioneering work, *The Interpretation of Dreams*, had been published in 1900 in an edition of only six hundred copies, and took eight years to sell out.

Hanns Sachs, one of the eight attendees, has left an account of Freud's lectures:

> [Freud] wore a short dark-brown beard, was slender and of medium size. He had deep-set and piercing eyes and a finely shaped forehead, remarkably high at the temples. Pointing to a row of eight or ten chairs which stood in a semicircle in front of the benches, close to the table of the lecturer where a few people were already sitting, he said in the politest way: "Won't you come nearer and be seated, gentlemen?" . . . The chairs had been placed in front of the empty benches because Freud disliked to strain his voice . . . the atmo-

sphere was intimate and informal. . . . All the topics and problems of psycho-analysis which existed then or were just in the process of development were discussed. Dream-interpretation, the unconscious and repression, the structure of neurosis were, of course, the favourite subjects. But the many new vistas opening before our eyes, the unexhausted possibilities for new fields, and the new methods of exploration in almost every branch of science added a great deal to the absorbing interest of those hours.

My newly married grandfather was a probationary teacher in Vienna. His supervisor's report says that his well-prepared lessons were received with "attention, understanding and interest" and that his ability to keep order and discipline in the classroom was "satisfactory." After his probationary year he was sent to the high school in Nikolsburg, a small town in Moravia between Vienna and Brünn where more than two hundred years earlier his ancestor Rabbi David Oppenheim had been a rabbi before being called to a more significant position in Prague. In Nikolsburg, on December 12, 1907, my mother was born. David's parents had asked that if the child was a girl she be named after David's deceased older sister, Cornelia. David agreed, but changed "Cornelia" into "Kora," which came from *kore*, the ancient Greek word for "girl." Then he gave her as a second name, the Latin word for "reborn," Renata. My mother's names showed her father's love of the ancients.

While teaching in Nikolsburg, David published his first scholarly work, an article on a work by the Roman poet Tibullus. In the passage David discusses, Tibullus presents himself as a lover who has, in a fit of anger, broken up with his beloved, but now wants her back. Unfortunately, an evil procuress has alienated her affections, and led her to a wealthy rival. The poet therefore pronounces a long curse on the procuress, and David seeks to explain the nature of this curse. He is able to do so, he tells the reader, because he has been investigating ritual nudity, and this in turn has led him to research ancient cults and forms of magic, which are invoked in the curse. The essay shows David's interest in the pervasive influence of sexual themes in mythology and literature.

The young family did not stay long in Nikolsburg. In 1909 David was appointed to the position of teacher of classical languages at the Akademisches Gymnasium, or Academic High School, in Vienna's historic First District. The appointment brought David and Amalie back from the provinces to the capital of the empire, and to the flagship of its state education system, intended for those who were academically inclined. Among the Akademisches Gymnasium's graduates were many of Vienna's current and future cultural celebrities, including the writers Hugo von Hofmannsthal and Arthur Schnitzler, the philosopher of law Hans Kelsen, the economist Ludwig von Mises, the physicist Erwin Schrödinger, and the future Czech leader Tomáš Masaryk. It was a plum appointment for a young teacher, and David could look forward to a promising future.

When David and Amalie returned to Vienna they could not have guessed that seven centuries of the Hapsburg monarchy were drawing to a close. The empire was at peace, and had been for decades. It seemed solidly based on the rule of law. It had a free, and lively, press, and was slowly becoming more democratic. The 1907 elections for the imperial parliament introduced a major new reform: all adult males were able to vote. The broader suffrage brought large gains to the Social Democrats and the Christian Socialists, while the German nationalists had their representation slashed. The empire's predominantly German-speaking ruling circles had made important concessions on the use of national languages. Granted, there was still ethnic tension in Bohemia, where a dispute between Czech and German members of the provincial parliament had led to flying ink bottles and the overturning of tables. That had sparked anti-German riots in Prague, and a brief period of martial law. But everyone expected that such ethnic problems would be overcome by reasonable reforms. Now, for all the nationalities of the empire, there seemed to be opportunities for both material and moral progress.

The most serious discord to this generally contented symphony came from the southeastern provinces of the empire. In 1878, as part of the settlement of a dispute between Russia and the declining Ottoman Empire, Austria-Hungary was given, without going to war at all, the right to occupy the province of Bosnia-Herzegovina. That region had—as it still has—a mixed population of Muslims and Orthodox Serbs. Though administered by Austria-Hungary, for thirty years the province remained in name part of the Ottoman Empire. Serbia opposed the occupation, for it was hoping to unite all the southern Slavs into a Greater Serbia. Its hostility, and that of Bosnian Serb nationalists, increased when, to mark the sixtieth year of the reign of Emperor Franz Josef, in 1908, the Austro-Hungarian government decided to annex Bosnia-Herzegovina and declare it part of Austria-

Hungary. There were also international protests about this unilateral breach of an international treaty, but in Austria-Hungary itself the move was welcomed, even by the liberal press. After all, what difference was there, in practice, between occupation and annexation? Most people thought that both the nationalist and the international opposition would soon fade away.

Whatever David might have thought about these matters, he had no real involvement in them. In Austro-Hungarian politics there was little room for people such as him. Around the time when he was born, the previously dominant liberals, whose universal-enlightenment values and belief in equal civil rights for all he would have shared, had been heavily defeated. They never recovered; instead, their place had been taken by German nationalists and the Christian Socialists, both of which were openly anti-Semitic. Of the major political parties, only the Social Democrats welcomed Jews, and David was no socialist. In any case, he was more interested in the intellectual opportunities that the city offered—and particularly in pursuing his quest to understand the secrets of human behavior and character.

Soon after taking up his new appointment in Vienna, David sent Freud a copy of a paper he had written, presumably the one on Tibullus, with a dedication expressing his appreciation of Freud's work. Freud replied, thanking David for the paper, which he says made him regret "that my knowledge of the ancients has grown so little since my time at high school." He then makes a suggestion that David must have been excited to read:

> For a long time I have been troubled by the idea that our studies on the content of neuroses could be drawn upon to explain the riddle of the way in which myths form, and that the nucleus of mythology is nothing other than what we speak of as "the nuclear complex of the neuroses"—which I was able to make clear recently in the analysis of the phobia of a five-year-old boy. Two of my pupils, Abraham in Berlin and O. Rank in Vienna, have dared to attempt to invade the region of mythology, and there, with the help of the psychoanalytical technique and its point of view, to make conquests. But we are amateurs and have every reason to fear errors. We don't have the tools. The confidence with the materials. Thus we are looking for a researcher who has developed from the opposite direction, who possesses the knowledge of the field, and wants to apply to it our psychoanalytical equipment, which we will gladly make

available to him—a native researcher, that is to say, who will be able to achieve something quite different from intruders who do not know their way around the place.

Would you like to be this man we are seeking? What do you know of psychoanalysis? And do you have the spare time and inclination to go into it further for these ends?

David responded positively and went to see Freud. In a letter written on November 11 to his close colleague Carl Jung, Freud refers to the meeting:

Chance recently led me to a clever high school teacher who is working on mythology with similar ideas, but fully equipped . . . decidedly intelligent, only so far he gives me the impression that he isn't really adept at taking on something that has up to now been foreign to him. At our first meeting I found out from him that Oedipus may have been originally a phallic demon, like the Idean Dactyls (!), the name means simply erection. Further, that the hearth is a symbol for the womb, because the ancients saw the flame as a phallus. The Vestal Virgins were like nuns, married to this hearth-phallus, and so on.

Freud invited David to join the "Wednesday Group," a group of about fifteen people who met on Wednesday evenings in Freud's apartment at 19 Berggasse. The minutes of the group show that Freud formally proposed David for membership on January 12, 1910. His name first appears among those attending on January 26. From then on he was a regular participant, attending thirty-nine meetings between January 1910 and October 1911. The group consisted largely of senior medical doctors of Jewish descent, and until April 1910, entirely of men. Freud, of course, was its center. His stature in the world had improved a little since the storm that had greeted the publication of his *Three Essays on the Theory of Sexuality* five years earlier. He had gained his first foreign—and non-Jewish—adherents, led by Carl Jung at the Psychiatric Clinic in Zurich. A journal devoted to psychoanalysis had been launched. In 1909 he had visited the United States to give a series of lectures at Clark University, from which he had received an honorary doctorate. Nevertheless, outside the small circle of his followers, Freud's claim that small children have sexual desires directed at their parents still provoked outrage. At the Congress of German Neurologists and Psychiatrists held in Hamburg in 1910, one professor reacted to the mention of Freud's theories by banging his fist on the table and shouting: "This is not a topic for discussion at a scientific meeting: it is a matter for the police."

After Freud, the most significant figure in the Viennese circle was Alfred Adler, a forty-year-old family doctor who three years earlier had published his *Study of Organ Inferiority*, a book about the ways in which a sense of physical inferiority can affect a person's psychology. Adler's own appearance could have served as a basis for such a study: in contrast to Freud's sternly elegant countenance, Adler had a puffy round face and piggy eyes; yet there was an intellectual energy about him that more than made up for this. David was among the youngest of the group. Otto Rank, who took the minutes, was the only member younger than David, while one other regular member of the group, Carl Furtmüller, was about the same age and, like my grandfather, was not a medical doctor but a teacher. The other non–medically trained member of the group was a former judge, Viktor Tausk.

At David's first meeting Eduard Hitschmann presented the case of a young male with anxiety problems traceable to his guilt about masturbation. The discussion that ensued must have showed my grandfather that this was not a forum for the thin-skinned. Paul Federn opened it by commenting that such cases "are already familiar to us and do not have anything essentially new to offer." Rudolf Reitler thought the case had been "rather superficially analyzed." My grandfather's first contribution is recorded as follows:

> OPPENHEIM can confirm Reitler's statement that a cursing of the penis (death-wish) is not alien to the popular mind. The sexual interpretation of forests and meadows in dreams has its analogy in Greek mythology, where the birth-goddess Artemis was worshipped on meadows. The sexual use of the key that opens closed doors is familar from the Bible. The South Slav symbolism of the penis as a bald head may be linked to dreams of decapitation.

The comment is typical of many David was to make at these meetings. He justifies the sexual interpretation of dreams or other phenomena by drawing on his knowledge of ancient Greece, of the Bible, and of folk traditions, where sexual symbolism is more readily apparent. Some of these suggestions are illuminating, while others read like comic parodies of

Freudian psychoanalysis in which everything takes on a sexual significance of some kind.

Only Freud and Adler went out of their way to say something positive about Hitschmann's paper, but their comments were also directed toward more significant targets. Adler stressed Hitschmann's diligence and honest work, and said that the shortcomings of his analysis were the shortcomings of all analyses, namely a failure to show what really lies behind neurosis. Freud praised the paper for the "correctness of the observations" before going on to criticize Federn and Adler for failing to appreciate that all neurotic phenomena are of sexual origin, and dismissing Adler's search for the roots of neurosis as a question "we take to be settled." From this exchange David might have gathered that he had joined the Wednesday Group at a time when differences between Freud and Adler were simmering just beneath the surface. The issue between them went to the heart of what psychoanalysis was about. Does it all, in the end, come down to unconscious sexual desires? Was the sexual origin of neurosis and other forms of mental illness to be taken as "settled"? Or could one consider other possibilities? But beyond this difference in explaining neurosis, there was also a question of how discussion in psychoanalysis was to proceed. Although Freud was clearly the founding figure in the discovery of the unconscious, the whole terrain was still unexplored, and it was by no means predetermined that Freud's own theories would prove to be the right ones. On the contrary, the field seemed ripe for those involved to put forward rival theories that would be judged on the basis of their ability to account for the evidence. If the differences between Freud and Adler had been tested and resolved in this kind of atmosphere of open scientific inquiry, the future of psychoanalysis would have been very different—and so, perhaps, would David's future as well.

In February Adler gave a paper on "Psychic Hermaphroditism"—that is, on people having both masculine and feminine traits—and immediately David found himself drawn into the dispute between Adler and Freud. Adler argued that the disposition to neurosis lies not in unconscious sexual desires, but in "the feeling of inferiority, the fear of being slighted." All of us have both masculine and feminine character traits, but we see the masculine as ideal and the feminine as inferior. The neurotic male seeks to repress his feminine side. The neurosis then arises from "the battle between the feminine foundation and the masculine protest." The minutes record David's comment:

OPPENHEIM wants to content himself with referring back to Tausk's question of what, in a psychological sense, is masculine and what is feminine. One can conceive of the masculine and the feminine only in an anatomical sense; their transposition into the psychological world is difficult. He would doubt that it is a scientific concept rather than a historical one, based on value judgments.

When Freud spoke, he remarked on this:

It is noteworthy that three speakers who were actually not psychoanalytically oriented—Tausk, Oppenheim and Furtmüller—placed their emphasis on what is decisive: that in the area of psychology we do not know what we should call masculine and what feminine . . . the concepts of "masculine" and "feminine" are of no use in psychology and we do better, in view of the findings of the psychology of the neuroses, to employ the concepts of libido and repression. Whatever is of the libido has a masculine character, and whatever is repression is of a feminine character. Psychologically, we can present only the character of activity and passivity.

Freud's remarks are concerned to show the differences between his own position and Adler's. His positive reference to Tausk, Oppenheim, and Furtmüller seems intended to suggest that they take his side, rather than that of Adler. But when Freud immediately goes on to identify the libido with the masculine, and the repressive with the feminine, he misses the point that David was making, for he is continuing to use "masculine" and "feminine" in a psychological sense, rather than an anatomical one, and has provided no scientific grounds for associating repression with the feminine, or libido with the masculine. David was questioning the whole basis for such "scientific" characterizations of what is "essentially feminine" or "essentially masculine," claiming, as he had done four years earlier in his letter to Amalie about Weininger, that they are merely disguised value judgments. Yet on this occasion David said no more.

At a meeting on March 16, 1910, David raised the issue of suicide in high school students, then a heated topic because a high school student from a high-ranking Viennese family had recently committed suicide after receiving a bad school report. This led to a press campaign against Vienna's high school teachers, accusing them of causing suicides by their excessively strict discipline and demanding examinations. Wilhelm Stekel proposed that a particular evening should be set aside for the discussion of suicide, especially that of young people, and this led, a month later, to David's presentation on this topic on his twenty-ninth birthday.

In response to the press accusations of excessive discipline, my grandfather argues that the suicide of children occurs in many different countries, and has done so for many centuries. The puzzle he presents to Freud and his circle, however, is how the strongest human instinct—self-preservation—can be overridden. Reporting on cases in which teenagers committed suicide after the death of the opposite-sex parent, David says that from the standpoint of Freudian psychology, one must suspect that teenagers experience erotic conflict, in the love of a girl for her father and of a boy for his mother. This makes it possible to understand how the child's desire to live is overpowered by the "biologically equivalent" sexual desire. But, David adds, not all cases of teenage suicide have such conveniently Freudian explanations, and he offers as an example a case in which a child heard of someone else committing suicide, and was thereby led to imitate the deed. This leads him back to his original target, "the new despot in the realm of the spirit, the press." He then goes on to accuse the press of sensationalism and hypocrisy, reporting each new child suicide with a great show of grief and accusing the child's teachers of having "murdered" the victim—while the publicity the press gives to these events actually leads more children to commit copycat suicides. That, of course, gives the press new material for more sensational reports, and so the story feeds on itself.

Then David comes to the problem that, he says, "concerns my own life so painfully." He poses the question whether conditions in the schools, such as strict discipline or the pressure of exams, drive schoolchildren into suicide. His answer is that they do not, and to prove his point he quotes statistics showing that the proportion of children committing suicide is no higher among those attending high school than among children of the same age who do not attend high school. He defends firm school discipline, saying that secondary school "would fail in its highest purpose, that of being a preparation for life, if it did not have in itself a part of this life, of this hard life with its constant struggles, its heavy defeats, and its hard-won victories."

After David's talk the group took its customary fifteen-minute break. Martha, Freud's wife, entered with cake and black coffee, and then the discussion began. Freud expressed his appreciation of the paper, but he disagreed with David on what schools should be like. They should not, he said, be like life, with all its harshness. Children are not mature individuals, and the school should serve to ease the transition they must make between the parental home and the harsh reality of life.

This led Freud to make a striking comment on homosexuality in school-teachers:

> Teachers concern themselves too little with the question of the child's sexuality. . . . The reason why so few teachers nowadays are adequate to this task . . . is connected with the growing proscription of homosexuality in our time. In suppressing the practice of homosexuality, one has simply also suppressed the homosexual direction of human feelings that is so necessary for our society. The best teachers are the real homosexuals, who actually have that attitude of benevolent superiority toward their pupils. If, however, a teacher with suppressed homosexuality comes face to face with this demand, he becomes sadistic toward the boys; these teachers hate and persecute the children because they make those "sexual demands," thereby irritating the teachers' sexuality. Just as the homosexuals are the best teachers, so the repressed homosexuals are the worst, and the strictest.

After this there was time for only a few brief comments before Adler proposed that, in view of the late hour, the discussion should be adjourned to the next meeting, and raised the question "whether the valuable suggestions and conclusions of this discussion should not, under the direction of a committee, be published as a pamphlet." This suggestion was carried. At the meeting on May 4 it was resolved that my grandfather should write an introductory chapter specifically about the suicide of students. According to the minutes, he expressed some doubts, "but finally declares his willingness, with the proviso that he might possibly write under a nom de plume."

On Suicide, in Particular Student-Suicide appeared before the end of the year. David's introductory chapter is a substantially revised version of his presentation to the Wednesday Group. The new material includes an attack on school reformers, who think that the schools must change to fit their students, including the less capable ones. If this happens, he writes, "our students may still kill themselves, since their concerns are not limited to school. What is certain, however, is that the intellectual life of the people will have been killed." David then suggests that "without destroying the forms of schooling that have been handed down to us" we may be able to institute some general rules to guard against the suicide of students, and suggests some practical ideas to this effect. These suggestions, though made in Austria-Hungary in 1910 rather than the United States at the start of the twenty-first century, have a familiar ring: they include better communication between the parents and the school, and making it more difficult for students to get hold of guns. Freud's commentary repeats some of the remarks he made in the discussion of David's paper in the Wednesday Group, but omits any mention of homosexuality. Then come essays by Adler, Furtmüller, and other members of the group, and some "Concluding Remarks" by Freud.

As David had foreshadowed during the discussion of plans for this publication, his essay appears under a pseudonym: "Unus multorum," Latin for "one of the multitude." The phrase comes from a passage in Horace that reads:

> "Today is the thirtieth—the Sabbath, you know.
> Do you want to affront the circumcised Jews?"
>
> "I have no religious objections."
>
> "But I have. I'm a somewhat weaker brother—one of the multitude."

Was David indicating that he was just an ordinary person, one of the "silent majority"? Or, since he must have known the source, was he describing himself as "a somewhat weaker brother" of the observant Jews? Dr. Erwin Ringel, one of David's pupils and later a personal friend, considers both the use of a pseudonym, and the particular pseudonym chosen, a sign of David's "enormous modesty," which made him feel, as an ordinary schoolteacher, unworthy of having his name appear as the author of the article. On the other hand, the fact that Carl Furtmüller also used a pseudonym suggests a prudent desire by the two high school teachers to ensure that their careers did not suffer from their association with the notorious man who claimed that children had sexual desires directed at their parents.

13

David's Choice: Freud or Adler?

THE SECOND INTERNATIONAL Psychoanalytical Congress, held in Nuremberg in March 1910, was another step in a sequence that had a decisive effect on the direction of David's life. Freud had Sandor Ferenczi, a close friend from Hungary, make an extraordinary proposal. He suggested the formation of the International Psychoanalytical Association, with its headquarters in Zurich and Carl Jung as its president—not for any fixed term, but for life. Moreover, Ferenczi continued, all papers written or addresses delivered by any psychoanalyst should first be submitted to the president of the association, who would decide if they were to be published. Freud's attempt to counter the contention that psychoanalysis was a "Jewish science" was one factor in his plan to give greater prominence to Jung, but another was his desire to shift the levers of power out of Vienna, where Adler had his supporters.

Not surprisingly, Ferenczi's proposal provoked an angry response. Adler and Stekel both spoke bluntly of "censorship" and "restrictions on scientific freedom." Freud saw that he had to compromise. He said that he would step down from the presidency of the Vienna Psychoanalytical Society and nominate Adler as his replacement. On this basis Adler and Stekel consented to the nomination of Jung as president of the new international association, but only for a two-year term, and without any power of censorship. Freud also agreed that Adler and Stekel could found a new monthly periodical, to run alongside another periodical that would be edited from

Zurich; but he persuaded Adler and Stekel that he should have the title of "publisher" with the right to veto the publication of any article.

On the first Wednesday after the congress, the Vienna society met as usual in Freud's rooms. David was there to hear Freud open the session with a review of the congress. The Vienna society, he said, must now constitute itself as a branch of the international association. As agreed in Nuremberg, he proposed Adler as president, and offered his cooperation as a member of the society. The arrangement whereby the group met in his rooms, however, he considered "no longer feasible." Many members urged Freud to accept some position that made him more than a mere member of the society, and in the end he agreed to accept the position of "scientific chairman," to which he was elected by acclamation. He then again proposed Adler as president of the Vienna society, and Adler too was elected by acclamation. A committee was appointed to run the society, and a separate editorial committee of four was elected to assist Adler and Stekel with the new monthly periodical, which was to be called the *Zentralblatt für Psychoanalyse*. David was elected to the editorial committee.

Under Adler's chairmanship, meetings continued more or less as before throughout 1910, though in the autumn the venue switched to Vienna's College of Physicians. New members were admitted, and the number of people taking part in the discussions grew to twenty or more. Gradually, however, disagreements between Freud and Adler sharpened. In November the Vienna society agreed that Adler should be invited to speak on a theme that would shed some light on the differences between his and Freud's views. Adler was flattered by the fact that he, rather than Freud, would for once be the focus of attention, and he genuinely hoped that Freud would be ready to listen to what he had to say, and perhaps even to accept some of his ideas. Freud, however, had other plans. In December he wrote to Jung:

> It is getting really bad with Adler. . . . The crux of the matter—and this is what really alarms me—is that he minimizes the sexual drive and our opponents will soon be able to speak of an experienced psychoanalyst whose conclusions are radically different from ours.

At the first meeting for 1911, Adler presented a paper called "Some Problems of Psychoanalysis" to the Vienna Psychoanalytical Society. After pay-ing tribute to Freud's work for providing "the ground for the examination of all these problems," Adler argued that neurosis is caused by a sense of inferiority. In response, Federn accused Adler of having "aligned himself with the opponents of Freud's teachings" in denying that neurosis stems from the child's repressed sexual instincts. Freud remained silent—a very rare event in these meetings. Others criticized Adler, and no one is recorded in the minutes as speaking clearly in support of his views. David did not speak.

In a second installment, on February 1, Adler went further. Pointing to feelings of inferiority and fears of having to take "a feminine role," he said that the desire of young boys to have sexual intercourse with their mother is a result of the boys' masculine desire to be "on top" and to debase their mother in order to deny the feminine side of their nature. Going to the opposite extreme from Freud, Adler denied the primary role of sexual libido not only in infantile sexual desires, but also in "affairs with servant girls and governesses." These also should be understood as ways of asserting one's masculinity and superiority. The primacy of this drive explains, Adler argued, why some patients who have known about their Oedipus complex do not get better. The problem is not that they have repressed their sexual desires for their mother, but that the Oedipus complex is just one component of the masculine protest.

Freud held back no longer. "This is not psychoanalysis," he thundered, and then launched into a devastating two-hour critique. Adler, he said, was only doing "surface psychology," ignoring the unconscious; his views were "scientifically unsound" and would "do great harm to psychoanalysis." Adler's response was brief, maintaining that he was not denying sexual desires, but rather was trying to get behind what we see as sexual, to the more significant relationships that take on the guise of sexuality. Stekel made a final comment, both praising and criticizing Adler, and then the debate was adjourned until February 22.

Although my grandfather had been present for both of Adler's papers, the conclusion of the Freud-Adler debate on February 22 was one of the few meetings he did not attend during his membership in the group. Perhaps he knew what was coming, and did not wish to be forced into the position of taking sides between Freud and Adler; or, after the exchange on February 1, he might have found the whole scene so unpleasant that he decided to stay away. That this preference was not without a basis is clear from accounts given by others. Freud sat at the head of the table. The discussion began on his right, and everyone at the table had to say whether he agreed with Adler, or did not agree, and why. Most of the speakers were on Freud's side, including several who, at the end of their critiques, added positive remarks about the value of Adler's work. As the meeting neared its close, Maximilian Steiner spelled out the implications of Freud's earlier statement that "This is not psychoanalysis." If the group were to accept Adler's views, he said, "we would have to rename our association, into whose program and framework Adler's ideas do not fit at all." The suggestion was clear: Adler's views made him unfit to be a member of the society. Adler had the closing word, and said that if he had been in Steiner's place, "he would not have found the courage to make such a speech." But his replies to more substantial points of criticism are those of a shaken man.

At the next committee meeting of the society, Adler resigned his position as chairman. Stekel followed suit, resigning his position as deputy chairman. A Special General Meeting of the society was held on March 1, and this time David was present. Freud, having declared himself "not unwilling" to accept the chairmanship, was elected to that position by acclamation. On March 3 Freud wrote to Jung:

> Since the day before yesterday I have been chairman of the Vienna group. It had become impossible to go on with Adler. . . . There was strong opposition to Adler among the older members, whereas the younger and newer men showed considerable sympathy for him.

Adler and Stekel were still editors of the *Zentralblatt*, but Freud had plans about that too. On March 14 he told Jung:

> The palace revolution in Vienna has had little effect on the *Zentralblatt*. Naturally I am only waiting for an occasion to throw them both out, but they know it and are being very cautious and conciliatory, so there is nothing I can do for the present. Of course I am watching them more closely, but they put up with it. In my heart I am through with them.

Though Adler had resigned as chairman, he remained a member of the society, and attended ten of the twelve meetings held during the spring of 1911. Previously one of the most vocal members of the group, he spoke only once during that entire period. Occasionally Furtmüller defended an

Adlerian approach to a question under discussion. Freud did nothing until the end of May, when the society went into its summer recess. Then he wrote to J. F. Bergmann, the head of the company that produced the *Zentralblatt,* urging him to dismiss Adler as editor. Again Freud told Jung all about it:

> I have finally got rid of Adler. After I had pressed Bergmann to dismiss him from the *Zentralblatt,* he twisted and turned and finally came up with a strangely worded statement which can only be taken as his resignation. . . . The damage is not very great. Paranoid intelligences are not rare and are more dangerous than useful. As a paranoiac of course he is right about many things, though wrong about everything. A few rather useless members will probably follow his example.

LESS THAN THREE MONTHS earlier Freud had referred to David as "a very good and serious classical philologist." He made that comment in a letter telling Jung that, together with David, he was "preparing a small piece" for the periodical Jung was editing: "It will be the first foray into folklore: 'On a certain type of indecent dream in comic stories.' " As late as May he told Ferenczi that he was working on "the little folkloric thing with Oppenheim."

The collaborative work that Freud had so enthusiastically proposed to David in his initial letter was now under way. Freud and my grandfather decided to begin, not as Freud had originally envisaged, with a psychoanalytical treatment of ancient myths, but with popular folk stories. Freud rarely used a coauthor—only with Josef Breuer, who had then been the senior partner, had he written significant joint works. For a young high school teacher, therefore, to be invited to coauthor a work with Freud was a mark of great distinction, and one that could have set David's career on an entirely new trajectory. The stimulus for the article seems to have come from David's report, at the meeting of the Vienna Psychoanalytical Society on November 16, 1910, on "material from folklore of relevance to the topic of dream symbolism." The references to dreams in popular tales show, David argued, that ordinary people are aware that dreams involve sexual symbolism. At the next meeting he continued his report, giving examples of popular tales that refer to dreams, and asking whether these dreams could be interpreted in accordance with Freud's teachings. Freud, in discussion, gave an affirmative answer to David's question, saying that dreams reported in folktales could be interpreted in the same way as other dreams.

The third edition of Freud's *The Interpretation of Dreams*, published in the spring of 1911, has this new footnote:

> Professor Ernst Oppenheim* of Vienna has shown me, from the evidence of folklore, that there is a class of dreams in which the prophetic meaning has been dropped even in popular belief and which are perfectly correctly traced back to wishes and needs emerging during sleep. He will shortly be giving a detailed account of these dreams, which are as a rule narrated in the form of comic stories.

Freud's willingness to refer to the work shows that he had no doubt that it would be satisfactorily completed; but meanwhile the dispute between Freud and Adler was reaching its climax. David had powerful reasons for siding with Freud. First, he seemed to have more in common with Freud, who, like David, came from a highly educated Moravian Jewish family and was an enthusiast of the ancients. Freud's rooms at 19 Berggasse contained bookcases filled with the results of his passion for collecting antiquities, among them statuettes, bronzes, and terra-cottas from Egypt, Greece, and Rome. Freud and my grandfather also shared a love of German literature, and particularly of Goethe. Adler, on the other hand, was the son of a Jewish grain merchant. He had grown up on the outskirts of Vienna in a district with few well-educated families, and throughout his life his German showed traces of the Viennese working-class dialect. As a young man he had been baptized in a Protestant church, possibly in the hope that he would thus avoid the consequences of anti-Semitism.

David's political leanings might have provided a second reason for my grandfather to align himself with Freud and against Adler. Freud's biographer, Ernest Jones, suggests that politics played a decisive role in the dispute between the two:

> . . . most of Adler's followers were, like himself, ardent Socialists. Adler's wife, a Russian, was an intimate friend of the leading Russian revolutionaries;

---

* In his early publications, my grandfather uses his second name, the characteristically German "Ernst," rather than the more obviously Jewish "David."

Trotsky and Joffe, for instance, constantly frequented her house. Furtmüller himself had an active political career.*

Freud's teachings were uncongenial to socialists, for he saw civilization as a necessarily repressive force locked in perpetual conflict with our sexual drive and our basic instincts. Individuals might be helped by analysis, but ideas of a better society, without repression or neurosis, were no part of Freud's vision. Adler, in contrast, saw repression not as inevitable, but as influenced by the kind of society in which one lived. He supported the reforming policies of Austria's Social Democrats, and Furtmüller and Dr. Margarete Hilferding, the first woman member of the Wednesday Group, were members of the Social Democratic Party. David's political leanings at this time were more to the conservative side, as shown by his hostility to school reform.

The third—and for most people it would have been the weightiest—reason for David to take Freud's side was that the work on which they were now jointly engaged would be more far significant than the minor scholarly articles that David had published up to that time. More enticing still, once that work was successfully completed, was the prospect that Freud had held out to David in his first letter to him: combining their knowledge and talents they would "invade the region of mythology" and explain it from a psychoanalytical perspective. David's whole life and education up to that moment—his love for the classics, his empathetic understanding of the diversity of human sexuality, and the task he had set himself of unlocking the secrets of the human soul—seemed to have been designed precisely in order to equip him to aid Freud in this task. Working together with the man credited with discovering the unconscious, a figure some were already hailing as a genius, David could explore classical mythology from a psychoanalytical perspective, discovering its universal, but hidden, sexual significance. (Imagine, being the first to plow so virgin a field!) As Freud's coauthor, David could expect international renown, invitations to speak at important conferences, perhaps to accompany Freud on a lecture tour of America, and in the end that "comfortable academic throne" of which he

---

* Trotsky lived in Vienna after escaping from Russia in 1907 and remained there until the outbreak of the First World War. He frequented the Café Central, and Klemperer recalls meeting him in the Adler household. My grandfather probably met him too, but there is no record of it.

had written to Amalie when he was thinking about the choice between staying at university or becoming a high school teacher.

What, then, could have been pulling David in the opposite direction? He told his daughters many years later: "I admired Freud, but I loved Adler." So perhaps a kind of love for Adler drew David toward him. Another member of Adler's circle, Paul Klemperer, recalls that during the crucial summer of 1911, Adler and his wife met with their friends every evening at the Café Central, then as now one of Vienna's finest coffeehouses. Klemperer mentions my grandfather as being there, along with Furtmüller and two or three others.

David's own psychology suggests a second reason that might have drawn him to Adler. David's letters to Amalie reveal that he himself, at times, had feelings of inferiority, both as a philologist and more generally. In a letter he wrote during his military service, after he was not included in the first round of promotions, he says that these feelings of inadequacy "are never absent." Though David appears to have overcome these feelings, his own fine psychological sensitivity would have made him aware of them, and of the influence they could have on him. And from that he could have had an understanding for the mental life of others who perhaps had such feelings in a stronger form. Thus, he would have responded from a position of personal knowledge to Adler's emphasis on the importance of the drive to overcome feelings of inferiority, and he might well have thought that Adler was right to assume the universality and significance of such feelings. Maybe he even saw in Adler, who had been a sickly, clumsy child and had grown into a stocky man with a pudgy face and piggy eyes, a kindred spirit who had triumphed over his own inferiority problems.

A third possible factor influencing David's choice might have been growing doubts about some of Freud's views, at least in the strong form in which Freud and his close followers put them at the meetings David attended. He cannot have agreed with the way Freud, in the discussion following Adler's paper "Psychic Hermaphroditism," categorized libido and repression as "masculine" and "feminine," respectively. Moreover, his own discussion of suicide suggested that some suicides, committed both by adults and by students, have nothing to do with neuroses of a sexual nature. Here, as in his later work, David seemed to be taking a line that was based more on commonsense empirical observation of the data than on speculative interpretation about unconscious motivations. Perhaps David had doubts about such speculations even at his first meeting with Freud, and that explains why Freud found him not "really adept at taking on something that has up to now been foreign to him."

For some members of the Psychoanalytical Society, the choice between Freud and Adler was not a question of who was right about the causes of neurosis, nor a matter of politics, but rather a question of what kind of a body the Psychoanalytical Society was to be. Hanns Sachs, a member of the society who remained with Freud, said that those who sided with Adler did so because of their conviction "that the entire proceedings violated the 'freedom of science.' " Here lies a fourth reason for David to decide against Freud. The language that Freud uses in his private letters reveals that he often thought and behaved more like the leader of a religious sect than as a scientist should think and behave. In a letter to Jung he described the new deputy chairman, Hitschmann, as "quite orthodox" and added: "I mean to be more careful from now on that heresy does not occupy too much space in the *Zentralblatt*." Freud's defenders might claim that his use of such terms was not meant seriously—but who was it who taught us to read the unconscious mind in the jokes people make? The exclusion of Adler and others who disagreed with fundamental tenets of Freud's teachings was a tragedy for psychoanalysis. It ensured that it would remain dogma, rather than science, because psychoanalysts would treat its central doctrines as truths that were immune to any kind of testing that might show them to be false.

When Adler's friends learned of Freud's maneuvers to oust Adler from the editorship of the *Zentralblatt*, they resolved to draft a declaration stating their view of the situation. The document describes Adler's departure from the Psychoanalytical Society as "clearly provoked" and expresses its approval of his conduct and the wish to continue to discuss scientific ideas with him. "We will," the declaration continues, in a clear hint of plans to found a new society, "no doubt find a suitable framework for this." At the same time, the signatories say that they "place the greatest value on continuing to be keen members of the Psychoanalytical Society, but only if we are welcome as members." They say that they are being open about their intention to continue contact with Adler, so that if the committee of the Psychoanalytical Society objects to this, the matter can be put before a general meeting for a decision by the members.

Seven members of the Vienna Psychoanalytical Society signed the declaration. My grandfather was one of them. While the declaration can be seen as an attempt to build a bridge between the Freudian and Adlerian camps by expressing the wish to remain members of both groups, David must have known that Freud was unlikely to respond favorably to that attempt. In putting his name to the declaration, he was placing in jeopardy the greatest scholarly opportunity he was ever likely to get. When, along with four other signatories, he was one of the founding members of the Society for Free Psychoanalytical Research, he confirmed that he was prepared to risk losing that opportunity.

Freud's response came at the first meeting of the Vienna Psychoanalytical Society after the summer of 1911, a special plenary session held on October 11 in the Café Arkaden. David was there, together with four other signatories of the declaration. The minutes state:

> PROF. FREUD then lets it be known that, since the last meeting of the Society, the following members have resigned: Dr. Adler, Dr. Bach, Dr. Manday, and Baron Dr. Hye.

At this point, Freud's prediction that a "few useless members" would resign along with Adler was accurate enough. None of the three who had resigned immediately together with Adler had played a significant role in the society. But then the minutes record:

> THE CHAIRMAN [FREUD] thereupon takes the floor to discuss the matter of internal affairs. Speaking for the Board, he confronts those members who also belong to Dr. Adler's circle with the fact that its activities bear the character of hostile competition, and calls upon them to decide between membership either here or there, since the Board regards their present position as being contradictory. The Chairman then presents the reasons for the Board's view and asks those members whose position is not yet known to him to present their decision no later than next Wednesday.

Furtmüller rose to challenge Freud. He demanded that the full meeting should vote on whether membership in Adler's circle should be incompatible with membership in the Vienna Psychoanalytical Society. Freud's authority was now at stake. Five of his followers spoke in favor of the view that there has to be "a clean-cut separation." Freud himself then took the floor. (The minutes here make no attempt to report what was said.) Furtmüller spoke again, saying that the real issue was whether psychoanalytical research should be free. At the conclusion of the debate, by eleven votes to five, the meeting declared that "membership in the 'Society for Free Psychoanalytical Research' is incompatible with membership in the Psychoanalytical Society." The minutes then state:

> DR. FURTMÜLLER thereupon, in his name as well as in the name of five other members (Dr. Oppenheim, Dr. Hilferding, Franz and Gustav Grüner, Paul Klemperer), announces their resignation from the Society.

With this, my grandfather's collaboration with Freud was irrevocably at an end, and his intellectual path was instead to follow the lead set by Adler. At the time, Adler was still relatively unknown and very much in Freud's shadow. Did David believe that Adler was about to emerge from that shadow and equal or even surpass Freud in the significance of his thought? Today there can be no question that Freud's ideas have been far more influential than Adler's, and that David's work would have been better known if he had continued to work with Freud, but that might not have been so evident in 1911. The idea that mental illness has its roots in feelings of inferiority is as inherently plausible as the idea that these roots are to be found in repressed sexual desires for one's opposite-sex parent. And as we shall see, there was a period, in the 1920s, when Adler's ideas actually were of greater practical significance than Freud's, at least in Vienna. David might then have been pleased that he had sided with the more effective thinker.

In any case, such calculations were probably not foremost in my grandfather's mind at the time he made his fateful choice. Later Furtmüller wrote that most of those who left Freud's circle with Adler did so not because they were committed supporters of Adler's theories but "because they believed him wronged and were indignant at Freud's treatment of him." Klemperer certainly was one of these—he later said that he was "enraged" by "the tyrannical attitude of Freud." That meshes perfectly with what I always heard from my mother and my aunt after I became old enough to learn of my grandfather's connection with Freud. He chose to side with Adler, I was told, because Freud had not behaved decently toward Adler. The record of Freud's thoughts and actions leading up to the break with Adler justifies David's judgment. David's decision was not based on his own scholarly assessment of the rival theories, still less on his personal ambitions. He was doing what he thought—with good grounds—to be right, whatever the personal consequences might be.

Freud never forgave Adler or those who left with him. Klemperer said that when he met Freud in the street while walking with a companion whom Freud knew, Freud greeted the companion and looked straight through Klemperer without a word of greeting, as if he did not exist. Even after World War I, when Klemperer's cousin, the staunch Freud loyalist Paul Federn, asked Freud to agree to a visit from Klemperer, who was no longer involved with the Adlerians, Freud refused. Since my grandfather remained an active member of Adler's group, his prospects of further contact with Freud would have been nil. The only person Freud ever permitted to attend meetings of both groups was Lou Andreas-Salomé, a vivacious woman of Russian origin with a remarkable talent for charming famous men.

After the breach, Freud set out to downplay the work of the "defectors." The footnote in the 1911 edition of *The Interpretation of Dreams* in which Freud acknowledged his debt to David for showing him that the evidence of folklore supports a sexual interpretation of some dreams was dropped from the next edition. Some references to Adler received similar treatment. For Freud the Adlerians had become nonpersons.

POSTHUMOUSLY, my grandfather did what neither he nor any of the other members of Freud's or Adler's groups could do while alive: he brought the Vienna Freudians and Adlerians back together. In June 1989 the first joint meeting of the Vienna Psychoanalytical Society and of the society founded by the Adlerians, now known as the Austrian Society for Individual Psychology, took place for the purpose of commemorating David Oppenheim and his involvement with both organizations. The principal speakers were former pupils of my grandfather at the Akademisches Gymnasium. One, Erwin Ringel, was a leading Adlerian, and the other, Ernst Federn, a noted Freudian and the son of Paul Federn, one of Freud's most loyal disciples. Before an audience that included David's two daughters, three grandchildren, and some of his great-grandchildren, as well as several surviving friends, the Adlerians and the Freudians discussed David's life, his work with Freud and Adler, and his death. In his memory, they spoke of ways of building bridges over a bitter division that had lasted nearly eighty years.

14

"Dreams in Folklore"

AT THE TIME of the final rupture between Freud and my grandfather, the manuscript of *Dreams in Folklore* was in David's possession, probably so that he could add a few notes. There it remained, unpublished and largely unkown, as Freud's reputation grew. Amalie brought it to Australia after the war.

Across the top of the first page of the manuscript, in Freud's handwriting, is:

Dreams in Folklore
by Sigm. Freud and Prof. Ernst Oppenheim
(Vienna)

Squeezed in between the title and the first line of the manuscript, in David's hand and in red ink that stands out from Freud's black, is a Latin quotation from Horace's *Ars Poetica* that means, roughly: "Haughty persons in authority disdain poems that are lacking in charm." The work itself begins with an explanation of how it came to be written:

One of us (O.) in his studies of folklore has made two observations with regard to the dreams narrated there which seem to him worth communicating. Firstly, that the symbolism employed in these dreams coincides completely with that accepted by psychoanalysis, and secondly, that a number of these dreams are understood by the common people in the same way as they would be interpreted by psychoanalysis — that is, not as premonitions about a still unrevealed future, but as the fulfillment of wishes, the satisfaction of needs which arise during the state of sleep. Certain peculiarities of these dreams, which are told as comic tales and are thoroughly indecent, have encouraged the other one of us (Fr.) to attempt an interpretation of them which shows them to be more significant and deserving of attention.

The manuscript enables us to see what each author did. David went through accounts of folktales in anthropological periodicals and copied out those that referred to dreams, especially dreams that seemed ripe for psychoanalytical interpretation. Some of this is in his handwriting, and some is typewritten. He gave his transcriptions, with a few brief comments, to Freud, who pasted them onto large sheets of paper, added a commentary to the material, and wrote an introduction and a conclusion. Freud then returned these sheets to David, who added one or two extra notes.

After the introduction comes a section headed *"Penis Symbolism in Folklore-Dreams."* It begins with a southern Slav story involving a girl who told her mother that she had dreamed of "some sort of long and red and blunted thing." The mother begins to interpret this as a road, but the father interrupts, saying, "It sounds rather like my cock." Freud comments on the way in which such stories "delight in laying bare the veiling symbols." Then come some Austrian folk verses in which a royal scepter is equated with a penis, and a Silesian folk song in which a girl lying on the grass dreams that her beloved has turned into a fat earthworm and crawled inside her stomach. Later she becomes pregnant, and the song warns girls not to dream on the grass, lest a fat earthworm should creep up inside them. This is followed by a Ukrainian peasant story in which a woman dreams that she is trying to pull a dagger out of its sheath, but wakes to find that she is pulling at her husband's cock. Freud comments that the representation of the penis as a weapon "lies at the root of numerous phobias in neurotic people." David adds a footnote referring to the German word for burglar, which means literally "one who breaks in." That there is a popular awareness of the double meaning of burglary is shown, David says, by the fact that the Berlin slang term for a strong penis is *Brecheisen*, a jimmy.

The section on penis symbolism runs to ten pages in the printed version, and is followed by a second part, three times as long, "Feces Symbolism and Related Dream Actions," which gathers together folk stories telling of dreams about shitting and pissing. The dreamers typically awake to find that they have defecated over their partner, and in some dreams they are also fondling or licking their partner's genitals.

Does the essay show that, as the introduction claims, the symbolism employed in the dreams "coincides completely with that accepted by psychoanalysis"? It might be better to say that it makes a start on that endeavor. The tale of a woman dreaming of pulling a dagger from a sheath, when she is in fact pulling her husband's penis, tends to support psychoanalytic interpretations of dreams about knives or daggers as also derived from sexual wishes or fantasies, because in the tale the dreamer actually awakes to find herself in the middle of a sexual act.

But other dream interpretations in the essay lack this explicit link with sex. In "The Peasant's Assumption to Heaven," a peasant dreams that the price of wheat in heaven is high. He loads up his cart with wheat, puts his horse in harness, and drives there, but the heavenly gate slams shut just before he can get in. He begs the angels to open it again, but they say that he is too late. Turning back, the peasant finds that the road has disappeared. The angels advise him to lower himself down a rope, but he has no rope. He uses the reins of his cart, then various other expedients, but always the rope is still too short. So the angels tell him to shit, and his shit turns into a rope. He climbs down that, but it still isn't long enough, so the angels tell him to piss. The piss turns into a thread, which the peasant also climbs down, but even that isn't quite long enough, and he has to jump the last part. In doing so, he wakes himself up, for he has jumped down from his sleeping platform above the stove. He calls out to his wife, who wakes and finds that he has shat and pissed all over her. It is plausible to see this dream as confirming part of my grandfather's second observation—that a number of dreams are to be seen "as the fulfillment of wishes, the satisfaction of needs which arise during the state of sleep." In this case, we would naturally assume, the sleeping peasant needs to go to the lavatory. But Freud eschews so simple an interpretation. He writes that the psychoanalytic experience of interpreting dreams tells us that objects that get longer are symbols for erection. He interprets the peasant's anxiety over the fact that the rope is not long enough as a sign that the peasant is making an effort to get an erection. Only when he fails does he turn to defecation. Thus, Freud claims: "Behind the excremental need of this dream, a sexual need comes all at once into view."

Freud also suggests that other elements of the dream have a sexual interpretation. The price of wheat is high. Wheat "probably stands for semen." The horse and cart are "genital symbols" that the peasant seeks to drive into the open gate of heaven. But the gate slams shut, showing that the object of the man's sexual desire is unreachable. His wife does not attract him, and he strives in vain to get an erection for her. The disappointed sexual libido finds release by way of regression in the excremental desire, which abuses and soils the useless sexual object. Freud says that one must assume that the action with which a dream ends is the one intended by the latent thoughts of the dreamer. So if the dreamer awakes to find he has defecated over his wife, this signifies that he rejects her.

Here Freud reads a sexual interpretation into a dream that, on its face, has nothing to do with sex, neither in the dream nor in what the dreamer is actually doing. Hence the tale does not provide any independent confirmation of Freud's interpretation, or of similar interpretations of similar dreams told by patients undergoing psychoanalysis. Moreover, if this is how the dream is to be interpreted psychoanalytically, then *Dreams in Folklore* fails to establish David's second observation, namely that "a number of these dreams are understood by the common people in the same way as they would be interpreted by psychoanalysis." For there is no evidence that the common people interpret this dream as related to *sexual* needs.

Here is another example of Freud's interpretations. A peasant dreams that it is wartime and he must bury his treasure in order to prevent soldiers' plundering it. He can't find a spade, so he digs with his hands and manages to bury the treasure. But after he has buried it, he wonders how to mark the spot. Suddenly the need to defecate comes on him, and so he has the idea of marking the spot with his shit. This he does, and then looks for some grass to wipe himself. As he is pulling up a clump, he gets a blow that nearly knocks him out. His wife is yelling at him: "You rude bastard, you miserable fellow, do you think I have to take everything from you? First you rummage around with your two hands in my cunt, then you shit on it, and now you want to pull all the hair off it!" Freud interprets this as revealing the dreamer's death wish against his wife, "hypocritically designated as treasure." But if the dream does reflect the latent thoughts of the dreamer, then here the fact that the dreamer has his hands in his wife's cunt suggests a sexual interest in her, which must coexist with the rejection that Freud says is shown by his defecation on her. That is not impossible, but it does give rise to questions about whether the interpretations offered are correct—and whether it is right to assume that what the dreamer actually does indicates his or her latent thoughts. *Dreams in Folklore* provides interesting and entertaining material about dreams, but it does not provide independent evidence for the sexual interpretation of dreams that are not themselves explicitly about sexual matters, or are not associated with sexual acts on the part of the dreamer.

THERE IS ONE final twist to the story of the manuscript's fate. After Amalie's death in 1955 my aunt entered into correspondence with the Freud Archives, in New York, and eventually sold it to them—or so she believed. The manuscript was subsequently published in a special volume, with the text in both English and German. But when I sought it among the other documents held by the Freud Archives—available through the Library of Congress in Washington—I found only a photocopy. The library suggested that I contact Dr. Bernard Pacella, a past president of the American Psychoanalytic Association and the author of the preface to the published text. He told me that the manuscript was in his personal possession, and that he had given it to his daughter and son-in-law. The son-in-law, Dr. John Oldham, director of the New York State Psychiatric Institute, was kind enough to allow me to see it in his Manhattan office. When I asked Dr. Oldham how the manuscript came to be the property of Dr. Pacella, he told me that his father-in-law, and not the archives, had been the original purchasers of the manuscript. Dr. Pacella subsequently said the same thing, in a letter to me. That assertion, however, seems difficult to reconcile, not only with the correspondence between my aunt and the Freud Archives at the time of the sale, but also by Dr. Pacella's own statement in his preface to the published text that the manuscript was bought by the Freud Archives. Because Freud destroyed all the original manuscripts in his possession at the time of the First World War, this is the only Freud manuscript from that period to have survived. My aunt had thought, when she sold it, that it would be in public hands, in the Freud Archives. She appears to have been misled.

15

Psychology, Free and Individual

DAVID SOON BECAME one of the most active members of the new Society for Free Psychoanalytical Research, later renamed the Society for Individual Psychology. Carl Furtmüller recalls that at first the group felt "a bit bewildered" and missed the routine of the Wednesday Group, but Adler was encouraging, and there was plenty of work to be done. Philosophers, writers, and teachers as well as physicians, of both sexes and mostly relatively young, joined the group, giving it an atmosphere that was much more open to new ideas than Freud's circle. The group was also more political, and this meant that David was suddenly part of a group interested in social reform. Adler was completing what was to be his major work, *The Neurotic Constitution,* in which he integrates his psychological theory of inferiority with a broadly Marxist view of the influence of social forces on the individual. From our schooling onward, he writes, we are discouraged from fulfilling our potential and making a meaningful contribution to society. We suffer from feelings of inferiority, unsatisfied strivings for superiority, and unfulfilled needs for involvement in a larger social whole. We feel powerless in the face of an uncaring world. Confronted by these problems, some people withdraw from reality and become neurotics. The rest of us may get disheartened, but we cope somehow—though not as well as we might if we had been brought up differently in a society that gave us a greater sense of our own worth and significance.

In keeping with the group's interest in social reform and the role of the school, the first collection of essays it published—edited by Adler and Furt-müller—was called *Healing and Educating*. It included David's essay on student suicide, previously published by the Vienna Psychoanalytical Society, as well as other essays on educational issues. The linking of the two ideas represented in its title gave a new meaning to what David was doing as a teacher. He could now see his work not only as educating his students in Greek, Latin, and the culture of the ancient world, but as preparing them to be psychologically sound human beings, ready to contribute to building a better society and finding meaning in their own lives by doing so. He must have begun to reconsider his political conservatism and especially his hostility to reform of the schools.

The records of the meetings held during the first two years of the new society have not been preserved, but the diary of Lou Andreas-Salomé shows that David gave two lectures on Goethe's *Faust*. On November 7, 1912, she recorded the following:

> With Adler during Oppenheim's lecture on Faust, Part II, second lecture. Good and interesting. Furtmüller also led a stimulating discussion (of Faust as the example of inferiority in quest of compensation, to be satisfied only by the unattainable); but it was already clear that the distinguishing boundary between creativity and neurosis was obliterated and with it the problem. Adler's group could be very stimulating if only he stayed *outside* psychoanalysis.

David might have agreed. His interest in Adler's psychology was not in helping patients overcome neurosis or other forms of mental illness, but as an aid to understanding literary texts, and through them, the nature of human beings. Records from late 1913 and the first half of 1914 show that David spoke three times in this period, on Thomas Mann's *Death in Venice*; on Plutarch's life of Quintus Fabius Maximus Cunctator, the Roman consul whose evasive tactics led to the defeat of Hannibal's army in Italy; and on the play *Cyrano de Bergerac*, by the French playwright Edmond Rostand. His concern in *Death in Venice* was to discuss the psychology of the protagonist, Gustav Aschenbach, who he noted had been a weak and sickly boy, but had overcome this by his determination to become a successful writer. Interestingly, the report of his talk does not mention the issue of the love of an older man for a beautiful boy, which the novel also raises, although this question was brought up in discussion. There is no report of what David said in his two other talks, but his theme is not difficult to guess. Plutarch tells us that Quintus Fabius Maximus Cunctator was slow in speaking and learning, and bore the nickname "Verrucosus" because of a wart on his upper lip. *Cyrano de Bergerac* is about a gifted man who believes that no woman will ever love him because he has an enormous nose. David was pursuing the Adlerian theme of how people compensate for a sense of inferiority, arising from a physical blemish or weakness.

Before David could take his interest in Adlerian themes in literature any further, however, external events interrupted the work of the new society, and confronted David with a personal test of his own ability to overcome his sense of inadequacy. The secure and prosperous world in which he had grown up was about to come to an abrupt end.

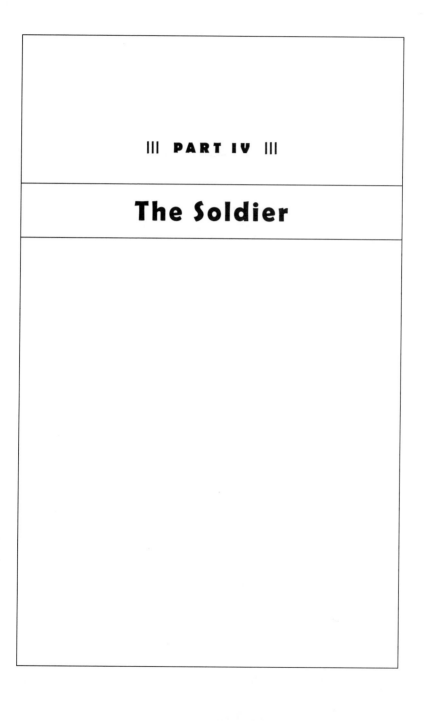

||| PART IV |||

The Soldier

16

The Eastern Front

ON A BEAUTIFUL SUNDAY in late June 1914, Stefan Zweig went to a spa town near Vienna where people came to sip the waters and stroll in the park. He was sitting in the park, reading quietly, when he became aware that the music of a band, which had been wafting to him through the trees, had stopped. He looked around and noticed that people were no longer strolling by. He went to the pavilion where the band had been playing. The musicians had left. People were gathered around a notice that had been put up. It announced that His Imperial Highness the Archduke Franz Ferdinand and his wife, Sophie, had been assassinated in Sarajevo.

The imperial couple had been unlucky. The Bosnian Serb conspirators had bungled an initial attempt to shoot the heir to the Austro-Hungarian throne, and one of them, Gavrilo Princep, was standing in a state of deep despondency on a street corner, lamenting the failure of the plot, when the open car carrying the couple drove right past him. The driver had taken the wrong route. Realizing his error, the driver stopped and turned the car around, giving Princep an unexpected opportunity to step up on the running board, pull out his pistol, and shoot the defenseless archduke and his wife at point-blank range.

Shocking as the assassination was, Vienna took the news calmly. Franz Ferdinand was widely regarded as an arrogant man with terrible artistic taste, so few tears were shed at his death. No one thought that the assassination might lead to a war among the major European powers.

As these events were unfolding, David and Amalie Oppenheim were enjoying their usual summer vacation outside Vienna, relaxing by a mountain lake with their daughter Kora, now six years old. The pleasure they would normally have taken in the particularly fine summer of 1914 must have slowly become overshadowed by concern about political developments. But this concern itself was double-edged, since for David, now thirty-three years old, there was something thrilling about the prospect of being personally involved for the first time in world-shaking events.

The Austrian authorities had evidence that Serbian officials had supplied the arms and trained the assassins. Urged on by Germany, the dual monarchy's leaders saw this as a chance to settle accounts with Serbia, which had already played a central role in two Balkan wars, and had been supporting nationalist movements among the Slav peoples of the empire's southern provinces. On July 23 Austria-Hungary delivered an ultimatum to Serbia, demanding that the Serb government dismiss officials at the behest of the Austrian government, after the provision of evidence of their involvement. Austria-Hungary also insisted that the Serbs accept the participation of Austrian police in the suppression of anti-Austrian subversive groups. The demands themselves were not unreasonable in the circumstances, but Austria-Hungary's belligerent intentions are shown by the fact that Serbia was given only forty-eight hours to respond. When Serbia accepted most of the demands but demurred on some details, Austria-Hungary broke off diplomatic relations and, on July 28, declared war on Serbia.*

Even then it was widely believed that the conflict would remain localized, without intervention by other great powers. But the Austro-Hungarian declaration of war on Serbia was followed by Russia's announcement of the mobilization of its army, and on August 1, in the face of the threat of a mobilized Russian army on its borders, Austria-Hungary announced the mobilization of its own army. With Germany committed to supporting Austria-Hungary, and France and England linked with Russia, two great alliances faced each other. The German military was determined to avoid facing hostile armies on both its east and west. Its war plan for such circumstances was to strike first at France, scoring a quick knockout blow—as Prussia had done in 1871—before turning to deal with Russia, whose mobil-

---

* Austria-Hungary was, however, no more belligerent—and certainly was more respectful of diplomatic niceties—than the United States was toward Afghanistan after September 11, 2001.

ization was bound to take several weeks to complete. That strategy made it impossible to limit the conflict to the Balkans. A European war could no longer be prevented.

———

TODAY IT IS HARD to imagine anyone reacting to these events with anything but horror and dread. But in 1914 no one expected a war that would last four years and cost more than nine million lives. Stefan Zweig was in Vienna during the first days of the war:

> A city of two million, a country of nearly fifty million, in that hour felt that they were participating in world history, in a moment which would never re-cur, and that each one was called upon to cast his infinitesimal self into the glowing mass, there to be purified of all selfishness. All differences of class, rank, and language were swamped at that moment by the rushing feeling of fraternity. Strangers spoke to one another in the streets, people who had avoided each other for years shook hands, everywhere one saw excited faces. Each individual experienced an exaltation of his ego, he was no longer the isolated person of former times, he had been incorporated into the mass, he was part of the people, and his person, his hitherto unnoticed person, had been given meaning.

David must have been caught up in these feelings. Nine years earlier, he had done his year of military training, in the army barracks in Brünn, the city of his birth. As a university student he was able to opt for a special one-year officer training program. He had not been keen to go, and had hoped that a friendly doctor might rule him unfit. When that did not happen, he fortified himself by reading the *Meditations* of the Roman emperor Marcus Aurelius, appropriate reading because the *Meditations* were, as he wrote to Amalie, written in an army camp by "a man who was also a soldier without having the inclination for it" and "a loner, in the middle of his army crowd." At first David had a very hard time. He told Amalie that the lieu-tenants in charge of drill knew nothing of "the most sacred of human rights, the right to natural ineptitude." He confessed that since elementary school he had been unable to do physical exercises, and now he was "cer-tainly one of the most inept, and in some exercises, even the most inept of all." His captain tried to improve him by verbal abuse and punishments of various kinds, mostly extra chores and confinement to the barracks. On one occasion during parade-ground drill when David's thoughts were elsewhere, he remained standing while his companions marched away. The captain attributed his deficiencies to the fact that he was a Jew, saying that it was impossible to get anything military into "these people." David fumed at being typecast: "I, who through my historical studies have long seen in war 'the driving force of human destiny,' and therefore have had the most lively interest in military studies . . . am supposed to have no interest." He admitted that many of his fellow trainees lacked interest, and even that this was more prevalent among the Jewish ones, but insisted, "I am just different from the others." His military blunders stemmed, he thought, not from his Jewishness, nor from a lack of interest, but from the fact that his personality was "little suited not only for military service, but for practical life as a whole, a personality the originality of which lies in its confused mix of talents and incapacities."

Despite his many difficulties, David managed to find something positive in his military experience: "I can recognize the greatness of the entire army institution, and feel a certain satisfaction in belonging to it." After participating in a military ceremony in which the entire Brünn garrison took part, he wrote that when a large body of troops is assembled together, "one feels oneself a member of an important whole that is united down to the last stride." This created in him "a genuinely democratic pride, one is pleased just to be *unus multorum*."

David was not included in the first batch of trainees promoted to lance corporal, but he achieved that rank three months later, and when the time came for promotion to corporal, he ranked eleventh among forty-nine trainees. His determination to be a successful soldier made a difference once military studies became a more significant part of the training than parade-ground drill. At the completion of his military service he was promoted to platoon leader, the usual rank with which university graduates who elected to go into officer training completed their year of military service. By 1914, after taking part in summer training exercises during several of the intervening years, he held the rank of second lieutenant in the army reserve.

When Austria-Hungary mobilized, David received a summons "to exceptional active service because of the general order of mobilization." Now he would see "the driving force of human destiny" at first hand and play his

part in it, not as a mere foot soldier but as a junior officer, responsible for
the lives and deaths of his men. A photograph taken on August 19, 1914,
shows him with the First Company, Second Marching Battalion, of a reserve infantry regiment. He sits proudly upright, his saber across his knee,
flanked by his noncommissioned officers and surrounded by fifty soldiers
under his command.

≡

DAVID'S UNIT WAS sent to the eastern front in Galicia, then a province
of the Austro-Hungarian Empire, now the southern part of Poland and the
western part of Ukraine. They arrived at the front on September 18, 1914. A
disastrous miscalculation by the Austrian commander on the whereabouts
of the Russian army had already led to the loss of Lemberg, the largest city
in the province. In the first month of the war, one hundred thousand
Austro-Hungarian soldiers were killed and a similar number taken prisoner.
Much of Galicia was in Russian hands, and the incompetently led Austrian
forces were trying to relieve the besieged fortress of Przemyśl, the chief
stronghold of the entire region. The siege was raised, at the cost of ten thousand men, and Austrian troops set about clearing fifteen thousand corpses
from the perimeter of the fortress. Then the Russians regrouped and drove
the Austrians back, and Przemyśl was again completely encircled by the
enemy. On October 19, during this period of chaotic fighting, David was
hit by a bullet in his right thigh, and sent back to a hospital in Vienna.

Amalie heard of David's wound while she was staying in Brünn. She
traveled immediately to Vienna to join him, leaving the seven-year-old
Kora with David's parents. From Vienna she wrote to them with good
news. The bullet had passed clean through David's thigh, missing the
bone, and although it "certainly hurts a bit," it would heal. Apart from the
wound David was well and his appetite was "quite unrestrained, as he arrived completely starved." Amalie tried to reassure David's parents by writing: "Please do not be at all worried . . . he is being wonderfully well looked
after, as if in the most expensive sanatorium"; but she could not avoid noting that "the war has not been beneficial for his nerves, so for example his
crying out at night, in the war as well as here, has attracted attention."
David added a few lines, saying that his wound was "insignificant," his
overall state of health quite unaffected, that he was being very well looked
after, and looked forward to seeing his parents again soon. But he said noth-

ing about the state of his nerves, and it is hard to imagine that his parents were able to obey Amalie's injunction against being worried. By the end of the year—after only four months of fighting—nearly a million Austro-Hungarian soldiers had been killed, wounded, or taken prisoner. Nor was it only the soldiers who were suffering. Food shortages began to be felt as early as October 1914, when ten thousand horses were shot to provide horse meat. (No wonder that David returned to Vienna "completely starved.") The imperial government had neither expected nor planned for a drawn-out war, and the loss of Austria's breadbasket in Ukraine before the harvest had been gathered cut off Vienna from the source of much of her peacetime grain supplies.

A War Ministry document from this period shows that 96 percent of officers killed, wounded, or captured were from the infantry, three out of every four officers lost were lieutenants and captains, and officers from the reserve were four times as likely to be casualties as those from the regular army. As an infantry lieutenant from the reserve, David had all the characteristics that increased the odds against survival. The memo blamed lack of realistic prewar training, as well as Russian snipers who had learned to pick the colorful uniforms of officers of the Imperial and Royal Armies. The War Ministry itself wondered how long this loss of officers could be endured before the army collapsed completely.

━━

DAVID RETURNED to Galicia on March 12, 1915, just a few days before the Russians finally captured the supposedly invulnerable Przemyśl, taking 120,000 Austrian soldiers captive. Between the Russian army and the Hungarian plains now stood only the Carpathians, a long, low mountain chain about sixty miles wide and three thousand feet in height. David was involved in the bitter struggle to deny the Russians passage through the mountain passes, still in the icy grip of winter. A week after David's return to the front, a storm broke over the region with a ferocity that Colonel Georg Veith of the Austrian Third Army described as usually "found only in glacial regions. . . . Hundreds of soldiers freeze to death daily. Entire lines of riflemen surrender in tears to escape the pain . . . the infantry stands without cover and unable to move in front of the enemy's defensive works; the artillery is several days march behind." The cold was so intense that before an attack on enemy positions could be launched, infantry soldiers had to have their hands thawed in warm water. Under these conditions, Austrian sources calculated, the effective life of a soldier was no more than five or six weeks—after that he was likely to have been killed, captured, or wounded. Many committed suicide. Only those with "iron constitutions," Veith concluded, survived in the Carpathians; the others simply broke down.

David's military training had shown that army life did not come easily to him. In the nine years between that training and the outbreak of war he had lived quietly as a schoolteacher and scholar. His nerves were already strained by his first spell at the front. Now he endured a month of the bitterest winter campaign and a further two months of heavy fighting in the spring, a period in which the Hapsburg army was losing 170,000 men each month. Amazingly, David not only survived this campaign, he even did some scholarly work during it. In April 1915 he mailed Amalie an essay entitled "Horace in the Trenches." The title was justified, he told her, because although he had prepared it while marching, he had finalized his thoughts about it and written it down in the trenches. The chief interest in the essay is its preface, which David addressed to his fellow schoolteachers:

> Thinkers and writers have celebrated war as the father of all things, as the mover of human destiny. War has not had a fully valid claim to this title of fame, however, until the war that we are today fighting. For it alone is really all-embracing, a battle in which all humanity participates. And so all its creative and moving forces are visibly at work, to rearrange the world from the ground up. The new generation inherits a new world; it is the task of the school to ensure that it is worthy to grasp its possession. Consequently the school must take a position on the war.

David goes on to say that while every branch of instruction must breathe in "the fresh, strong air of the war," none will find this more natural than classical studies, since almost all of the classical works studied by young people are filled with battle and war. In leaving the school, he did not leave his beloved ancient writers behind: "they willingly and gladly have followed me into my life in the war," and his wartime experiences have transformed many passages from the classics into "reality at blood-heat." He tells us of the "bitter hour" of departure from his wife, when everything that he had in his heart was summed up in these lines of Horace:

*If you should wonder, you should not seek to know what destiny the
    fates will give to me, and what to you . . .
In this way, I will better bear it, whatever it will be.*

The nervous tension that flowed through him before battle is, David
says, well described by Xenophon's account of the preparations for the Battle of Cunaxa. From the winter campaign in the Carpathian Mountains he
gained an inner certainty that the endurance of a soldier, of which
Xenophon speaks, is not a passive endurance, as it has been mistranslated,
but one in which the bearer actively wills to endure many different kinds of
toil and danger. Recalling the descriptions in Tacitus of the hard work of
the soldiers digging trenches, David reveals that he too felt depressed when
"again and again, with my own hand, I had to dig myself some cover." He
was united with the legions of Germanicus by knowing the tedium of "end-
less marches on innumerable routes." But the last of his examples is the
most telling:

> And when curious questioners now assail me, at home, to tell of my war trav-
> els and experiences, then I feel deeply the truth of the elegiac: *Infandum,
> regina, iubes, renovare dolorem.* [Queen, you order me to relive unspeakable
> pain.]

Turning to his work on Horace, David maintains that "the deadly bitter
seriousness of the war . . . purifies and deepens the entire human being."
For two "peaceful school years" he had worked without success to understand the construction of Horace's first ode; now, he says, because of this
"purification and deepening" he has been able to solve the problem. He
concludes his preface with the hope that, even if the analysis of Horace is
not wholly original and is not as completely worked through as it might be,
its publication may be justified in that it can be seen as "an expression of intellectual life at the front."

David's idea of war as something that purifies was common at the time.
Thomas Mann described the previous era of peace as "foul with all its comfort" and wrote: "Morally and psychologically I felt the necessity of this catastrophe and that feeling of cleansing, of elevation and liberation which
filled me." Ludwig Wittgenstein wrote in his diary: "Now I have the chance
to be a decent human being, for I'm standing eye to eye with death." Nev-

ertheless, that David could still be so positive about the war, after he had seen seven months of carnage, is remarkable. Only in the single Latin line that portrays the request to tell of his wartime experiences as an order to "relive unspeakable pain" is there a reference to the suffering and death that were at the center of the war in which David was fighting.

———

IN MAY 1915 the tide of the war in the East turned. The German army, pushing down from the north, broke through the Russian armies and drove them back. The Russian troops in the Carpathians were in danger of being cut off, and they were soon in full flight. David was not involved in pursuing them, for by mid-June he was again on leave in Vienna. Compared to the front, this must have seemed a life of ease, but basic foods were now rationed, and the prices of almost everything else spiraled upward.

After nearly six months away from the front, David—now promoted to first lieutenant—returned to Galicia on December 8, 1915, and served throughout the worst of the winter. While he was there "The Ancients and War: Horace in the Trenches" was published in the *Journal for Austrian Gymnasia,* and the publication was briefly noted in the *Vienna Newspaper* as "a gratifying expression of intellectual life at the front." Amalie sent out offprints to many friends and colleagues, more than a dozen of whom sent back cards in return, thanking her for sending it to them and commenting briefly on it. Most of the cards are full of praise for the essay. In one, however—signed illegibly—the writer expresses wonder at how the experience of war "purifies and deepens the entire human being" and then adds tellingly: "Apparently we here lack the organ of empathy."

David was relieved from his tour of duty at the front on March 2, 1916.

17

The Battles of the Isonzo

IN MAY 1915, while the Germans and Austro-Hungarians were celebrating the Russian retreat, they suffered a blow from the south. Italy, originally allied with them as part of the Triple Alliance, and up to this time neutral, came in on the side of Britain, France, and Russia—induced to do so by the promise that once victory had been gained, it would be given the Austrian province of South Tirol. Because most of the frontier between Italy and Austria-Hungary was formed by the Alps, the bulk of the fighting took place along the rocky gorge of the Isonzo River, on the border between Italy and what is now Slovenia. After several costly Italian attacks had failed to dislodge the Austrians from the high ground, the Austrian high command might have sensed that here at last was a foe whose military incompetence matched their own. With the eastern front relatively quiet, they began to shift forces to the Italian front in the hope of winning a major victory there. On July 1, 1916, David was sent to the Isonzo, to face as a foe not the "eastern barbarians," but the inhabitants of the country where he had spent his honeymoon, a people whose language he spoke and for whose cultural achievements he had unbounded admiration.

David arrived in time for the Sixth Battle of the Isonzo. During ten days of fierce fighting the Italians scored their first real success against the Austrians, inflicting forty thousand casualties and taking the city of Görz, now the Italian city of Gorizia. In the Seventh, Eighth, and Ninth Battles of Isonzo, between September 14 and November 4, the Austrians held their ground, but at the cost of another one hundred thousand men. For his conduct in these battles, my grandfather was nominated for a decoration. The letter of nomination, only part of which remains legible, states that David served as tactical commander of the First Company of the 161st Battalion, where he directed the "technical work." He did this "excellently" at Meso Junction, in Brenta, where he was "in the immediate proximity of the enemy, under constant fire." During an engagement at Passumer, in the Riva section, he was made provisional commander of the same company, and proved himself completely suitable for this position. The nomination concludes with the comment: "Extremely reliable and conscientious officer." An additional note signed by another officer says: "The service of this fine and exemplary officer, who has faced the enemy for 11 months, must be rewarded." David was awarded the Bronze Military Service Medal and, on November 11, 1916, was officially given "the highest laudatory recognition for brave conduct before the enemy."

Austria-Hungary's reserves of men were now so diminished that David remained at the Isonzo front for more than a year, until August 1917. During this period he would have lived for two to three weeks in the trenches and then been relieved by another battalion, to spend a similar amount of time in reserve a few kilometers behind the front lines before returning to the trenches. Food and water had to be brought in to the trenches at night, the only time when it was possible to move around safely. Water was particularly scarce. Soldiers were given only enough for drinking, but officers also received one bowl of water per day for washing. The trenches were overrun with rats and mice, and lice were impossible to avoid. On the other hand, between major battles there was little to do. During daylight hours the soldiers had to remain in the trenches, and those not on watch were free to read, write, or entertain themselves as they pleased.

A faded and creased photograph shows David at this time, standing upright and looking well, in a trench that rises far above his head. He wears his cap, shading his heavily bearded face from the bright sun that is shining into one side of the trench, and he appears to have a large revolver in his hand. A small wooden structure is partly visible behind him. Underneath the photograph he has written, in faded pencil: "Trenches on the . . . stream near Castelnuovo. Taken next to my shelter. Me as commander of the section . . . delta I. Late September 1916."

═══

AMALIE MUST HAVE SPENT the war making sure that Kora had enough food to be well nourished and—since her own parents had died earlier—ensuring that David's aging parents were managing as well as they could. His father's poor health must have been an additional strain, on top of the constant worry that any day David's name might be added to the long lists of those who had fallen in defense of their country. Nevertheless, Amalie still found ways of helping other members of the family. In February 1917 David learned that his sister Hannchen was expecting a proposal of marriage. The suitor, Sandor Kunstadt, was the younger brother of the husband of one of Amalie's sisters, and Hannchen appears to have become acquainted with him while staying with Amalie in Vienna. Sandor Kunstadt was fourteen years older than David's sister, but in contrast to the age difference between Amalie and David, this appears not to have troubled David's mother, Ernestine. Joachim, David's father, was doubtful, but for other reasons: "Papa would have wished for a learned son-in-law," Ernestine wrote to David. Sandor Kunstadt was not learned, but he had something that in Ernestine's eyes was more important: "I have always had the wish that you would get a good, upright, wealthy man . . . so that in days to come you can lead a comfortable life by his side." Apart from that, in a passage that showed Ernestine's trust in Amalie's judgment, she wrote that Amalie "would never have accepted the frequent meetings, if she . . . had not found it good for your future happiness." So "Papa" was going to have to give up his dream of another scholar in the family, and "would not deny his consent." She added that she had written to David about these matters, but had not yet received an answer, and "his views are also important."

David's answer has not been preserved, but Hannchen did keep a letter he wrote to her six months later, in which he writes of their relationship. There has never been much companionship between them, he acknowledges. When Hannchen was young the fifteen-year difference in their ages was too great, and for the past three years, while Hannchen was ripening from a small girl into a bride, David was at war in alien lands. On the rare occasions when he was at home, their father's illness and other worries about the war prevented him from taking as much notice of her as he should have. Now that Hannchen is grown, and will be living in the same city as he is—for her husband lives in Vienna—David expects a closer relationship to spring up between them. He closes by thanking her for some sausage that she sent.

THE TENTH BATTLE OF ISONZO, from May 12 to June 6, was another disaster for the Italians. They threw 280,000 men, supported by 2,200 guns and 1,000 trench mortars, against 173,000 Austrians. The Italians succeeded in gaining three kilometers of barren rock, at a cost of 36,000 men killed and 123,000 wounded or captured. Of my grandfather's fellow soldiers, 7,300 were killed and 68,000 wounded or captured. The eleventh battle began on August 18. This time the Italians had assembled 51 divisions and 5,200 guns. The Austrian artillery was under such pressure from continuous firing that more than a third of its guns broke down. The Italians gained about ten kilometers, at a cost even greater than that of the tenth battle, but still failed to break through the Austrian front. Austrian losses were 40,000 killed or missing and 45,000 wounded. Among those 45,000 wounded was my grandfather. On August 31 a bullet struck him in the chest, failing to kill him only because a small book that he was carrying in his breast pocket deflected it into his shoulder rather than his heart. It was a missal, or book for use during mass, and why he was carrying it remains a mystery. It might have been standard army issue, and perhaps it gave him something to read, for he always took a scholarly interest in religious teachings. Later he joked that if he had not been an atheist, the incident would have made him convert to Catholicism. The wound was more serious than the one he had received three years earlier, and he was sent back to Vienna for treatment. He kept the missal and many years later gave it to his former student Friedrich Heer.

By this time David had spent a total of twenty-one months at the front. For risking his life for his country he was awarded the Karl Troops Cross and the Medal for the Wounded, with two stripes, in addition to his Bronze Military Service Medal, to which he gained the added distinction of two crossed swords. Granted, the Austro-Hungarian Empire handed out medals so readily that critics said the war might have gone better if only they had used all that metal for weapons, but no one could accuse David of failing to do his share in the defense of his country. The "most inept" of all the 1905–6 group of trainees in Brünn had turned out to be a brave soldier and an exemplary officer.

OVER THE NEXT THREE MONTHS my grandfather got over his shoulder wound, but his experiences at the Isonzo, living through a series of battles as pointlessly bloody as those of Verdun or the Somme on the western front, were to haunt him all his life. Among those killed was Werner, his personal orderly, with whom he had been together for three years, and who fell at his side. One of his students from the twenties recalls that during a class, while reading a passage in Homer he paused and said: "I will never forget how, during a charge that I had to command, people were falling to the left and right of me, shouting 'Comrade, Comrade.'" Twenty years later the war remained his standard of the worst that could happen to him. When awaiting major surgery, he wrote that he had lived through worse things, "for example, waiting through the night for the intense bombardment that would set in the next morning." After the operation and its painful consequences he wrote that "only the experiences of the front provided anything comparable in kind and intensity."

On November 24, 1917, David petitioned a military committee of review for classification as unfit for service at the front. In the petition he states that he is making the application "under the orders of the officers' convalescence assembly post," on the grounds of "heart disease and neurasthenia." On November 28 David was examined by military doctors. The doctor responsible for the physical examination found him to be "tall, medium strength, fairly well nourished" and drew no conclusion on his fitness for service, but the report on his nervous condition found various abnormalities, and said that he experienced "paroxysm-like attacks" during which he "does not react to calls, completely uncontrolled, but soon responds when talked to vigorously." This was taken as a sign of a nervous disorder, and he was found not fit for service in the field, but fit for office work.

David applied for, and received, a posting to the government's Censorship Department, where his knowledge of Italian would have been useful, for the Austro-Hungarian Empire had a significant number of Italian-speaking subjects, living mostly in Trentino, whose correspondence had to be checked. The department was a large one, employing a thousand people to monitor more than eight million postcards and letters every month. The censors did not merely censor; they also sampled public opinion, as reflected in the mail they were reading, and reported on it to the government. David joined the department at a time of growing opposition to the war. Many workers knew that Lenin's successful revolution in Russia had taken that country out of the war, and some wanted to follow his example, but it was food more than politics that was the immediate cause of discontent. The markets ran out of milk, fat, eggs, and vegetables. A further reduction in the flour ration in January 1918 triggered strikes at motor, locomotive, and aircraft factories across the Austro-Hungarian Empire. Some workers began demanding not only more food, but an end to the war. The censors reported that 14 percent of letter writers welcomed the strikes, and a third saw them as revolutionary acts. The letters were filled with complaints not only about the lack of food, but also about call-ups for military service, and government inefficiency.

David's condition was reviewed on July 7, 1918, and he was found still unfit for service in the field. He could not, however, have been entirely unwell, for around this time, and despite the hardship of war and the uncertain future, Amalie conceived their second child. As this new life began, an older one came to an end: David's father died in August. The war-weary Austro-Hungarian Empire did not long outlive him. On October 14 the Provisional Government of Czechoslovakia was proclaimed, and it was promptly recognized by the Allies. Within its boundaries lived not only Czechs and Slovaks, but also more than three million German speakers. Suddenly both David's and Amalie's childhood homes, and many members of their families, were in a foreign country. The formation of Czechoslovakia was soon followed by that of Poland and Yugoslavia. Croatian, Czech, Hungarian, and Romanian army units simply left their posts at the Italian front and headed home. With the German army also unable to continue the war, Germany and Austria-Hungary accepted an armistice on November 11. The next day the German-speaking members of the Austrian parliament followed the lead of the other nationalities of the empire and proclaimed the "Republic of German-Austria." Outside parliament, on the Ringstrasse, a vast crowd of people celebrated the new republic and the bloodless transition from six centuries of Hapsburg monarchy to a new, democratic era. They rejoiced too because they had been through the bloodiest war Europe had ever known, and were still alive.

My mother used to say that she and Doris had had different fathers. Her father was a cheerful young man who, in the seven years before the war, delighted in playing all kinds of games with her. Doris, born after the war, had a father who was "severely depressed, and no longer the same young rascal that he had been when I was a child." Doris recalls her father as emotionally unstable, a man who, while usually thoughtful and calm, could also be very emotional and excitable, and have "fits of rage." During these rages, which were very brief but occurred relatively often, he would thump the table, and shout "very, very, very loudly." Although as a follower of Adler, David was opposed to the physical punishment of children, and never hit her, Doris still felt that he was "uncontrolled."

The attacks of fear and crying out in the night about which Amalie had written in 1914 did not stop when the war ended. From 1921 until 1931 David frequently sought and obtained a reduction of his teaching hours on the grounds of ill health. Medical examinations during these years found him to be between 20 and 35 percent incapacitated, in part because of "a high degree of nervous weakness" or "neurasthenia," although also because during these years he developed diabetes. As late as 1931 a government medical report said that he was "a war invalid with more than 35% disability."

Politically, after seeing the carnage on the Isonzo, David told one of his army friends: "I am becoming more and more red." Instead of the positive view of war he had expressed in the preface to "Horace in the Trenches," he became a pacifist. He was no longer a political conservative. He joined the Social Democratic Party, the great Austrian party of the Left for which roughly four out of every ten Austrians voted in every election between 1918 and the end of Austrian democracy in 1934. He was not an active member, but he took part in their huge marches on May 1, the international workers' day.

Despite his new political beliefs, David remained proud of his military service. Nothing better illustrates this than a story told by Eva Berger (formerly Eva Hitschmann, my mother's closest childhood friend). In the dark years of Nazi rule in Vienna, after my mother and aunt had emigrated, Eva, who was not Jewish, often visited my grandparents in their flat. On one of these visits she found him in a highly emotional state. He had received a letter from the Nazi authorities telling him that because he was Jewish he was unworthy of military service. "Unworthy of military service! Unworthy of military service!" he repeated, evidently quite dismayed. Eva was baffled at his reaction—how could he possibly want to serve in the Nazi army? But he saw only a rejection of the worth of what he had done in the previous war, and that wounded him deeply.

||| PART V |||

The Scholar and Teacher

18

The New Republic

In November 1918 Vienna ceased to be the seat of an imperial court ruling over fifty-five million people, and instead became the top-heavy capital of a tiny, landlocked, mostly alpine republic with a population of less than seven million. Of the innumerable adjustments that needed to be made, the most urgent was providing food and fuel. The armistice had ended the fighting, but the Allies kept in place, pending a final peace settlement, the harsh blockade they had imposed during the war. Vienna had depended for its food supplies on imports from the former provinces of the empire. These were now separate states, their borders still to be settled. The political leaders of Czechoslovakia, Hungary, and Yugoslavia were well aware that restricting food exports to half-starved Austria was a powerful bargaining tool. The result was a winter that made the severe rationing of the war years a time of comparative plenty. In the middle of Europe, people of all ages were dying from malnutrition-related diseases.

From these desperate circumstances, David, Amalie, and Kora could not have been immune, especially as Amalie was expecting her second child in March 1919. They did have a way out. Since all of them had been born in what was now Czechoslovakia, they could have become citizens of that country. Though it too faced difficult times, Czechoslovakia was not subject to the blockade, and the shortages were not nearly as bad as in Vienna. But David and Amalie were thoroughly German, in language and culture, and they had spent almost all of the past twenty years in Vienna.

Despite the terrible hardship, Vienna was still Vienna, and more attractive to them than any Czech-speaking city could be. They chose Austrian citizenship.

As reports of starvation in Vienna reached the rest of the world, assistance programs were organized, and families in several European nations offered to take in needy children from Vienna. Tens of thousands of Viennese children were sent to foreign countries. David and Amalie, worried about how they would care for the new baby, and whether Kora's health would suffer from the food shortages, sent my mother, then eleven years old, away with the other children. She went to Stockholm, where she spent more than a year living with a Swedish family. David returned to the Akademisches Gymnasium, but employment provided money, not food. Viennese went into the countryside to find peasants with surplus food, taking with them the family silver and linen because the peasants did not trust the devalued currency. Maybe David and Amalie's relatives in Czechoslovakia were able to help them (although it was during this period that David's mother, Ernestine, died after an illness).

The peasants were wise not to trust the currency. The Austrian kronen were no longer those "bright gold pieces" of which Stefan Zweig wrote, and the security and predictability of the Hapsburg era was just a memory. Both the krone and the German mark had begun falling in value during the war. After the war this decline turned into a previously unimaginable form of inflation. In 1918 a ride on a tram in Vienna cost less than half a krone. Two years later this had risen to 3 kronen. By January 1922 it was 60, and in January 1923, 1,500 kronen. By 1924, a meal that cost about 1 krone in 1918 could not be had for less than 30,000 kronen. David's pay was regularly increased, but it still failed to keep up with the cost of living. The salaries of state employees sank to between a quarter and a half of their previous real value. The hardest hit were retired people who had planned to live on money safely invested with a bank. Now their life's savings would not buy them a plate of goulash. The inflation was finally curbed in 1924 by a hard-currency loan guaranteed by major foreign powers, and a switch to a new currency, the Austrian schilling. In this suddenly quite unstable situation the leaders of extremist political parties found new adherents.

Immense as these problems were, for social democrats it was an exciting time to be in Vienna. The city became the first great metropolis in the world to put its municipal government democratically, but unequivocally, in socialist hands. "Red Vienna" lasted from 1919 to 1934. Moreover, from 1922 the city, which held a third of Austria's entire population, constituted a *Land*, or province all on its own, with wide powers of taxation. David was now living and working in a laboratory for new social ideas. Progressive-minded people came from all over the world to study Vienna's social programs. New public housing was built for almost 10 percent of the population. Public health was also a priority, and once the famine was over, infant mortality fell dramatically. "In Vienna," wrote one social democrat, "we lived with the great illusion that we would be the generation of fulfillment, that our generation would establish democratic socialism in Austria . . . this illusion was constructive and enriching to life."

Red Vienna's vision of socialism was one peculiarly well suited to a person of David's training and interests, for the vision of Austrian socialists differed from that of Russia's Bolsheviks precisely in that the Austrians saw culture and education as transforming agents that could bring about socialism. In this active political struggle, Adler's psychological theory was well positioned to play a key role. Since the war, Adler had made his position even more attractive to the Left by emphasizing that we all strive to be part of a community, to belong and to work with others for a common goal. A misguided upbringing and a hostile social environment may suppress our natural sense of community, and instill in us the false belief that we can find fulfillment by thinking only of ourselves. If education can change the way in which children are reared, they will cease to see work for the common good as an obligation imposed from outside. Working with others for a common goal will instead be the natural result of following our need to belong to a community.

By the mid 1920s the meetings of the Adlerian society were, according to Furtmüller, "one of the living centers of intellectual Vienna," and David was one of the leading members of that society. He lectured frequently and was a member of the editorial board of the *International Journal of Individual Psychology*; and when in December 1925 two specialist working groups were set up, one dealing with medical questions and the other with research in the humanities, David was elected chair of the humanities group. Four months later, when the society held its first formal postwar election of officers, Adler was elected chairman, and David became one of two deputy chairmen.

In keeping with his view of the role that upbringing and education can

play in avoiding neurosis, Adler opened a child guidance clinic in which
he gave advice to the teachers and parents of problem children. This
proved so successful that the city government took up the idea and established twenty-eight clinics, mostly based in schools. Suddenly child psychology, especially individual psychology, was making a real difference in
the lives of ordinary people. Red Vienna also saw an immense upsurge of
adult education, in which the Adlerians participated enthusiastically. For
example, from October 1923 to January 1924, Adler directed a "Seminar for
Mass Psychology" at the *Volksheim* in Leopoldstadt, just a few blocks from
where David lived. Vienna had many of these "people's homes," meeting
places or clubs that were used for lectures and discussions. The theme of
the "Mass Psychology" series was community feeling, and how making it
real can overcome feelings of weakness in the individual. David's contribution to the series was a talk called "Mass Psychology in Schiller's *Tell*," in
which he spoke about the varying ways in which, in Schiller's play, the
Swiss national hero William Tell deals with the union of individual and
community.

Most of the lectures David gave to Adler's group were on literary subjects—on Goethe's *Faust*; on the contemporary play *She-Devil*, by Karl
Schönherr; on Schiller as an individual psychologist; and a more general
one entitled "Individual Psychological Fruits of Reading." At the First International Congress of the Society for Individual Psychology, held in Munich in 1922, David spoke on "Shakespeare's Knowledge of Human
Beings," and in 1925 he traveled to Berlin for the Second International
Congress for Individual Psychology, where his topic was "Women's Struggle for Social Position as Reflected in Classical Literature." Occasionally,
however, he ventured more directly into psychological matters, giving
three lectures on aspects of Adler's idea of "masculine protest," one on the
feeling of inferiority itself, another called "The Psychology of Slaves," and
even a lecture on the possibility of intervening in case of a breakdown.

My grandfather's enthusiasm for the new democratic age is shown by a
speech he gave to his school on the fifth anniversary of the founding of the
republic. Austria was then what some called "the republic without republicans"—a reference to the fact that for all the political parties, the Republic
of Austria was a second-best choice. Some preferred union with Germany,
others longed for the return of the monarchy, another group wanted a
Soviet-style socialist society, and some favored a fascist dictatorship of the

kind Mussolini had just established in Italy. In that context, to give a talk called "Speech on the Celebration of the Republic" was to make a political statement, and this lecture is my grandfather's most explicitly political work. How, he asked, can a republic, defined as a union of the people concerned to advance the general welfare, become a living reality? David takes from Plato the idea that the state must raise the citizens that it needs. The young Austrian republic, therefore, has not really arrived yet. It will come into existence to the extent to which it attracts republicans to it. Here he finds a role for educators such as himself and his colleagues. We should seek a republic, not in the sense of a mere aggregation of free citizens, but of a union for a living community. This involves renunciation of our isolated individuality, for the benefit of the community; thereby we make the whole real, become its limbs, and serve it. But we can do this best by educating ourselves to become proficient in diverse fields of specialization. The work of education is therefore construction work in the service of the republic.

David then goes on to consider in more detail the nature of the republican "soul." He links the striving for political freedom with the child's striving to be free of the authority of parents and teachers. He illustrates the scorn of the young for old age by a lengthy passage from Goethe's *Faust*, from which he takes the idea that the youthful striving for freedom can, like cloudy apple juice in the first stage of fermentation, eventually become a fine, clear cider. But there is also another possibility: the juice can burst its container, and instead of the hoped-for clarity, the darkness of death may pour out.

David's speech raises important philosophical questions but does not probe the difficult issues that the Republic of Austria was soon to face. What are we to do when freedom of speech is used to advocate overthrowing the republic and denying freedom to others? This dilemma was to prove crucial for the future of the republic, beset as it was by enemies ready to take advantage of its freedoms in order to bring about its downfall. The Hapsburg Empire had had the trappings of democracy, but to the end, the emperor had retained far more power than, for example, the British constitutional monarchs. Austrian intellectuals led the world in a host of fields from logical positivism to psychology, literature, and economics, but few were active advocates of liberal democratic ideals. Many of them were alienated from politics altogether. Most of the intellectuals who were politically involved were socialists who, while democratic in their methods, were more interested in bringing about a socialist society than in defending democracy for its own sake. It takes time to develop a tradition strong enough to make a return to authoritarian leadership unthinkable, and the young republic was not given that time. The republican ideal failed to grip the masses in the way that other ideologies, both Left and Right, did. That, tragically, was why on one point David did turn out to be absolutely right. The cloudy juice of youthful freedom can turn into the darkness of death.

19

"The Secret of the Human Soul"

THE LETTERS David wrote to Amalie before they were married show that, even then, he knew that his life's work was to bring to light "the secret of the human soul," by examining his own life and the lives of others, "whether they lived thousands of years ago or are my closest contemporaries." He had started keeping folders of documents into which he filed Amalie's reports on her conversations with Lise, adding them, no doubt, to earlier ones on Martina, on his own observations of his relationship with Victor, and on what he had learned from Soyka. His attendance at Freud's lectures, and his subsequent membership in Freud's circle, as well as his research for *Dreams in Folklore*, can all be seen as part of this search. Choosing Adler over Freud did not change this; it merely gave David a different psychological framework for the same end. The 1920s was the most fruitful period for this work. He wrote sixteen articles, of which ten were published, as well as a substantial book.

David had set himself a huge task, nothing less than, as he wrote when it was all over, "to enlarge knowledge of humanity." As I began to read David's published works and the unpublished typescripts I found among his papers, I was curious to see how far he had been able to get with it. The phrase "knowledge of humanity" comes from his English summary of his life's work, so it is David's own translation of the idea of *Menschenkenntnis*, the key concept for what he is trying to achieve. Elsewhere David says that to gain understanding of our fellow human beings we need, not the analytical approach of the natural sciences, but intuitive insight into the nature of the person. Consider Socrates, unjustly condemned to die by drinking hemlock. A friend comes to him and offers him the opportunity to escape and go into exile, but Socrates refuses. Why? Here the natural sciences cannot help. To understand Socrates' decision, David says, I need to understand the whole person, and to know that Socrates regarded it as an ethical duty to accept even an unjust judgment, for otherwise he would himself be committing the wrong of breaking the law of his community.

The distinction David is making here owes a lot to Wilhelm Dilthey, the late-nineteenth- and early-twentieth-century German philosopher whom David calls the founder of a new method of psychological investigation. Though he was largely unappreciated during his own lifetime, Dilthey's preoccupation was to preserve the uniqueness of the humanities by resisting attempts to apply to them the methods of the natural sciences. Consistent with this view, in "My Scientific Work" David contrasts academic psychology with "knowledge of humanity" by saying that the former seeks to *explain* human behavior, and the latter to *understand* it. We understand something that is meant, or intended, by making it coherent with what we know of human ways of thinking, acting, and living. That is the task of *Menschenkenntnis*. Explaining, on the other hand, putting something into a series of causes and effects, is a task for academic psychology. Thus, *Menschenkenntnis* belongs to the humanities, and academic psychology to the natural sciences.

To understand our fellow human beings is not, David wrote, something that can be summed up in a book. It is more like a skill. Instead of analyzing a character into its parts as a botanist might do in studying a new plant, those who seek knowledge of humanity must put the parts together to understand the whole. For this reason we do not gain *Menschenkenntnis* by a series of controlled experiments in artificial laboratory conditions; instead, it comes from a kind of intuition, dependent on putting oneself in the place of the person one is trying to understand. Direct knowledge is possible only about our own self; we gain indirect knowledge of others by analogy with our own inner life. At the core of this method of understanding others, therefore, lies an understanding of oneself, and David's preoccupation with self-examination served as the essential starting point for his lifelong quest. Moreover, this quest comes around in a circle: knowledge of others is impossible without some self-knowledge, and conversely, complete self-knowledge is only attainable with the help of knowledge of others, for it is only by means of a comparison with others that we can gain a clear picture of our own nature.

David's search for knowledge of humanity is thus the pursuit of the two mutually dependent and intertwined interests that figure so prominently in the letters he wrote to Amalie from 1904 to 1906: understanding himself, and understanding others. At the First International Congress for Individual Psychology, David explained why this field was so important to him: "For life is after all living together, and what could be more essential for that, than at all times to know with whom we are faced, and who we ourselves are."

There are two important differences between David's researches into the nature of human beings during the period of his correspondence with Amalie, and during his involvement with the Society for Individual Psychology. The first is that in the earlier period, he was collecting material on real people—Victor, Martina, Soyka, Lise, and no doubt others. Now he is focusing on characters from literature of all kinds: folk stories, fables, fairy tales, the sayings of founders of religion, and of statesmen, and the works of great writers and poets. All of this he sees as a vast storehouse of knowledge of human nature. The second important distinction between David's early and later work is that during the 1920s everything he writes is based on Adler's theories.

Adler has established, David says in the preface to his book, *Fiction and Knowledge of Humanity*, that we have a "biologically grounded inadequacy." As isolated individuals we are too weak to have a secure existence. To do well we must be part of the community, and this leads us to feel the need to belong to a community. On the other hand, we also have a desire to achieve superiority as an individual. This arises from a sense of inferiority that exists because the various weaknesses spread across the human species give everyone sufficient grounds for feeling in some way inferior. Everyone strives to overcome the disadvantages that they believe they have. We construct an ideal self in which we are big, strong, and on top. In unfavorable circumstances, if the feelings of inferiority are extreme, our ideal self becomes godlike. We then strive to make this ideal self real, thus putting ourselves at odds with our own desire to be part of a community. The nature of that tension, and also the greater or lesser courage with which we pursue our endeavors, form our character. When the need for community is weak, and other opportunities for overcoming feelings of inferiority do not exist, a person may become a criminal. Where demoralization goes deeper still, a person may flee from reality, engage in childlike behavior, or develop a neurosis.

It is striking how far David has moved from Freud's teaching. In the preface to his book, his summary of our knowledge of human character does not even mention sexuality. David spoke more explicitly about his differences with Freud in 1930, in a talk entitled "The Goal and the Path of Knowledge of Humanity." Here he returns to the topic of love, which occupied him so much in his younger days:

> To love women is . . . to the highest degree a social feeling. Whoever loves a woman as a means to gaining pleasure, like wine, or as a kind of instrument on which he skillfully plays, counterfeits love in practice; whoever accepts its counterfeit as the original, falsifies it in theory (Freud's theory of the libido). The confusion becomes still worse if one does not clearly distinguish love for the beloved from love for the mother. The one is *eros*, or *amor*, the other *agape*, or *caritas*.

Here David rejects the foundation of Freud's entire psychological edifice, saying that his theory of the libido is based on the false idea that love between a man and a woman is to be understood in terms of a search for sexual pleasure, when it is really a desire for social contact, companionship or a sense of belonging. Moreover, Freud fails to distinguish love between men and women from the love of a child for his or her mother. David could not have held this view—or at least, not openly—at the time he worked with Freud on *Dreams in Folklore*. Any hint of heresy about such a core notion would have led to Freud's ending the collaboration immediately.

Although David rejects Freud's view of human beings, he offers no positive evidence for accepting Adler's, beyond the fact that Adler is a doctor who has observed his own patients and been able to help them. David's approach is that of a humanist, not a scientist in the modern sense of someone who subjects hypotheses to rigorous testing. In that, he is no different from Freud and Adler, neither of whom—even though they were both medically trained—was much interested in putting his theories to the test.

20

My Grandfather's Book

Melbourne, March 1999

AT HOME IN Australia, with some time off from my university work, I have read all of my grandfather's articles, published and unpublished. There is only one of his scholarly works still to read: his book, *Fiction and Knowledge of Humanity: Psychological Rambles through Old and New Literature*. Had I kept strictly to chronological order I would have read it before reading his last few articles, for it was published in 1926; but its 346 pages of dense German prose were intimidating. After nearly a year immersed in my grandfather's life and works I can now read David's German with sufficient fluency to follow his thoughts, appreciate his style, and be amused by the occasional humorous aside. His book is the last terra incognita, the exploration of which is at once an exciting prospect and a formidable task.

I have two copies. One was in my home when I was a child. Its tattered cover, a buff-colored piece of stiff paper, is unadorned except for the book's title, the name of its author, and the publisher's name and logo. Inside, my grandfather has written his name and address. There are a few penciled annotations in his handwriting. This is a copy he read over, so I'd like to use it, but the pages are coming loose from the spine, and reading will damage it further. The other copy, a hardback with a properly sewn-in binding, belonged to my aunt. Perhaps she had it bound, to stop it from falling apart. That's the copy I read.

The book begins with a Latin dedication to Amalie, both his "dear spouse" and his partner in research. Then comes an introduction on questions of method, followed by the core of the book, five studies of characters in literature: Achilles from Homer's *Iliad*; Dido from Virgil's *Aeneid*; Shakespeare's Othello; Gustav Aschenbach, the central figure in Mann's *Death in Venice*; and the husband from Schönherr's play *She-Devil*. In each case David shows how the character fits with Adlerian psychology.

The centerpiece is a one-hundred-page study of *Othello*. That my grandfather had a deep knowledge of entire realms of literature, in Greek, Latin, and German, I already knew; what I did not expect was the depth and breadth of his reading of Shakespeare. He draws not only on well-known plays such as *Julius Caesar, Richard III, The Merchant of Venice,* and *Measure for Measure,* but also on *Titus Andronicus, King John, Henry VI,* and *Henry VIII.* His interpretation of *Othello* is striking because he treats it not as a play about jealousy, but as one about race and—to use a currently fashionable term—"otherness." Othello is a Moor, and Shakespeare provides ample evidence that he is despised because of his race. Perhaps it is not surprising that an Austrian Jew should be sensitive to this, at a time when the major English-speaking Shakespearean critics barely noticed the race issue. But David does not make this point simply in order to highlight the importance of race in the play. Instead, he sees Othello's race as the basis for a sense of inferiority that is central to his motivation and hence his downfall. In this, Othello is not, as David points out, unique among Shakespeare's characters. Richard III has his physical deformity; Edmund, in *King Lear,* is a bastard; and Shylock is another victim of the racial prejudices of the Venetians. But while both Shylock and Othello are abused because of their race, Shylock at least has the support of the Jewish community. Othello is all alone, and his position is therefore more desperate. He strives for recognition from the Venetians, but the honors bestowed on him are unsatisfying because Othello knows that the nobles are honoring him not for what he is, but because they need him to wage their wars. Only a woman's love can make him feel accepted for himself. Thus, he needs and loves Desdemona. Yet as an aging, proud, black soldier, he is worried about being dominated by his beautiful young white wife. And these feelings are not without some foundation: Desdemona says to Cassio that she will "tame" her husband, and Othello tells her that he will deny her nothing. Since his principles do not allow him to break ethical standards by being unfaithful to her, he can save himself from this domination only by finding that she has been unfaithful to him. Thus we have an Othello in whom, as David puts it, "the demon that guides him is not Iago but his own ethos."

I reread *Othello*. My grandfather has made me see a familiar masterpiece of English literature in a new way, as a play about the impact of a racially charged setting on a proud man. I wonder if David's view really is new, or only strikes me as so because of my own limited knowledge of the play. In the library I find the work of A. C. Bradley, the leading English Shakespeare scholar at the time David was writing. Bradley writes that "the action and catastrophe of *Othello* depend largely on intrigue." Nowhere does he contemplate the impact on Othello of the racist remarks made by Venetians in the play. Even twenty-five years after David wrote his essay, F. R. Leavis, then the dominant figure in English literary criticism, does not ask whether racial ostracism might be a factor in producing Othello's character. Another quarter century had to pass before, in the 1970s, critics began to give the racial issues involved in the play their proper place. David was ahead of his time.

━━━

IN A BIOGRAPHY of Alfred Adler written by Phyllis Bottome, I stumble on the following passage:

> One of these scholar friends of Adler's, Professor Oppenheim, published a book of which he was inordinately and perhaps unjustly proud. A review promptly appeared in the International Journal of Individual Psychology, of a slight and rather damning nature. This was ascribed to Manès Sperba,* and Adler did nothing to counteract the impression made by the review. He did not even read the book. No one knows the exact cause of this neglect, though when the author asked Professor Furtmüller, associated with both Adler and Professor Oppenheim, why Adler did *not* read his friend's great work, he replied: "I myself tried hard to read that book, but found that I could not; it was unreadable."
>
> Usually Adler, though he seldom had time to read his friends' books, un-

* A young protégé of Adler's, who often caused friction in the group—the correct spelling is Sperber.

less they were on the direct track of his own work, took the deepest interest in their success. This particular friend's book *was* on the track of Adler's work, and the friend in question was one of Adler's oldest and most intimate friends. Professor Oppenheim therefore had grounds for his bitter disappointment. The end of this deep and devoted friendship came with a resounding crash. Professor Oppenheim, a highly emotional man, ran through the streets of Vienna with tears streaming down his cheeks, asserting to the friends who crossed his path that Adler had been cruelly unkind to him, and that all was over between them.

I am moved by this vivid image of my grandfather, and saddened by the thought that his book should be treated with disdain by those he considered to be his close friends and coworkers. But I have read several reviews of his book and I don't recall any that fit the account Bottome gives. The review in the *International Journal of Individual Psychology*—the official journal of the Adlerian society—is signed by Dr. Rudolf Pick-Seewart, a well-known member of the Vienna group. So how could it have been "ascribed" to Manès Sperber? And it recommends the book as one that could be read "with profit" by "every Individual Psychologist," adding that the section on *Othello* "brings the uneasy military commander as close to us as a human being as perhaps only Goethe's Wilhelm Meister has brought us near Hamlet." For David there could be no higher praise than to be compared with Goethe. So what review could Bottome be talking about?

Nor can Bottome be right when she says that the friendship between David and Adler ended around the time David's book was published, in 1926. In David's papers there are several postcards Adler wrote to him when on his various tours of America, in 1927, 1928, and 1929, some of which discuss possible publishers for an English translation of David's book. And on my mother's bookshelves there is still the one-volume edition of *The Complete Works of William Shakespeare*, in English, that I used to read when I was a teenager. On the flyleaf it bears an inscription: "To Professor D Oppenheim, in steadfast esteem as his most splendid comrade-in-arms in times of need. Dr Alfred Adler, New York, March 26th, 1929." So it is unlikely that Adler failed to read my grandfather's book, and simply not possible that anything around the time of its publication caused an irreparable breach in their friendship. Whether anything else connected with Adler or the book ever caused him to run through the streets of Vienna with tears streaming down his cheeks, I do not know.

The book did not, however, achieve the success for which David must have hoped. There were some other reviews, but apparently none in any major newspaper or magazine. In July 1927 my grandfather wrote to J. F. Bergmann suggesting further efforts to obtain reviews in specialist journals, and also encouraging him to reduce the retail price of the book so that more of those interested in individual psychology could afford it. Perhaps the study on Othello would have had more impact if, as Adler suggested, the book had been published in English, but that did not happen.

———

Fiction and Knowledge of Humanity seeks to show that people are driven by feelings of inferiority to strive for recognition and success, and that this has been an important theme in some of the leading literary works of the Western tradition, from Homer to modern times. My grandfather wants, as he says in the introduction, to understand the range and diversity of human character. He has succeeded in showing only a part of that range and diversity. Nor has the method David advocated become widely accepted as the best way of achieving that understanding. From the evolutionary perspective that I favor, it is easy to see that both Freud and Adler were onto something important about human nature, but that they both missed the larger picture. Sex and the struggle to overcome inferiority are two sides of the same phenomenon. Those of our ancestors who were not interested in sex were less likely to leave descendants in future generations. Hence sexual desire does, consciously or unconsciously, underlie many of our actions. But for most of our evolutionary history social status has correlated strongly, especially for males, with access to sexual partners, and with the chances of offspring surviving to maturity. Hence an evolutionary understanding of human behavior explains why both sexuality and the drive to overcome inferiority are so important to us.

21

Independence

As THE 1920S DREW to a close there were ominous signs that the Adlerians, like the Freudians twenty years earlier, were becoming intolerant of independent thinking. Several prominent members resigned, among them Rudolf Allers, who with David was a deputy chairman of the group, and Viktor Frankl, who after the war went on to develop his own school of psychology under the label "logotherapy." Later Adler cut his former protégé Manès Sperber out of the group. Erwin Ringel, a high school student of David's who continued to be a friend after he had left school and later became a leading member of the Society for Individual Psychology, said:

> Oppenheim was an immensely tolerant person. He embodied tolerance. I will not hide the fact that this damaged his relationship with Adler in the final years of the '20s and the beginning of the '30s. Adler's conflict with Allers and especially Adler's conflict with Manès Sperber affected him deeply, and—let's put it this way—Adler's brusque way of proceeding somehow estranged and oppressed him.

If David had decided in 1911 to side with Adler largely because of the way in which Freud had behaved toward Adler, the rerun of these events, with Adler playing Freud's role, would have left him feeling distinctly uncomfortable. On February 3, 1930, at a special meeting to mark Alfred

Adler's sixtieth birthday, David gave a talk called "The Goal and the Path of Knowledge of Humankind." David's speech begins in a challenging way, given that this was a celebration for Adler, by referring to the danger of a cult of personality. Indeed, anyone who reads what Adler's followers said about him can see that the danger was very real, for the constant admiration for what Adler did or said rapidly becomes cloying. That David was alert to the sycophantic way in which Adler's followers treated him is the first clue as to why he might have begun to disengage from the Adlerians. Nevertheless, David says that a sixtieth-birthday celebration is a special occasion and we are justified in praising Adler, as long as we do it on account of his achievements. Then he himself becomes lavish in his praise, applying to Adler words from Seneca, saying that he is "the discoverer of souls, holds the key to hearts, and is the teacher of humanity." After exploring what these terms mean, David concludes by asking how someone like himself can contribute to the task of creating a "culture of humanity." He finds his answer in the idea that despite the importance of feelings of inferiority, which Adler has shown, there is a fundamental equality in all human beings that consists in the fact that each one of us "can form himself in accordance with his own plan." If we take responsibility for the kind of being we are, "the burdensome feeling of being less, being able to do less, and counting for less than others will disappear" and will be replaced by "a joyful eagerness" to prove that one is equal to others, by contributing to the general task of helping to bring about "a culture of humanity."

This can be read both as philosophy and as autobiography. As philosophy, it expresses David's ideal society: one of free, responsible individuals working together to build a common human culture. Such a culture would transcend the divisive ideas of nation, race, and class that were becoming more prominent in Europe at the time. Though David does not explicitly address the triumph of fascism in Italy or the increasing popularity of the Nazi Party in Germany, his references to a "culture of humanity" would, to his audience, have been a very clear indication of his opposition to, and concern about, these nationalist tendencies. That this passage is also autobiographical is evident from the parallel between David's account here of "the burdensome feeling of being less, being able to do less, and counting for less than others" and the accounts he gave Amalie, a quarter of a century earlier, of his own constant feelings of inadequacy. Read in this way, the passage tells us that David has himself learned to take responsibility for his own life and now feels that he has found the path toward throwing off his feelings of inferiority.

Another essay, written in the same year and contributed to a Festschrift* dedicated to Adler, reveals more about how David was thinking of taking his destiny into his own hands. Under the title "Seneca on Educating One-self and Being Educated by Others," David offers an exposition of the Ro-man philosopher's views on whether true education comes from another person, a teacher, or is something one must work through for oneself. The subtext of the paper, however, is a sorting out of David's own relationship to Adler. What we learn from Seneca is: "The human being must be guided, until he begins to be able to guide himself." David is aware that he can now guide himself; and in another self-referential remark, he writes that anyone who aspires to lead his life in the right way must "renounce the freedom of dallying and bumbling through life." This renunciation, David says, is "a fundamental act of self-education, especially when, after long, painful wrong turnings and confusions, it derives from a clear insight into one's own inadequacy." Here is my grandfather, nearing fifty, after spending twenty years in close association with the man who developed the theory of the inferiority complex, still confronting his own feelings of inadequacy. But what are the wrong turnings and confusions to which he refers? The answer becomes apparent when David discusses the different ways in which a pupil can relate to a teacher. On the one hand, one can relate to one's teacher in a way that comes close to "the sworn duty that compels a soldier or gladiator to grant inviolable validity to every word of his supe-rior . . . to stick with [his] chief through thick and thin." That is the wrong way; but there is also another way, which involves "freedom of thought and critique." Once our character is properly formed, we can choose this sec-ond way: where we previously acted to please our teacher, in the future we will act out of respect for our own character.

This essay is David's declaration of independence, his way of saying that he can think for himself, and will not take Adler's words as the inviolable truth. He does this, not in a bitter or hostile tone, but in a way that empha-sizes the crucial influence that Adler has had on him, and expresses his

---

*A Festschrift is a volume of essays presented in honor of an eminent scholar by friends and students or former students.

thanks to Adler for having helped him to achieve, after such long struggles, this hard-won independence. The essay is nevertheless a thinly veiled rebuke of Adler's followers for turning the Society for Individual Psychology into a cult—and, to the extent that Adler had allowed or encouraged this to happen, of Adler himself. That David should make this rebuke by drawing on Seneca gives it a nice touch, for Adler had used Seneca's words as the motto of his most important book, *The Neurotic Constitution*.

Such a declaration of independence should be followed by a new line of fresh, independent writings. Instead there is silence. David found his independence, but not his way as an independent scholar. His essay on Seneca is his last published work. The reasons for this are unclear. Perhaps he had no outlet for his work, now that it was no longer suitable for the journal of the Society for Individual Psychology; or possibly it was because he felt he could better contribute to the creation of a society of free individuals by focusing more intensively on educating his own students.

22

The Teacher of Humanity

DAVID'S ESSAY on Seneca tells us that his ideal of a good teacher was not one "absorbed in dry academic learning, which cuts him and his adherents off from active life," but a teacher who is "all concern for the ethical progress of his pupils, on whom his personal example works more effectively than his word." Here I found the fuller statement of the point that had struck me fifteen years earlier when reading my aunt's essay on her father. My grandfather's idea that what one teaches cannot be divorced from the way one lives is also my own—though I held it long before I read anything by or about my grandfather. Nor did I obtain it from him indirectly, through my mother, for it was not my view until I was a long way from home, at Oxford University doing a postgraduate degree in philosophy. There I found myself unable to justify the total disregard of the interests of animals that precedes their appearance on our plates at mealtimes. It struck me then that, if I was going to spend my life studying and teaching ethics, I needed not merely to think and write about the ethics of our treatment of animals, but to change what I ate. Afterward I applied the same principle to other issues, for example the ethical obligations of those living in abundance to people elsewhere in the world in danger of starvation or death from poverty-related illnesses. It seems that my grandfather and I independently reached a similar view of the connection between ethics and how one lives, and also between teaching as passing on academic learning, and teaching as making a difference to how one's students live.

What was David like as a teacher? Erwin Ringel recalled:

. . . in the *Akademisches Gymnasium* we had a series of magnificent teachers, and the grandest of all was Oppenheim. He was a humanist of the most intensive kind. He taught us Greek from 1934 to 1938, and with the Greek he conveyed to us not only the vocabulary and so on, but also the humane ideals of the Greeks. Beautifully and well. And that, we have to say, is the ideal teacher . . . that he doesn't teach just one subject, but that he teaches the humanity that is really in every subject.

In his book *The Austrian Soul* Ringel adds another significant detail: of the twelve students who remained in his class after the Jewish students had been excluded from the school, five were subsequently arrested by the Gestapo. This he sees as evidence of the influence of their teachers, Oppenheim among them, "who with clarity and firmness informed us of the inhumanity of the Nazis." If Ringel is right, David's teaching did make a difference to how at least some of his students lived when they were tested in a manner more severe than we would ever want or expect our students to be.

Among the students who subsequently attracted the attentions of the Gestapo was Friedrich Heer, who was later to become an influential writer and critic in postwar Austria. In August 1938, after the Nazis had taken over Austria and the school's Jewish teachers had been dismissed, Heer wrote to David:

I am now looking back over a major part of my years of education. And I can quite simply say just one thing: nowhere, least of all at university, have I found a teacher like you. . . . You were a teacher through and through your entire life. I think truly a teacher possessed. Possessed by the desire to form unformed shoots and to give them shape, to create form out of chaos, and to create clarity and light out of confusion and fog—to create together with the students. . . .

Perhaps you have asked yourself (I am sure you have) the anxious question, whether something of your mind will really get through, in a formative and creative way, to the often confused and turbulent thoughts of young fellows. Perhaps this question has arisen in a particularly pressing way in these days in which the old "humanitas" appears to have so completely lost its formative power over people. I have often thought of you during these days. And today I am very sure of one thing: that, so long as I live, I will bear witness for you, my greatest teacher, and for the world in which you live.

These were brave words to write, under Nazi rule, to a Jewish teacher recently dismissed by the Nazis, but Heer was as good as his word. He took part in the only significant public demonstration in Austria against the Nazi regime. For this he was arrested by the Gestapo, but soon released. After the war Heer, a Catholic, wrote a book exposing Catholic anti-Semitism. His postwar essay "Austrian Genius and Judaism" begins with a dedication to David Oppenheim in which Heer briefly outlines his teacher's life and his death, and then states simply: "He taught me humanity."

Not all of David's students, however, were enthusiastic about his teaching. Peter Schramke, who was in the same class as Heer, says that he sometimes gave lectures in which he got carried away into realms of thought where most of the students could not follow him. Then students in the class would start to misbehave. Suddenly David would come back to earth, see what was going on, and display "flaming anger." Walter Friedmann, another pupil from my grandfather's last years as a teacher, also recalls outbursts of temper that, coming as they did from a usually mild-mannered man, were embarrassing to the whole class. In one case, where a student was poorly prepared for a class, "He shouted at the student and told him that he should go to a trade school and not waste his time at the *Akademisches Gymnasium*."

David was renowned for his reluctance to fail his students. He introduced a new grade, "just satisfactory," to enable him to pass students who might not have achieved a "satisfactory." Fritz Schopf, to whom David taught Latin in the early 1920s, said that "justice was one of his most striking characteristics, on which one could always depend, whether in the matter of marks or in general human judgment." On the other hand, David expected a lot from his students. When they could not translate texts properly he could be indignant, because he saw it as a kind of disrespect of the ancients. In translation he was always searching for exactly the right word. Schopf remembers one such incident:

> He would stop in the middle of a sentence and, like someone dying of thirst, would, with outstretched arms, strive for the word, which his audience was to call out to him, as if he needed to be helped out of a fix. . . . I remember, for example, that once someone offered, or better, suggested to him, the apparently quite correct word "horse," and he replied loudly and indignantly: "Horse, horse! — it has to be *steed*!"

For all his lofty expectations, however, Schopf says the students valued highly the fact that David was a teacher "with whom we could, at any time, talk openly about our concerns and worries."

Schopf describes David as looking like a rabbinical scholar, with "a beautiful long beard . . . wavy hair, lightly streaked, which was mostly rather wild, as if in motion." He had a strong, resonant voice. Some thought his lecturing style "exaggeratedly theatrical," but Schopf found it effective in getting his students absorbed in what he was saying. The most vivid portrait of David as a teacher, however, comes from a newsletter put out by the 1937 graduating students. It is in the form of a poem, in the classical style, and while it should not be taken too seriously, it is unique in that it is not colored, as postwar comments may be, by knowledge of David's fate:

> Valiant, I call the man who taught many students Latin,
> Howling and spitting at the same time in sheer unspeakable effort.
> Grant me the strength, O Muse, to sing his praises. . . .
> If a sentence that a pupil translates for him seems false,
> With a fearful gaze at the heavens he moans softly to himself.
> Soon however the voice is raised in the breast of the old schoolman
> And the word of thunder flows from the bearded lips:
> "Today it is again splendidly revealed how null and void your
>   ability is.
> If you cherish the assumption that you will squeeze through with such
>   atrocious ignorance, you are completely astray.
> An honest peasant can understand that! It's inconceivable!"

The poem goes on to describe David's general appearance: his goatlike beard, his streaked, graying collar, his tie "drawn together, like the hangman's rope," and one of his trouser buttons left undone. It concludes with this image of my grandfather leaving at the end of the school day:

> Oh, he really resembles a homeless tramp
> From cradle to grave his coat is bound to him
> And his once gray scarf, that he often forgets.
> Protected by his hat and armed with his bag,
> He calls simply "Farewell" and disappears through the open door

In December 1998 I walked through the entrance of the nineteenth-century neo-Gothic building that houses the Akademisches Gymnasium, knowing that my grandfather must have walked through this doorway thousands of times between 1909 and 1938. Inside is a fine arched foyer, with columns and a classical statue. A wide staircase led me up to the first floor, where the staff room and the principal's office was. I had written to the principal, Harald Feix, telling him that I was writing a book on my grandfather and would like to see the school where he taught for so many years. The building had survived the war—and the wear and tear of another fifty years' use as a school—and was in remarkably good shape. Feix received me warmly and introduced his colleague, Hedi Weindl, who had led a school program to mark the sixtieth anniversary of the dismissal of the three Jewish teachers at the school and the expulsion of all Jewish students, who made up 43 percent of the total school enrollment. I was shown a series of large, blue bound volumes that contained handwritten class lists, which included the names of the teachers and pupils for each class, year by year. I went through a few years in the 1930s, noting the classes David had taught—usually one class in Greek and one in Latin. The class records for the classes he taught bore his familiar signature. I noticed that he did not teach the same year level in consecutive years, but instead he would teach, say, Greek to 1A in 1931, to 2A in 1932, to 3A in 1933, and so on. Did this mean, I asked, that he would have the same students for the same subject year after year? Yes, I was told, that was—and to a large extent still is—the usual practice in Austrian schools. For better or worse, the students and teacher are bonded together for as long as they are doing the subject. That helped me to understand how my grandfather could have had such a profound influence on some of his pupils. Together year after year, they would get to know each other much better than I ever got to know my high school teachers, most of whom taught me for only one or two years.

Before I left, the principal asked me if, on another visit to Vienna, I would be willing to talk to the students about my ethical views on animals and bioethics. I was surprised—I had never mentioned my academic work, and I did not know that he knew about it. In October 2002, I went back to the Akademisches Gymnasium. There, in the school's neo-Gothic ceremonial hall, where David would have delivered his speech on the fifth anniversary of the Austrian republic, I spoke to an audience of sixty final-year students. I began by talking about my grandfather, his values, and his fate.

Then I moved to my own work in ethics. Afterward the students asked questions and we had a lively discussion. In the dark years between David's dismissal from the school and his death, he would have been comforted, I thought, if he could have known that one day his grandson would be able to have this kind of free, open conversation at his old school.

23

The Secular Jew

CONSIDERING THAT David was the descendant of innumerable rabbis, the son of the secretary of a Jewish community organization, and the husband of a rabbi's daughter, being Jewish seems to have been of remarkably little importance to him—until Hitler made it the crux of the last four years of his life. His letters to Amalie are full of Greek and Latin, but devoid of Hebrew. His German shows no trace of any Yiddish influence. (Yiddish, in his time, was not used by Jews in Moravia.) All those who knew him agree that he was either an agnostic or an atheist. The clearest indication of David's attitude to being Jewish is his refusal to have a son of his circumcised, a decision that rejects the mark of the Jewish people's covenant with God.

David's universalist values led him to oppose those who emphasized national or ethnic identity. His solution for anti-Semitism involved not only greater tolerance, but also assimilation into the larger community, so that being Jewish would become less significant. Hence he never wavered in his opposition to Zionism. Doris recalls that when she was thirteen or fourteen, around the time the Nazis came to power in Germany, Zionist youth groups were popular in her neighborhood. They would meet in the homes of their members:

> I was a fairly lonely child and the singing and dancing I heard when walking past their homes had a strong emotional and social appeal for me; however,

my father was a devout social democrat, and although I was brought up in a very liberal atmosphere where few things were directly forbidden, his feelings against "National" and for "International" groups were so strong that my joining would have been an act of defiance.

David wrote very little about Judaism. Early in his scholarly career, in 1908, he reviewed a book entitled *The Rise and Development of Anti-Semitism in the Ancient World.* He begins by pointing out that whereas modern anti-Semitism denies Jews equal rights because it sees the Jews as racially inferior, in Greece and Rome hatred of Jews arose from the incompatibility of the specifically Jewish culture, organized on religious and national lines, with the system of public order in the Greek and Roman states. This important distinction, David thinks, the book under review fails to explain. It matters because where Jews were prepared to merge into the Greek or Roman public order, they were accepted as equals. David would have had no doubt that the viewpoint of the ancient world was less objectionable than the racist form of anti-Semitism that had emerged as a political force only in late-nineteenth-century Europe. David himself had no objection to giving his allegiance to his community. But to the new, racist anti-Semites, no matter what risks he had taken and what injuries he had suffered in the defense of his country in the First World War, no matter how strong his support for the fledgling Austrian republic, no matter how pure a German he spoke or how well he knew and loved the works of Goethe and Schiller, no matter how much he distanced himself from Vienna's Jewish community, or that he did not believe in or practice the Jewish religion, he would always be a Jew.

———

THE ONLY OTHER PIECE David wrote about the religion of his ancestors would probably never have been written had not, in October 1925, a Dr. Josef Heymann written to Alfred Adler objecting to his statement, in *The Neurotic Constitution,* that some Jewish religious customs devalue women in an odious way. "In reality," wrote Dr. Heymann, "not a trace of such devaluation can be found in Jewish law." Dr. Heymann's letter was in my grandfather's papers, with a response from David that begins by explaining that Adler is too busy to provide a lengthy reply, and has instead asked David to do so. David begins by assuring Dr. Heymann that individual psychology wants to lead people to a closer community, and does not wish to offend religious feelings. Nevertheless, he continues, if it sees "obstacles on this path to community," then it cannot remain silent. Hence it "demands the setting aside of that ascendancy of men, which is anchored in the foundations of our culture." This male dominance has two roots, David says, one in the Graeco-Roman ancient world, and the other in the Judeo-Christian religion. He then lists a number of ways in which Judaism supports the ascendancy of men, beginning with Genesis, where God is male, creates man in his own image, and creates woman from man and for man. Then woman irreparably harms man by enticing him to sin, and as punishment God puts her under the rule of her husband. That rule still prevails. A Jewish woman cannot even free herself from the rule of her husband by divorce, because only the husband can bring about a divorce. A widow must seek the permission of her late husband's brother before she can remarry. The birth of a son is greeted with greater joy than the birth of a daughter. Only a boy is instructed in the Torah, and therefore it is incumbent only on a boy to be called at puberty to accept the law. The ten people needed for holding a communal divine service must all be men—for this purpose, "women count as little as children who cannot talk." Next David refers to the anxiety evident in Jewish teachings about the "seductive power of the woman." This is so great, he says, that when a Jewish woman enters marriage she must have her hair cut off, while particularly religious men do not even touch hands with a woman who is not their wife. To clinch the argument David reminds Dr. Heymann of the prayer that a Jewish man should say every morning, thanking his creator that he did not make him a heathen, a slave, or a woman. David closes by saying that the goal is to give women what is due to them, but "our time is still very far from this goal and will probably remain so for a long time, if we do not all, instead of quarreling over our greater or lesser fault, each call out for ourselves: 'I have sinned' and do everything to improve ourselves and others."

═══

HITLER ENSURED THAT for some Jews living in Europe before 1945, Zionism was a lifesaving choice. Are my grandfather's universalist values thereby proven wrong, or naively utopian? I do not think so. The postwar experience of Australia, the United States, and the countries that make up the European Union makes it still possible to hope, as my grandfather did, for a future in which racial differences cease to lead people to hate one another, and in which nationalism, of any kind, becomes a waning force in political life. Admittedly, the confidence with which one can hold to this hope wanes with each flare-up of ethnic hatred, for example in Bosnia and Kosovo, and waxes when more moderate views prevail. More recently—I am writing this in the spring of 2002—continuing suicide bombings by Arab terrorists show that while Zionism saved some Jews from Hitler, it has not brought peace and security to their children; and we have all seen on our television screens the cost that it has inflicted on Palestinians, including many who have nothing to do with terrorism. My grandfather might have thought that, in a tragic way, his opposition to Zionism has been shown to be right after all.

24

Sexual Equality

MY GRANDPARENTS SOUGHT an equal relationship, one in which they remained "self-sufficient personalities even in the union." Doris believes that they achieved this: "My parents' marriage was probably the best marriage I have ever encountered. . . . It foreshadowed the modern marriage, built on a sharing and respecting of each other's beliefs, on a spiritual partnership." Yet, no matter how much they might have tried to be entirely equal partners, David and Amalie did not break the pattern in which the man's career takes priority over that of the woman. David's career as a schoolteacher determined when the couple left Vienna for Nikolsburg, and when they returned to Vienna. At that time, which coincided with Kora's birth, Amalie appears not to have been working, although she might have done some private tutoring. Sometime after 1918 she became the secretary—that is, the executive officer—of the Association of Austrian Banks and Bankers. This was a position of responsibility that drew on her administrative skills. Unusually for the period, she worked part-time, "job-sharing" the position with a man. She showed her independence by declining to style herself "Frau Professor Oppenheim," as a woman married to "Herr Professor Oppenheim" normally would have done. Instead, she used "Frau Dr. Oppenheim," emphasizing her own academic qualification. Nevertheless, she did not pursue physics or mathematics at a higher level, though she clearly had the ability for it. Joan, my sister, recalls her saying that she had never really wanted to go further in her studies. Whether this was truly her feeling in 1905, when she formed and then abandoned the plan to spend a year in Berlin, I cannot tell. What is clear is that it was David, not Amalie, who pursued a scholarly career as well as a profession, and that Amalie assisted her husband in his research. She no doubt did this because she wanted to do it, not because either she or David believed that it was a wife's duty to sacrifice her career to that of her husband. Nevertheless, even if this was so, it is surely not a mere accident that despite her outstanding abilities, it was the woman who was the more willing to give up her career.

All those who knew my grandparents agree that Amalie was the practical partner in the marriage, the one who tackled "the many great and small issues of daily life," and was the "load-bearing pillar of the household." In the extended family she played the role of the wise one to whom others came for advice with a personal problem. By the 1930s, when young relatives came to dinner, they found David, seated at the head of the table, largely silent, an aloof and intimidating figure. Amalie, in contrast, had a natural warmth that made everyone love her.

BETWEEN 1923 AND 1925 David wrote and talked intensively about sexual equality, characteristically in the context of discussions of literature. In September 1923 he gave two talks to the Adlerians on Karl Schönherr's play *She-Devil*. The central character of this play is a man who, driven by feelings of inferiority and a consequent need to demonstrate his success, acquires a grand house and a beautiful wife. When the wife falls in love with another man and begs her husband to set her free, his response is not that he loves her or needs her, but: "My wife is my chattel; and I will not let my chattel be taken from me." Thus David draws the issue of the status of women into what has been the major theme of his work since he left Freud's circle, namely the way in which a feeling of inferiority can lead to a damaging desire to dominate. The social and educational message of the Adlerian school is implicit in the idea that if boys can be brought up in ways that do not produce feelings of inferiority, men will cease to treat women as chattels.

A year later David published an essay on Dido, the legendary founder of Carthage and a character in Virgil's epic poem, the *Aeneid*. Dido founds the city after fleeing from her brother, a tyrant who has slain her husband. She rules it with a degree of valor and fortitude usually attributed only to men. Then Aeneas, the hero of Troy, is shipwrecked on the coast of her country. Dido falls in love with him, but Aeneas is commanded by Jupiter to sail on and become the founder of Rome. When he obeys the divine command, Dido commits suicide. David has an unusual perspective on the *Aeneid:* he sees the entire work as "a great allegory of the battle of the sexes," and takes the story of Dido to show that if women seek to have both the manly and the womanly virtues, society puts them in an impossible situation: "For in Dido we found the woman who tries, with masculine as well as with feminine means, to equal the man, to surpass him, and even to rule him, and for this transgression of sacred boundaries, she has to pay with her life."

In 1925, at the Second International Congress for Individual Psychology in Berlin, David opened a session called "Cultural History and Religion" with a paper entitled "The Woman's Struggle for Her Social Position as Reflected in Classical Literature." It opens like a feminist tract: "Women's struggle for social position is an expression of dissatisfaction with the conditions which the man, in accordance with his viewpoint, has created regarding the relations between the sexes. In the conviction that the woman is physically, mentally and morally an inferior being, he keeps her in lifelong bondage."

David then says that he will show the ways in which women try to defend themselves from this oppression, either resisting or adapting to male dominance. This leads to an unusual catalog of "female types," many of them based on sexual behavior:

> The "untouched," *"integra"* resists the love of a man, and married love, in every way. . . . Half-yielding is the manner of the *"semiintegra,"* who belongs partly to the wanton Aphrodite, partly to the maidenly Athena. Her conduct is thus inoffensive, if she refuses the man one thing, and grants him the other. In that case we call her the defenseless *"seminuda."* Now and then she becomes, in order to save only her anatomical innocence, *"perversa,"* who either lets herself be used as a boy, *"paedicata,"* or lowers herself even to *"fellatrix."*

David continues in this mode, over three pages, until in the final two paragraphs he returns to the theme of his opening:

Fundamentally distinct from all the types mentioned so far is the *"communis,"* who is not oriented in opposition to the lords of creation, but to the community that links women to one another, and is active in mutual aid over both small and large matters. Closely related to the *communis* is the *"aequalis,"* which demands from men recognition of equal worth and equal rights for herself and those like her.

This last type, *aequalis,* or the woman who is an equal, is David's ideal woman. In marriage she wants not only that her partner should "honor the sanctity of the community of the flesh," but that they should share "a community of the intellect and the union of their destinies." She should also be able to participate in the governing of the state, something that has become possible only in the modern era, ushered in by the French Revolution.

Among my grandfather's papers I found an expanded version of this lecture. In the introduction to this version David points out that the cultures of ancient Greece and Rome were so masculine that it is rare for us to be able to hear the voice of a woman directly; but male writers found ways to express the sufferings of those who were not able to speak for themselves. He then draws on classical literature to give examples of the female types that were so fleetingly mentioned in the published version. Whereas the published lecture is sometimes so brief that the discussion of female types that involve particular forms of sexual behavior verges on the merely salacious, in the longer version it is clear that David is trying to show how women with no means of determining their destiny except through their sexual desirability and their indispensability for childbearing found different means of using these sources of influence. The longer version of the essay could easily have been the basis of a book on images of women in the ancient world, a work that would have served as a valuable source for the later growth of feminist studies. But David seems to have done nothing further with his research in this area.

Throughout my childhood, I had before my eyes one significant product of David and Amalie's shared ideal of sexual equality. Soon after I started going to school, in the early 1950s, I learned that something I had taken for granted was not at all "normal." When I was invited to my friends' homes after school, their mothers were there to give them a glass of milk and a treat. If I invited them home, my mother was at work, and there was a housekeeper at home to look after me when I got back from school. Not only did my mother work, when my friends' mothers did not, but my mother was a doctor at a time when there were few women practicing medicine. Her choice of career and her commitment to continue working after her marriage and the births of her children were a reflection of her parents' attitudes toward sexual equality.

25

Vacations and a Wedding

IN JULY OR August each year the family left the city for a summer vacation. Often they would visit relatives in Moravia, but they usually also went for three or four weeks to one of Austria's many mountain-ringed lakes. Other members of the extended family joined them there. In a group photo taken at Velden on the Wörther See in 1931, David stands at the back dressed in a light-colored loose-fitting outfit that resembles—but is surely not—something you would wear for classes in one of the oriental martial arts. His sister Hannchen stands next to him, and her husband, Sandor Kunstadt, sits in front of them, both in bathing suits. Amalie is the only person in the picture wearing normal street clothes. Sitting in the front row are Hannchen and Sandor's children, with Doris between them. Kora is not there. Two years later, however, she was with the family during August on the Klopeinersee, staying at a villa owned by a major Austrian bank, something that was presumably possible because of Amalie's work for the Association of Austrian Banks and Bankers. She describes the scene in a letter to Ernst Singer, my father, to whom she was not yet married. The villa is on the edge of the forest, about three minutes from the water. She is spending her days swimming in the scenic lake with her father, sunbathing in the meadow, going for walks with her cousin Alice Pollak, or, at five o'clock, going to the tea dance.

In July 1934 David, Amalie, and Doris returned to Velden, this time with Kora, for a vacation that was not to pass with the usual tranquillity. Eighteen months earlier, Hitler had come to power in Germany. In local elections in Austria, the Nazis were winning votes from the Christian Socialists. With the Social Democrats holding on to their traditional supporters, the Christian Socialist chancellor, Engelbert Dollfuss, looked likely to lose the next national election. Taking his lead from Mussolini, he swept parliament aside and turned Austria into a fascist state. In response, in February 1934 the Social Democrats called a general strike. The army, the police, and the Heimwehr, a fascist militia, went on the attack against the workers, whose strongholds were the big apartment blocks built by the "Red Vienna" government over a decade earlier. The army used artillery against residential buildings inhabited by the workers and their families, and within a day or two, all resistance was over. Dollfuss's "Fatherland Front" became the only legal political party.

Dollfuss thus destroyed the political movement to which David had belonged, and with it the hopes he had expressed a decade earlier that the Republic of Austria might become a true democratic community. David's attempt to educate his students for citizenship in that kind of community must have seemed in vain. Yet many Austrian Jews, including some who had been Social Democrats, now supported Dollfuss. They believed that firm measures were necessary to stop the Nazis from creating chaos and thus providing a pretext for Hitler to annex Austria. The Austrian Nazi Party was suppressed along with all other political parties, and Dollfuss sought to unite all Austrians against the Nazi threat. To that end he censored anti-Semitic propaganda and protected Jewish university students from violent attacks by organized Nazi student groups, and when some resort towns refused to accept Jews, he made it clear that such discrimination would not be permitted. (This is another instance of the complexity of Austrian anti-Semitism, for in this respect Austria was ahead of the United States, where at the time, and for decades afterward, many vacation resorts excluded Jews.)

On July 25, 1934, Austrian Nazis seized the chancellery, murdered Dollfuss, and proclaimed a Nazi government. Kora wrote to Ernst about how the news reached the Oppenheims in Velden:

> I found out about the events in Vienna on Wednesday evening at the dance, when around 10 the music suddenly stopped because of the death of the Chancellor. We rushed in great excitement to the nearest radio,

where we waited for the sparse reports from Vienna. We also tried to call Vienna . . . but lines were continually engaged. Yesterday morning an acquaintance of ours succeeded, after waiting an hour, in having a quick conversation with Vienna, which calmed us somewhat.

The calming news was that the putsch had failed and the Nazis in the chancellery had been surrounded and shot. Mussolini moved troops to the border to protect the independence of Austria, and Hitler tried to save face by disavowing the actions of his Austrian supporters. Dollfuss was replaced by Kurt von Schuschnigg, a member of Dollfuss's cabinet who was expected to continue his policies.

=====

MY MOTHER WAS now twenty-six years old, had done well in her medical studies, and was working as an intern at Vienna's celebrated General Hospital, the institution in which, thirty years earlier, her father had listened to Freud's lectures. By this time she had had a number of romances, including one with a young doctor from an aristocratic Roman Catholic family that owned a castle and estate in the South Tirol. She would have liked to marry him, and her parents would not have objected to such a union, but his did, and the relationship was broken off.* She met my father, a handsome young businessman from an assimilated Jewish family, while skiing with friends. The relationship became serious, but on more than one occasion it was nearly broken off because of my father's interest in other women. In June 1934 this problem became evident to David and Amalie, who, like any parents, must have taken an interest in the love life of their older daughter. Ernst took a steamer down the Danube to Varna, a beach resort in Bulgaria, with a friend called Mitzi. There they were seen by someone who knew them, who told my father's parents of it. As Ernst was on his way back to Vienna, my mother wrote to tell him that his father had called her parents, full of concern about the news of Ernst's behavior. Kora said that her parents, however, "considerately remain silent, as do all the others too." These difficulties were eventually overcome, and my par-

---

* Or should I say, interrupted? When my mother and her former boyfriend were both in their seventies, and alone because of the deaths of their spouses, they renewed their friendship and spent several summers traveling together in Europe.

ents were married on May 30, 1937. On the day before, my mother wrote in her diary: "I love E. very much, does he feel the same? I hope so!" The next day's entry says that the wedding was "very lovely." After a midday wedding banquet, David and Amalie bid farewell to their daughter and new son-in-law as the couple left for their honeymoon in Rome, Naples, and Capri.

The new member of the family came from a social milieu quite different from that of David and Amalie. My father's parents did not live in an apartment, but in their own house with a garden in Pötzleinsdorf, a leafy outer suburb of Vienna. The family's money came from making and selling umbrellas. Ernst, the oldest of three sons, did not go into the family business, but worked for a firm that imported coffee. As befits a businessman, his politics and lifestyle were conservative. Perhaps David privately echoed the sentiments of his father over Hannchen's marriage to a businessman, twenty years earlier: "Papa . . . would have wished for a learned son-in-law." But Kora was much too independent to be influenced by her parents on her choice of husband.

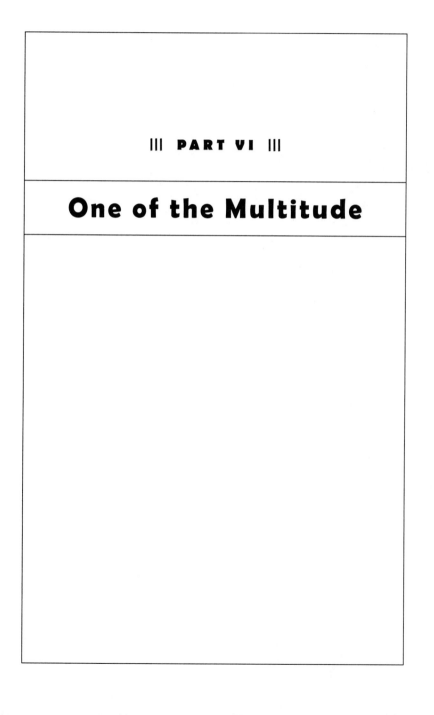

||| **PART VI** |||

One of the Multitude

26

The End of Austria

FOR THREE YEARS after the murder of Dollfuss an uneasy calm prevailed in Austria. In defiance of the Treaty of Versailles, Hitler rebuilt the German army, then sent it into the demilitarized Rhineland. The French and British governments protested ineffectually. It became apparent that if Hitler were to tear up the clause of the treaty forbidding the union of Germany and Austria, France and Britain would again send protests, not troops. Nor could Mussolini be counted on to come to the defense of Austria again, as he had in 1934. British and French opposition to his bloody conquest of Ethiopia had pushed him closer to Hitler. In February 1938 Hitler increased economic and political pressure on the Austrian government. Schuschnigg met Hitler at Berchtesgaden, where he was bullied into several concessions, the most serious of which put Austria's police and internal security forces into the hands of Arthur Seyss-Inquart, a leading Nazi sympathizer. It was expected that Hitler, in turn, would acknowledge Austria's independence in a speech that he was due to give to the Reichstag on February 20. Many Austrian Jews spent that afternoon clustered around the radio listening to Hitler's three-hour rant, anxiously hoping for some indication that Austria would be allowed to continue to exist as a separate nation. None was forthcoming.

The red-and-white flag of Austria began appearing everywhere, and Austrians of all political persuasions, other than the Nazis, took part in rallies for Austrian independence. On March 9, Schuschnigg announced that a referendum on the issue of Austrian independence would be held the following Sunday. It seemed a bold stroke, for all observers predicted a two-thirds majority in favor of independence. Hitler demanded that the referendum be canceled. Schuschnigg made an emotional speech in which he explained that to avoid pointless bloodshed, he had bowed to the demand for the cancellation of the referendum, and was resigning. That night the German army rolled across the Austrian border, meeting no resistance. The Roman Catholic archbishop, Cardinal Innitzer, ordered the church bells to be rung in celebration of Hitler's arrival in Vienna.

Suddenly every Austrian Jew was living in fear. In the week following the invasion, Austrian Nazis allowed free rein to their pent-up resentment, plundering Jewish property, and humiliating and beating up Jews. Jewish women were forced to scrub pro-Schuschnigg slogans off the streets with toothbrushes, and to clean the toilets of the barracks used by Nazi storm troopers. Children had to paint "Jew" across the windows of their fathers' shops. In the largely Jewish Second District, where David and Amalie lived, Jews were forced to call one another insulting names in the street, and Jewish shops and apartments were looted. The police either ignored complaints from Jews, or arrested and assaulted the complainants. At the end of the week, the Nazi authorities stopped the random acts of violence, and began a more systematic program of expropriation and degradation.

David's student Friedrich Heer has described my grandfather's experiences during that traumatic week:

> Dressed in his uniform as Captain of the Imperial and Royal Army, Dr. Oppenheim awaited the SA [storm troopers, the Nazi paramilitary forces] louts who stormed his apartment (fresh-faced youths, as he later described them to me). The lads ripped the medals of war from his chest.

Doris was also directly affected. She recalled the first day of Nazi rule vividly:

> Vienna turned out to be full of jubilant anti-Semites . . . hysterically jubilant. It all came out. It was the greatest shock of my life. Like when the guy stopped me: "Miss, are you Jewish?" "Yes." "Come here! Wash the windows!" Other people were there too. I tried to wash the windows. I was no good at it. After half an hour: "On your way!" . . . Nothing happened to me. A great deal happened to me. I went home and said that I was not staying in Vienna.

In my mother's diary Hitler's entry into Vienna, his triumphal reception at the packed Heroes Square, and the proclamation that Austria was now a province of the Third Reich all go unremarked except for the single comment "Frightful mood! Much excitement!" The entry for Saturday reveals that my parents are thinking along the same lines as Doris: "We are learning English." On Sunday, my parents go to see my father's parents, and then David and Amalie come to visit them. At the end of the week Kora writes: "Everyone comes to us, just to see other human beings." In the next week there is more learning of English. The end-of-week comment is: "Still without consolation."

On April 10 Hitler had his own referendum on Austrian independence. The Nazi Party waged a major propaganda campaign for a vote for union with Germany. There was no opposition, for all other political parties were banned, and Cardinal Innitzer issued a pastoral letter urging all Austrians to vote yes. Those voters who remained unconvinced had good reason to fear that anyone voting no would be detected and punished. My mother's diary reads: "On the day of the vote we stay at home, and have very many guests." The official result was a vote of 99.75 percent for union with Germany—an unbelievable result, given that only a month earlier, polls had shown a majority for Austrian independence.

From the day after the Anschluss, David was no longer allowed to set foot in the school where he had taught for nearly thirty years. The Jewish students were sent to a school for Jews only. Among my grandfather's papers is his official letter of dismissal, dated May 13, 1938:

> Since, in accordance with the decree of the Führer and Reich Chancellor regarding the swearing-in of public servants . . . you are, on account of your Jewish descent, not able to be sworn in, you are permanently incapable of carrying out the duties of your position in accordance with the regulations. It is therefore anticipated that you will be placed in permanent retirement with effect from the end of May.

This was a fine piece of Nazi logic. Public servants were required to swear an oath of allegiance to the government, but Jews were deemed incapable of swearing such an oath. Hence Jews were not eligible to retain their positions.

Reluctantly, David and Amalie accepted Doris's decision to leave her home and country. She was only seventeen years old. "My parents were not very happy about it," Doris recalled. "I was still a very young, inexperienced, impractical child. But they said: If you want to, then you must leave Vienna." Kora and Ernst were also quick to decide to go. In May my mother wrote that she was learning to cut gloves, and Ernst to sew them—this was to ensure that they had a skill that would enable them to earn a living in another country if my mother could not practice medicine and there were no business openings for my father. But where would they go? In the last week of April an entry reads: "Always the same—we are waiting until the end of next week." They were waiting for news about obtaining a visa to go to the United States. To get one it was necessary to have a U.S. citizen guarantee that the immigrants would not be a burden on the state. My father had written to an uncle there, hoping that he would provide the guarantee. When the uncle's reply came, however, it contained an offer to provide a guarantee for my father only; Ernst's wife, the uncle explained, was not known to him, and so he could not make any undertakings for her. My father declined the offer. Trying every possibility, no matter how unlikely, my mother wrote to an Australian she had met a year or two earlier, named Jerry Donovan. Some friends of hers had got to know him while skiing, and planned to take him to one of Vienna's famous *Heurigen*, a typically Austrian wine tavern. They invited my mother along because she spoke some English. Donovan, a Roman Catholic, sent her a card after he returned to Australia, and she kept it because getting a card from a place as remote as Australia was a novelty. Now she described the situation in Austria and asked him if he would possibly be willing to provide the guarantee necessary for her immigration to Australia—along with that of her new husband. Within six weeks, my parents had a visa to go to Australia.

As the day for my parents' departure drew closer, the Oppenheim family went to a hilltop restaurant in the Vienna woods and had photos taken of them all together. The actual farewell was recalled by Ernst's mother, Philippine, in a letter written to her son six months later:

> Every detail of that 22nd August on which you left us seems so distant, and yet every detail is still vivid to us. We see still in our mind's eye the gloomy station hall, we still see in front of us the friends, who wanted to shake your hand once more—there were 14 of us who came to bid you farewell. We still hear your words, dear child: "We are not saying 'Goodbye' we are saying 'Until we see you again.'"

It isn't hard to imagine how sad the remembrance of those parting words made my father in the years to come. The train took them across the mountains they loved to Genoa, in Italy, from where they boarded a ship for Australia.

A month later Doris left too, traveling first to England, where she had a temporary visa to work as a domestic servant. David gave her a parting gift that she kept with her all her life: a copy of Goethe's *Faust*, with a dedication telling her to turn to it when she needed consolation and faithful friendship. Unlike Kora, Doris forbade her mother to come to the station, telling her that her presence would make the parting too difficult, and she might jump out of the train window and stay.

The younger generation of Austrian Jews could see no future for themselves in what was now a part of Nazi Germany. Businesses run by Jews were being boycotted or expropriated; Jewish employees in schools, banks, and insurance companies were dismissed; and Jewish doctors were prohibited from treating non-Jews, which meant, since a disproportionate number of Austrian doctors were Jewish, that many of them would be unable to find sufficient patients to make a living. On top of that there was always the risk of physical violence at the hands of Nazi hooligans, and the unnerving sense, as my father later put it to me, of living in a country in which the government seemed to have fallen into the hands of gangsters. Those who could get permits to go elsewhere did so, as fast as they could. With the older generation it was different. Until their daughters left, David and Amalie showed no interest in emigration. Erwin Ringel recalls visiting his former teacher:

> I said to him, Professor, I beg you, I implore you, to leave this country, for your life is under threat. And I will never forget his reaction. He gave an affectionate chuckle. . . . "But Ringel, what an idea, what are you thinking of? Nothing at all can happen to me. I have risked my life for this country. I have the Gold Medal for Bravery. I have the Medal for the Wounded. I have given everything for this country. They can't do anything to me." So I left, unsuccessful . . . and what I didn't know was that two of my classmates, Herbert Christian and Peter Schramke, had independently been to him on two separate occasions and pleaded with him in the same vein. But there was nothing to be done.

Though David's war decoration was bronze, not gold, the essence of the story rings true, at least of David's attitude during the crucial first six months after the Nazi takeover. David's nephew George Kunstadt recalls that during these months "the Jewish population of Vienna went frantically from foreign embassy to foreign embassy to discover possibilities of emigration—except your grandfather. He felt that his distinguished military service would make him untouchable." Ringel suggests that there was another reason David was so reluctant to go. He lived and breathed German and European culture to such an extent that he could hardly imagine surviving in another country, let alone another continent, with an entirely different culture. It would have been, Ringel said, "like tearing a tree from its roots." Here Ringel gets wrong, if not the pain David would have felt in leaving his cultural roots, at least his willingness to be uprooted. In the very first letter Amalie wrote to her children in Australia, she wonders whether to book a passage for herself and David. With one daughter already away and the other about to go, the reality of being separated from their children must have overpowered David's sense of the impossibility of a life outside the German-speaking world. Still, the effect of even a slight drag on Amalie's interest in leaving might have made a vital difference to the eventual outcome. Whereas Kora and Doris had got away as soon as they could, Amalie's comment conveys no sense of urgency about leaving. My grandparents did not sense that their lives were in danger.

Many years earlier, in his speech at the First International Congress for Individual Psychology, David had said that the object of *Menschenkenntnis*, the attempt to understand human beings, was both self-understanding and "to know with whom we are faced." In several subsequent essays he had described how feelings of inferiority can lead to obsessive, bizarre passions with lethal consequences. This should have made him alert to the dangers of Nazism, a movement led by a rejected artist who had spent years on the margins of society, actively supported by those who were socially and economically at the bottom during the Weimar Republic, and fueled by a deep resentment against the more successful German and Austrian Jews. Yet now, in the hour when he needed it most, David's understanding of his fellow human beings failed him. Perhaps it was too theoretical, too remote from the world in which he was living. Others with less education had a better gut feeling for those with whom they were faced.

27

New Life and Old

AS MY PARENTS' SHIP SAILED away from Europe, south through the Suez Canal, into the Indian Ocean and then east for Singapore and Australia, Hitler was threatening war on Czechoslovakia in defense of the German minority in the Sudetenland, allegedly suffering under Czech oppression. Britain and France had a defense treaty with Czechoslovakia, and another European war seemed close. Neville Chamberlain, the British prime minister, was desperate to prevent a repetition of the carnage of 1914–18. "How horrible, fantastic, incredible it is," he said, "that we should be digging trenches and trying on gas masks here because of a quarrel in a faraway country between people of whom we know nothing!" (My father always remembered that speech with his own sense of incredulity. For him, Czechoslovakia was anything but "a faraway country," and it wasn't difficult to find out quite a lot about the quarrel between the Nazis, who could scarcely boast of their concern for minority rights, and the democratic Czechoslovakian government.) Seeking a way out, Chamberlain proposed a conference to settle the dispute. In Munich, on September 30, 1938, Britain, France, and Italy agreed to Hitler's demands and told the Czech government that if they did not hand over to Germany the lands Hitler sought, they would have to defend them on their own. Chamberlain flew back to England, waving a piece of paper with Hitler's signature on it which, he said, meant "peace in our time."

Three days after the Munich Agreement, David and Amalie received a telegram from my parents marking their safe arrival in Australia. David wrote back:

> My Dear Ones,
>   When we, who are used to hearing sad news constantly, suddenly get a happy message, the joy is twice as great. . . . That is how we felt about your telegram . . . now that everything is working out so well, not the least being the quite unhoped-for securing of world peace, we are now for the first time really confident and we hope that all our wishes that we bear in our hearts for your new life will be fulfilled quickly and completely. . . . A thousand greetings and kisses.
>
> Always in heartfelt love,
Your loyal father David

Until the outbreak of war in September 1939 letters traveled regularly and reliably between the Oppenheim and Singer parents in Vienna and their children in Melbourne, their new home. My parents kept the letters they received, and nearly all of them still exist. They wrote a single weekly letter to both their parents, to be shared between the Oppenheims and the Singers in Vienna. Amalie and David also kept the letters that came to them, and many of these have survived too.

From the moment my parents land in Australia they are delighted by the warmth with which they are welcomed by Jerry Donovan and many others—all of which makes an especially pleasing contrast to their recent experiences, since most of the people who are going out of their way to be kind to them are not Jewish. Ernst starts to explore the possibilities of setting himself up in business as an importer of coffee. He is advised that this is a pointless venture, as Australians drink only tea, but since he knows little about tea, he decides to stick to what he knows. Kora's medical degree from the internationally renowned University of Vienna is not recognized in Australia, so she seeks work as a laboratory assistant or a schoolteacher in math and sciences. Another urgent priority is applying for immigration permits—initially for Doris and my father's younger twin brothers, Fritz and Hans, but later for David and Amalie, Albert and Philippine, and other friends and relatives.

The letters from Vienna reveal the steady deterioration in the situation of Jews there, although since everyone knew that mail might be opened and read by the Gestapo, what their parents could say was limited. The first letters my parents receive after arriving in Australia contain news of the "Aryanization" of Ernst's family's umbrella business. First non-Jewish "managers" are installed, and then a fortnight later the complete confiscation of the business is confirmed. Though the letters refer to it only obliquely, soon Jews have to give up their radios, and are forbidden to go to the theater, concerts, and the opera. Many cinemas put up notices saying that Jews are not welcome. The words "Only for Aryans" or "Jews Prohibited" are stenciled onto benches in public parks. At the tram stop closest to the Vienna woods, Nazi storm troopers stand turning back Jews who want to go for a stroll.

On November 8 Ernst asks David what he is doing, now that he can no longer listen to the radio. Part of the answer David gives is that he is studying English. That letter was sent just before Kristallnacht, the pogrom against Jews across Germany that took place on November 9–10. In Vienna almost every synagogue was burned down, thousands of Jewish shops were looted and plundered, two thousand Jewish families were summarily evicted from their apartments, and many other homes were raided by Nazis, who took whatever valuables they could and destroyed those they could not take with them. Twenty-seven Jews were murdered, and more than six thousand were arrested and sent to Dachau concentration camp. For many German and Austrian Jews, Kristallnacht was a blessing in terrible disguise, for it ended their uncertainties about the need to leave.

The application for an Australian entry permit for Doris was swiftly granted. On her voyage to Australia she spent a day in Singapore, and in describing it to her parents she mentioned that Europeans never walked, in part because it was too hot, but also out of consideration for their standing. Here, because she is white, she is a member of the superior race. This is, she says, "one of the great charms that the East offers to the European," but she quickly adds that the value that is assigned to her personally is "questionable." That is not enough for David, who reminds Doris that "anyone who, having themselves been reduced to a pariah, finds consolation in regarding someone else as still lower, basically sanctions what is done to him."

The next Nazi move against the Jews was a law to "solve the housing shortage"; under this law, Jews were evicted from their homes and forced to live together with other families. In January David writes that both Marianne, a daughter of Amalie's deceased brother Jakob Pollak, and Sara Lustig are staying with them, although later Marianne finds another place to go to. The next month the Singers are forced to sell their fine house for a price that Ernst finds "shocking," but he tries to console them, saying that a house is "just a lifeless thing, ensouled only by the people who live in it." He hopes that they will one day have another in Australia.

In this atmosphere of constant crisis, Amalie increasingly takes over the decision making. She has, David writes, "a lot to do with her advising work," not only in her own household but for her wider family and friends. In May, Amalie begins to type her letters because her "writing work has really already become too great to be managed by hand." The Nazi occupation of Bohemia and Moravia, in March, has brought many more members of their extended family under Nazi rule. As well as keeping in touch with a large family, now rapidly dispersing to different parts of the globe, she is also writing on behalf of friends and other relatives, seeking ways in which they might be able to find a refuge. David tells his children not to mourn the loss of the intimate charm of handwriting—he and Amalie have, in any case, had to develop "the hide of a rhinoceros." He says that he would learn to type, were it not for the fact that he prefers to pursue one thing at a time, and considers learning English more important. Amalie says that they have just returned from Pötzleinsdorf, where the Singers are still living, though now only in a part of the house they once owned, and the four of them have spent a beautiful afternoon in the garden. Amalie adds, "This is for us the only possibility we have of getting into the open and the fresh air." There is a splendid park, the Augarten, just two blocks away from their own apartment in Krafftgasse, but Jews are now forbidden to enter Vienna's parks. There is also a telling remark about Amalie and David's respective moods and temperaments:

> You have, praise G., no need to worry, we are, praise G., all well and more or less cheerful and in good spirits, according to our nature. That I am among the "more," doesn't need to be said.

The implication, of course, is that David is among the "less." That is not at all surprising, for in addition to the tightening restrictions under which he was forced to live, the German invasion of the Czech lands had shattered the hopes for peace he had expressed after the conclusion of the Munich Conference. Hitler's word had been shown to be worthless, and it could no longer be claimed that his ambitions were limited to the goal of uniting all Germans into one *Reich*, for now he was ruling over the Czechs. Nothing short of war was going to stop him from dominating Europe. Even Chamberlain knew that "peace in our time" was an illusion.

Though the question of war must have been on everyone's mind, the correspondence between Vienna and Melbourne usually focused on narrower (and safer) concerns. My father had sent David an essay on coffee that he had written for *Australian Grocer*, a trade magazine, in which he suggested that grocers might promote coffee sales by providing their customers with information on how to make a good cup of coffee—information that, from the sharp comments my father makes on the coffee he has been served in Australia, was urgently needed. David praises the essay effusively and offers to assist in the writing of advertising material, so as to "use my pen as a weapon in the struggle for existence." He is continuing to study English "desperately" and is optimistic about his progress, but adds: "Unfortunately, such an optimistic outlook only wins out in small matters; when I think about the future, I cannot muster up your confidence."

Ernst succeeded in getting a permit for his brothers. By April they were ready to leave, when disaster struck: they were detected attempting to smuggle a camera out of the country. Jews were forbidden to take money or valuables with them when they emigrated. The suggestion to bring a camera had originally come from my father. He had written: "Since the ship stops for a day in Genoa, one could perhaps arrange for a rendezvous with Ivo [a cousin who lived in Zagreb, in what was then Yugoslavia]. He could perhaps bring my camera there." I am not sure how my father's camera was supposed to reach Ivo; but perhaps my father was suggesting that Ivo should take it home when next he visited Vienna. Perhaps there was no such camera, and this was a coded suggestion that Ivo be given a camera to take out, as a way of getting some of his parents' money out of the country. In any case, instead of arranging this rendezvous in Genoa, my father's brothers bought a camera in Vienna and attempted to get it out of the country through an intermediary, whom they met at the railway station. Somehow they were caught in the act, and the intermediary confessed everything. For a time it looked as if they would not be allowed to go. Ernst writes on April 14, "As far as one can see, there is no prospect at all that the brothers will come soon," and he says that he is "trembling about how your situation will develop." Jews had been sent to concentration camps for less. But Fritz and Hans were fortunate. The Singer family had, remarkably enough, a connection to Seyss-Inquart, the Nazi whom Schuschnigg had, under pressure from Hitler, made minister of the interior. He had been a tenant of Albert and Philippine's, occupying one floor of their house in Pötzleinsdorf. (It is hard to imagine how such a man—later to become notorious as the Nazi ruler of Holland—could have been on civil terms with his Jewish landlord, but that nevertheless seems to have been the case.) Now Seyss-Inquart headed the provincial government of "Ostmark," the German province that Austria had become. The Singers appealed to him to intervene in the case, and he did: in May, the twins were allowed to go. They arrived in Australia in July 1939. David writes to wish them well on their arrival, saying that they have been "reborn." He justifies this term by saying that "it is surely justified to call the life that is now behind them, the life here, 'a death.' . . . To end such an existence of death agony and fear for one's life and nonetheless to live on, can well be described as a 'rebirth.' "

Amalie's letters continue to be filled with news of the efforts of relatives and friends to leave. The repetition of desperate hopes, only occasionally fulfilled, becomes numbing, but here is one that is typical of many:

> From our dear ones in Brünn the reports are less satisfying. Max and Ilke are . . . already very impatient, which says a lot with these phlegmatics! Hansi has already had the entry permit for a long time, but still doesn't have the exit permit, which is more difficult to get there. Fritzi still has no prospect at all, for Gyury there are only many rejections. Fritz and Anny K. are supposed to have applied afresh, as I have heard. Hannovers write that Mrs. Newman has informed them that no decision has yet been reached; I fear that your information that she has been rejected is the more recent news . . . she is just longing for Australia.

In July, Amalie gives another picture of the "accustomed quiet life" that the Oppenheims are living, with the visits to and from the Singers "the only entertainment." Though they can go neither to the cinema nor to the coffeehouse, they are not bored, because David is working on his English "with real fanaticism" and she is busy with family matters and her extended correspondence. Later that month David writes of the mounting crisis over Poland, saying that they are starting to become accustomed to the "suspense of awaiting what the immediate future will bring to the world and beyond that, to us." Borrowing from *Macbeth*, he writes:

> if the old witches' song: "Fair is foul and foul is fair" keeps on sounding, I am still always "morally outraged" even though I know that no lightning bolt of rage can rout the witches' work on the world stage, whose boards are shaken by the resounding steps of Macbeth and his heirs.

My parents would have been in no doubt about David's meaning, but the literary allusion was sufficiently ambiguous for David to be able to insist, if queried by the Nazi censors, that since Macbeth was king of Scotland, it was the British who were his heirs.

Ernst's brothers found settling into Australia difficult, probably because they had arrived with little English and could find only the most menial work, Hans as a domestic servant and Fritz selling eggs door-to-door. They wrote letters expressing their longing for home, to which David replied that "the land that their souls are seeking is no longer where they are looking." The Austria they knew was finished. Instead, David said, they must learn to speak English. Only then, he says, quoting from Goethe's *Faust*, will they be able to say in their hearts: "Here I am a human being. Here I am allowed to be one."

28

Enticing Hopes

WHEN MY PARENTS WRITE that they have attended a discussion organized by a Melbourne Jewish group on "modern Judaism," David wonders whether someone there, perhaps a learned rabbi, "would perhaps be
interested in me." He suggests that Kora might mention her father to such a
person, describing him as "an offshoot of the venerable House of Oppenheim" who is "carrying on the tradition of the family, as a scholar to whom
the Bible is as familiar as Homer and who has given expression to this intellectual direction in a book." If she would do this,

> then perhaps, perhaps, I could even talk about whether it might after all
> be possible to find some space for a creature like me to live, a living space,
> i.e. a feeding place, the most modest possible, but one that is nourished
> by my own work. I know that it is a utopia in the literal meaning of the
> word, and that in fact that there is no longer a place for me anywhere at
> all, and least of all in that land, very far removed from intellectual luxury.

In December 1938 Doris writes from London to congratulate her parents on their coming wedding anniversary—their thirty-second—and to express the hope that the next one will see the family reunited. David
describes this hope as "enticing" but warns that it "should not seduce us
into forcing its fulfillment, and thereby—God forbid—finally leading to
disappointment." To make this hope "a beautiful reality" they must all work

"cautiously" for it. Doris's part in this, he says, is to learn to "stand more and more on your own feet, and so to relieve our concerns for the future." The implication is clear: the Oppenheims plan to join their children in Australia, but—even after Kristallnacht—they are in no real hurry, and want to see their children established in the new country before burdening them with their presence. When Amalie says this again to my parents, my father replies sharply:

> Mother writes that she doesn't want to be a burden to us here. This sentence really makes us cross. You are a burden to us when you are in Vienna, when we can't think rationally here because of our worries about you, but not here.

By this time Ernst has already applied for entry permits to Australia for David and Amalie and for his own parents, and Kora is beginning to make inquiries about possible positions for her father—who at fifty-seven is not yet ready for retirement—at the University of Melbourne.

The prospect of emigration forces David to face the distressing issue of disposing of his most precious possession, his library. There are too many books to take with him, so he has to select which he will leave behind. His letter on this topic shows the excitement in which it was written—it is full of alterations, phrases crossed out and words added, and the handwriting is even less legible than usual. My father, concerned that David's attachment to his library will keep him in Austria, wrote disparagingly of too much worry over "torn books." David quotes the phrase back at him, recognizing Ernst's good intentions, but saying that the phrase "makes the hurt still greater." Even torn books are not worthless, but in any case, his library has much more than that. If Ernst could only see his illustrated books of art history, the collections of French novels, the translations of the classics of Russian literature, he would not refer to his library in those terms. Then David adds:

> One who can go without his children can easily go without other things too. . . . Without butter, if it happens to be in short supply. That is what my dear wife said, not long ago, in a shop where this unpleasantness was taken too seriously, and I was entirely of her mind. Groceries are fuel for maintaining the metabolic process in which organic life consists. As long as there is something there, to keep this process going, what does it mat-

ter if one material or the other does the work? There are greater pains. But a collection of books, that is . . . so lofty a value that it does not vanish, even when we are unable to satisfy the hunger for so completely different a value as that of the love for our nearest and dearest.

On March 7, 1939, my father telegraphs: "BOTH PERMITS GRANTED." They have the vital entry permits for both the Oppenheims and the Singers. They had almost given up hope of getting them—an Australian official had spoken disparagingly of those who, as soon as they arrive in the country, want to have an entire "rat's tail" of people following after him. In a letter following the telegram, Ernst expresses his delight that the permits have nevertheless been granted. But then he adds a paragraph that sits oddly with his and Kora's emphatic rejection, just three months earlier, of Amalie's idea that they should not come yet because they would be a burden on their children:

> Now you will have to decide when you will come. You know how happy we would be if you were to come as soon as possible, but there are reasons why it would nevertheless be advantageous to wait until my business situation was clarified and until the children [i.e., his younger brothers] have found some kind of job. This is of course only applicable if the conditions are bearable. If not, come as quickly as possible. For the journey November/December is the best from a climatic point of view. Dutch ships are preferable but the Italian ones are also quite good. . . . You four parents should of course travel together. For the Oppenheims it would be best to arrive here around December, so that they have 2 months' time to prepare themselves for school and to settle in.

Here is my father, writing in March 1939, and suggesting that the Oppenheims and Singers might delay their departure until November! Despite the proviso "if conditions in Vienna are bearable," the effect of these remarks could only have been to encourage both sets of parents to put up with the situation in Austria a little longer, rather than to leave as soon as they possibly could.

Within a month, after receiving distressing accounts of the conditions under which his parents are living, Ernst thinks better of what he wrote in March:

I see all the time that you are worried that you will be a burden to us here. That's ridiculous. So far no one has starved here. You are a burden to us only as long as you are in Vienna—not, it is true, a material burden, but a mental one, and that is much worse.

This seems to have some effect. Ernst's parents book a passage to Australia on the Dutch vessel *Christian Huygens*, sailing on August 16, and the expectation is that the Oppenheims will go with them. Amalie is already compiling a list of things to be shipped. On June 22 she writes a letter full of the practicalities of the impending move. Ernst has suggested to his parents that they bring their piano, a baby grand, because they know of another immigrant who sold such a piano for forty pounds. Amalie says that Philippine wonders why they should bring it, since it needs major repairs in order to be usable. Surely, Amalie says, what one needs is a good table and some chairs, and a cupboard to put the crockery in. She is thinking of bringing their old small sideboard that came from David's mother's family home.

In their next letter my parents write that Kora has a new job. Now, they say, it is clearer than ever that David and Amalie will not be a burden on them, so they should come immediately. Amalie replies:

But nevertheless we don't think it desirable, either materially or psychologically, for all four of us to descend on you at once. For the voyage it might offer some advantages, but in Melbourne more disadvantages. The parents [she means Ernst's parents] have booked for 16.8, but it is very doubtful whether they will be able to travel then. We ourselves have reserved with Cook for the English line. . . . For various reasons—not least that it is cheap—I would rather travel with this ship than with the Dutch one. Dates in November or December would I suppose be best for the journey, or are there November storms in these regions?

Amalie's comment that it is doubtful if the Singers can travel on August 16 puzzled me. Since they have their entry visas to Australia and have booked their passage, why should they be unable to travel then? Ernst replies that he has not heard anything about "November storms."

By early July, with tension mounting over Hitler's next round of territorial claims, this time against Poland, David is again pessimistic about the prospects of emigration: "That this transplantation will fall to our lot, I can hardly believe, given that the world situation is pregnant with decisions. But for this reason we should act as if we were getting away." Then he returns to the theme of his books, asking whether he should take only the books that he considers indispensable, or also those that he might be able to sell in Melbourne, for example, the art books and his academic books on Goethe, philosophy, religion, and the classics. He asks my mother to make inquiries about the market for such books. He adds that in addition to his study of English, he is again writing, this time "on a biblical theme" and in English, so that the work "may perhaps serve over there to introduce me to Jewish circles."

My mother has had enough of her father's anxieties regarding his books, and replies curtly:

> Father asks regarding the books: we cannot find time at the moment to inquire about selling any. Father should bring a few art and good foreign language books but not too many (just to put some kind of number on it, say in total 500 as the upper limit).

On July 21 David says that they have arranged to travel on the English ship *Ormond*, which departs from Naples on December 12; but he knows that they still have obstacles to overcome:

> May heaven provide that everything else that is necessary before we travel falls into place, above all that your dear parents, dear Ernst, have already gone ahead and are happily settled, and after that, that you already have such a firm foothold in your own careers that you can take us along on your rope for part of the ascent.

If David feels the need to call on heaven to make it possible for them to leave, it is because a new and serious obstacle has arisen. Amalie refers to it in her part of the same letter when she says that "in the matter of the [Singer] parents there has still been no progress." She adds that one has to be patient, especially because of the holidays. Around this time the letters from Albert and Philippine also contain references to an unnamed problem, for example: "In our current matter there is unfortunately no progress to be discerned. We don't yet have our passports and tax clearance." The letters from Australia too contain anxious but veiled questions about "the unfortunate Singer matter." A letter from Albert and Philippine dated July 7 refers to including a newspaper cutting, and in response my father writes back: "The interesting newspaper clipping made a deep impression on all of us." For a long time I had no idea what this was referring to. Then, among some old clippings my father had kept separately from the letters, I found an undated article from a Vienna newspaper with the following headline:

"PRIVATE EXCHANGE" AND THE CONSEQUENCES
DINAR AGAINST REICHSMARK—JEWELRY WAS TO BE SMUGGLED

The article states that a forty-three-year-old man named only as "Johann G." appeared before the provincial court charged with having illegally sold dinars, the currency of Yugoslavia, for reichsmarks, the currency of Nazi Germany. Johann G. lived in Varaždin, in Yugoslavia. In November 1938 Friederike Ernst, a Jewish resident of Varaždin, suggested to Johann G. that he should sell forty thousand dinars to her sister, Philippine Singer. He traveled to Vienna and exchanged the dinars for reichsmarks. Johann G. then made another illegal transaction with an unnamed person before, in February 1939, again seeking out Philippine Singer, "whose two sons gave him various pieces of jewelry, a painting and a camera, to bring out of Germany." Johann G. was arrested before this undertaking could be carried through. He confessed and was sentenced to five months in prison and a fine of five thousand reichsmarks.

No wonder that reading this clipping made a "deep impression" on my father! He was speaking vaguely, to avoid saying anything that could cause more trouble for his parents, but the news was devastating. The problem that his brothers had with the camera was only part of it. His parents were in grave danger. If he had been able to read the statements that they made to the customs police—now available in the Austrian court records—he would have been even more heartbroken. Beneath the dispassionate surface of the official record of Philippine's testimony it is possible to grasp the nightmare in which this very proper middle-class woman found herself involved. At first she tells the interrogator that "Johann G."—his real name was Gams—came to her house in February with a gift from her sister, in Yugoslavia, of half a pound of butter. She had never seen him before, but her sons asked him when he was going back to Varaždin, and whether he could take a camera back with him. Questioned further—and presumably presented with other evidence—she admits that her sons had also given Gams a pocket watch, two rings, and two gold chains. The interrogator then states that he knows that Gams visited her on other occasions, and specifically in November of the previous year, when she personally gave him four thousand marks in cash. Philippine admits that this is correct, and tells a complicated story about how the money was part of an inheritance from her parents that she owed her sister but had not yet paid over to her. Finally, she is forced to confess that this too is false, and that the money came, not from an inheritance, but from the sale of stock, and was intended to be used by her sons when they emigrated.

Albert, Fritz, and Hans Singer were also interrogated, and the customs police sent the papers to the state prosecutor's office with a recommendation for prosecution. Although Fritz and Hans were soon allowed to go, presumably because of Seyss-Inquart's intervention, the older Singers had to give up their passports. That they were not sent to a concentration camp might have also been due to Seyss-Inquart's assistance, but he either would not or could not help them get their passports returned in time to leave as they had planned. They tried everything. On August 4, they wrote that they had hoped to be able to start packing their furniture for shipping, but still did not have their passports and tax clearance—although they had paid the heavy "exit tax" that the Nazis imposed on Jewish refugees. They were now employing an "Aryan" lawyer, in addition to the Jewish one they had originally, but he too was unable to get the case dealt with. Similar despairing comments appear regularly in later letters. They are "clueless" as to what they can do about this "calamity." By September the *Christian Huygens* has sailed, and they write, "All our plans have been in vain. Now we have to wait again. But the question is, how long."

The calamity affected the emigration plans not only of Albert and Philippine, but also of David and Amalie, for the Oppenheims did not wish to leave Vienna before the Singers. Albert had developed an eye condition that made him almost blind, and with her children gone, it was not easy for Philippine to manage everything by herself. But the Singers' problem was not the only barrier to the Oppenheims' departure. On August 2, as Hitler's threats against Poland became increasingly menacing, Amalie wrote to her children of a new impediment to their departure: David needed a prostate operation. He had often had blockages that prevented him from urinating, but previously these had been short-lived. Now these blockages had become more severe, and his doctor had told him that he needed an operation. They had obtained a second opinion from the leading specialist in the field, Professor Rubritius, who agreed with the first doctor. Rubritius was willing to perform the operation himself, and promised that "the operation will be completely successful, and that father will easily be able to make the trip in December."

David then writes, in a tiny, scrunched-up, barely legible script:

> The thought of how sad this letter must make you and how many worries it will cause you for a long time to come is one of the troubles that has now come upon us. But for this very reason we must also consider how immeasurably more upsetting it would have been if my condition had worsened on the journey or at a time when the operation became incompatible with leaving at the right time. The worst possibility of all would have been to become ill in the new country. I have to be at least halfway healthy and fit when I am with you. It is bad enough that I shall have to give up my English lessons.

Before the operation can take place, David's level of blood sugar, elevated because of his diabetes, has to be reduced. His anxiety about the operation exacerbates the problem. Days pass. David is in the hospital and anxious about the amount of money that his illness is costing, since his health fund pays for only a fraction of the cost; but of still greater concern to him, Amalie writes, is "his great anxiety that he will not be able to travel to you at the time planned, and that he will not be as fit for work as he thought he would be." Finally, after ten days in the hospital, David writes that his sugar level has come down, and the operation will take place on the next morning. But now David's thoughts are overshadowed by the mounting tension over Poland:

> It would be better not to think about the future at all. It looms before us all shrouded in black. And that I should be in this situation at precisely this time, I find particularly cruel. But when I think back, I see that I have survived many other things, some worse still, for example a night awaiting an artillery barrage the next morning, and I will know how to get through this time too.

The next day Amalie sends a telegram with a simple message: "OPERA-TION SUCCESSFUL." On the following day David writes that the operation and the first day of convalescence have "gone as well as can be expected [but] the objective satisfaction of the doctor and the subjective suffering of the patient are worlds apart!" David's state of mind cannot have been helped by the startling news that Hitler and Stalin, hitherto the deadliest of enemies, have signed a nonaggression pact. Now if Hitler attacks Poland, he has nothing to fear from the Soviet Union. France and Great Britain may still declare war, but they are too far away to help Poland.

On August 28 Amalie writes that David's incision is healing more slowly than expected, that he is in pain and has various other complaints, "which because of his special sensitivity, he feels twice as badly." Worst of all are the nights, during which he sleeps either not at all or only a little. Amalie says that she is now going to spend the night sleeping in his room at the sanatorium, partly to try to calm him, and partly to avoid the need for the "frightfully expensive" additional nurse. But Amalie herself is not finding it easy to be calm. The illness is costing a princely sum, she admits, and they are drawing on money that was intended for shipping their belongings to Australia. In addition, Jewish emigrants are no longer allowed to withdraw their pension funds, and this has upset her financial calculations. After telling her children that they still plan to pay for their tickets on the *Ormond*, Amalie writes:

> May G. grant that this will all be possible. Apart from father's health, there is still the question: war or peace, which depresses us, along with several other worries! I hope for peace!

Three days later—the day before the outbreak of the Second World War—Amalie no longer dares to hope, or plan:

> The burden of worries is sadly too great! . . . I do not have the inner peace to write more to you! Hopefully you are all healthy and content! When I think that I should be wishing you well for Rosh Hashanah [Jewish New Year], my heart grows heavy. We now see how little wishes can achieve! You have been away for a year now, a sad and fateful year for us, but hopefully the beginning of a better life for you! I dare not make plans for us at the moment!

29

"Best to Stay"

AS HITLER'S ARMIES ROLL triumphantly across Poland, a rare note of despair enters Amalie's letters, especially moving given her previous coolness under what have already been extraordinarily trying circumstances. She doesn't know if her letters will reach their destination, and she doesn't like to "speak into the wind." But above all it is the physical, emotional, and financial strain of caring for David that has brought her close to the breaking point. On September 17 she writes that she has been at David's bedside "all day, every day" since August 4. His illness "fills our lives completely." She had to give up her plan of staying in his room overnight, because she got very little sleep, and was too exhausted to be of any use during the day. Now the night nurse is back, with the consequent additional expense. As for David, he cannot sleep at night because of pain and discomfort, and if he takes a sleeping tablet, it only makes him more confused and agitated. As a result he is severely depressed. Amalie consoles herself with the thought that "maybe it is good to devote oneself totally to something. That way, the other worries fade into the background." But David's illness does not fill her life so overwhelmingly that she can avoid adding that in other respects too, "life is not so rosy, and we look into the future with trepidation." That remark may have been prompted by a new round of measures against Jews. On the eve of the war, the Nazis requisitioned all precious metals, leaving Jews with only their wedding rings, watches, and table service for two. By the end of September, Jews were forbidden to visit the few remaining public places still open to them, or to go out after 8:00 P.M. The curfew facilitated arrests, which often occurred at night.

The outbreak of the Second World War did not necessarily spell the end of David and Amalie's plans to join their children in Australia. Many Jews left Germany in September and October 1939. In November the flow slowed, and from the end of that month only another two thousand Austrian Jews managed to get away before November 1941, when the Nazis prohibited Jewish emigration completely in order to implement a different "final solution" to the Jewish problem. But of that, David and Amalie knew nothing. A more immediate cause of distress was the interruption to the precious correspondence that had been the only source of good tidings for them. By the time Amalie was ready to post her letter of August 28, airmail service from Germany had been canceled. She sent the letter by surface mail, knowing that it would take two to three months to reach Australia. Later she found a better route. Hungary was not yet at war, and so she wrote to David's cousin, Margit Brügler in Budapest, who forwarded the letter to Australia. My parents wrote back to Margit, who again passed on the letters. In the same way Ernst's parents wrote via Philippine's sister, Friederike, in Yugoslavia.

During this period optimistic moods are short-lived. "The incision finally looks like healing," Amalie writes on September 10, and she tells her children that David is getting out of bed for a few hours each day and even walking a little. But two weeks later the wound is still open, and David again must lie on his back waiting for it to heal. As for the travel plans, they "have naturally been indefinitely postponed, and it is better not to think about them at the moment." Amalie suggests that Ernst and Kora should apply to extend the entry permits that were granted in March, and were valid for one year. On October 12, almost two months after the operation, she writes again that the wound is still not healed, and "the Professor too has no other advice than 'patience.' " When she is with David she puts on a brave face, but she confesses to her children that she is nearly at the end of her strength.

Then on October 21, David writes once more, though by dictation to Amalie rather than in his own hand, that he is still in the sanatorium, and had to be operated on a second time, because the wound had not healed. His sufferings, of "body and soul," have led him to ask himself "the question asked by Job, 'Why?' " But he goes on to say that the question only has meaning for those who—unlike him—believe in "an almighty Providence." Instead, he tells his children:

> A less elevated, more commonplace, idea appeals to me more: that of "repaying" a great good fortune by a bit of misfortune. I find your success a great good fortune, over which I have shed tears of joy.

Another two weeks pass, filled with pain and discomfort for David, and fears that the second operation has not helped, because urine is still leaking through the stitches in the bladder. Finally, on November 11, Amalie can report that the bladder wound seems to have healed. David is still "very weak, and can barely walk three steps," but at last there is hope that he may be able to go home in a few days. In the same letter Amalie tells her children of the death of her sister: "Sara's most fervent wish has been fulfilled, she sleeps the eternal sleep. Sad as this is for us, one has to grant her this longed-for good fortune." Sara was one of thousands of Jews who, finding life under the Nazis not worth the struggle, committed suicide. Before forwarding this letter from Budapest, Margit adds a note saying that the Oppenheims are now in such difficult financial circumstances that they are gladly accepting food packages from Budapest, which they refused only six months earlier.

Four days later Amalie can write that they are again home. But she is still far from taking up again their plans to emigrate, and not only because David is so weak, but also because the "Singer affair" remains unresolved and "they just have to wait patiently." Hence Amalie writes that "at the moment unfortunately a trip is out of the question." David tries to write as well, but his handwriting is so weak that Amalie has to rewrite it:

> I am now finally sitting at my longed-for desk again. . . . Almost $3\frac{1}{2}$ months have passed, and if this is not a particularly long time even in terms of a short human life, this letter is separated from my previous ones by a confusion of sufferings of body and soul of the strongest, most incessant, and most varied kind. I would never have believed that I could somehow get through it. . . . Naturally, it is due to [Amalie's] work alone that I hung on, and did not refuse the food, which I found disgusting, or end up in a psychiatric clinic. If you think that worthy of thanks, it is her

that you should thank. I myself feel that from now on I am no longer my own person but rather her creation.

At the end of November David writes, more legibly this time, that he is back at work on his English, "although I hardly dare to hope that I will still get the opportunity to use it in practice." He keeps it up, nonetheless, because it makes him feel closer to his children. Only since his own recovery has he found out about the death of his sister-in-law—since this took place when David was in a poor state, Amalie kept the news from him. All this has changed his perspective, and now, when he looks back on his earlier worries about storms during their voyage, such concerns seem ridiculous. "How completely different are the storms that beset our ship of life, on an angry sea."

On December 6 Amalie writes that she has heard that all permits for entry into Australia have been canceled, and that they will have to reapply. The elation with which my parents wrote of getting the permits has come to nothing. But Amalie is less perturbed over this dismaying news than might be expected, saying only, "But that's a long way off." A letter from Philippine Singer to her children, written in the first few days of 1940, shows that David has made a surprisingly good recovery: he goes out alone and "also when necessary makes himself useful in domestic matters." So the prostate operation is no longer an obstacle. Instead, the Oppenheims have tied their fate to that of the Singers, who are still without their passports. Philippine's letter makes this momentous comment: "We have told the O. parents that given the situation, it would be more sensible if they were to go earlier, but they seem now not to want to hear anything of it."

At this point my anxious father begins to consider every possible way out for his parents. He writes to his aunt in Yugoslavia asking if they could stay with her, without a visa. She writes back saying that "an illegal stay here is no problem. But I don't know how one escapes from the beasts. One hears of people who get away illegally, but they have to be young and agile. . . . They have to jump from a moving train and walk for hours through forests and fields . . . so for Papa quite impractical."

Amalie's sister Ernestine had, like David's sister Hannchen, married a member of the Kunstadt family. Their son, Hans Kunstadt, was now settled in New York. He offered to try to obtain a visitor visa for them so that they could stay in the United States until they got permission to join their children in Australia. Yet this route too Amalie declines to pursue. In a letter written to Margit to be sent on to her children she writes:

> I don't see it as useful, because we 1.) have not registered, 2.) have no idea when the further trip and entry to Melbourne would be possible, 3.) don't know who would keep us in New York. So it is best to stay in the country and feed ourselves here honestly, to which end God helps in many forms, not least in yours, dear Margit.

Of the three reasons Amalie gives, only the first is serious. Tens of thousands of Jews had rushed to register an immigration application with the American embassy. There was a quota on the number of immigrants taken from each country each year, and so some of those who had registered much earlier were still waiting for their turn to come. If David and Amalie were to register now it would be a long time before they were eligible to be considered. Still, why not try? Registration was not difficult, it was always possible that the quota would be increased, and they had nothing to lose, and much to gain, by trying. Hans's suggestion was, in any case, to try to get a visitor visa, which he seems to have thought might be easier to obtain than an immigration visa. Amalie does not respond to this idea. The other two reasons for not taking up her brother-in-law's suggestion now seem trivial. What would it matter how long they had to wait in America for permission to go to Australia, as long as they were out of the clutches of the Nazis? And if their relatives had to support them for a while, or their children had to send them money, did that really matter, in comparison to the danger they were in? Given how much David and Amalie were evidently longing to be reunited with their children, there must be another explanation for Amalie and David's refusal to pursue the idea of a temporary refuge in America.

30

Good Austrians

IN THE MORAL DARKNESS of Nazi Vienna, a few non-Jewish visitors defied the propaganda of anti-Semitism and the risk of political suspicion, and stood by David and Amalie, visiting them in their apartment in the heart of the Jewish section of the city. Most frequently mentioned in the letters are Kora's old school friend, Eva, and her mother. They are here "often," Amalie writes, and in several letters she notes that they have just left, or if their visits coincide with the writing of a letter, they add a short greeting. Sometimes Eva's mother—"a good, faithful soul," David calls her—comes by herself, sometimes Eva comes alone, and sometimes they come together. Eva, a schoolteacher, was told that if she wanted to advance in her career, she must join the Nazi Party. She refused, and was not given the promotions awarded to her more compliant colleagues. Another visitor mentioned in the letters is Marie Spott, who for many years had been my grandparents' live-in maid. Nazi law prohibited non-Jewish women from working as maids in Jewish homes, but Marie continued to see her former employers, and help them when she could. As late as January 1941, David says that he is very fortunate to be "tirelessly cared for" by both Amalie and Marie. Particularly satisfying for David were visits from some of his favorite non-Jewish students:

> The visits that I receive from loyal friends, among them some quite surprising ones, are always a joy. That I have been able to win their esteem

has an extremely healthy effect on my severely threatened self-esteem, and refutes the derisive old saying that only those whom the gods hate become schoolteachers.

All the visitors brought food, and one, a medical doctor, provided David with insulin.

David's most unlikely relationship, however, was with a member of the SS. Albert Massiczek, the son of a rural police officer, was brought up with the anti-Semitic prejudices common in that milieu. He joined the Austrian Hitler Youth at the age of sixteen, and by 1936 was one of the leaders of this then illegal organization. In 1937 he moved on to the equally illegal SS. The joy with which he greeted the advent of Nazi rule in Austria, however, soon turned to disillusionment. Party membership, once a daring adventure, now became a series of highly disciplined meetings in which orders were handed down from higher up, and obeyed without question. Massiczek's doubts about Nazism were increased by a young woman who was a relative of a former chancellor of Germany, General Kurt von Schleicher. Schleicher, a conservative military man but no friend of the Nazis, had been murdered by the SS in 1934. Learning of this murder from someone personally affected by it opened Massiczek's eyes to other abuses. Six months after the Anschluss he became part of a resistance group associated with a Catholic priest, Roman Karl Scholz, who, like Massiczek, had been a member of the Nazi Party when it was illegal. Massiczek had studied together with, and become a friend of, Friedrich Heer, who invited him to come along on one of his visits to his revered former teacher. Thus Massiczek, now in his early twenties and still a member of the SS, found himself in David and Amalie's apartment.

Listening to my grandfather, Massiczek was at first embarrassed by the deep emotion with which David spoke. In Massiczek's circles one strived to follow the Prussian ideal of repressing emotions, to make oneself "hard." Gradually Massiczek came to feel differently. He was not able to express it at the time, but later he put it like this:

> I realized that the words of the Oppenheims carried more weight than mine, more feelings and more experience. Especially the emotional connotations of the terms *man, mankind* and *humanity* seemed to me multidimensional. They conveyed warmth and depth and an extension that can only spring

from strong human relationships. I began to sense that there was a great difference between the responsibility many Jews felt for their fellow human beings and the irresponsibility that exists among a lot of young non-Jewish people.

Massiczek returned to the Oppenheims several times before he was drafted into the army, an event that provided him with the opportunity to leave the SS and become a regular soldier. When he returned to Vienna on leave, he came again to see the Oppenheims, wearing his army uniform. During the invasion of Russia he lost his right eye when the tank in which he was the radio operator was hit by a shell. After he recovered he wore a black patch over the socket, which made him easy to recognize, but even this did not deter him from continuing to visit my grandparents. During these visits Massiczek and David talked at length about Judaism, Christianity, and anti-Semitism. Massiczek made no secret of the fact that he had turned completely away from the Nazi ideas he had held previously. Like Eva, Friedrich Heer, and others who visited, he brought gifts, items of food that Jews were unable to obtain on the meager rations allowed them during the war. When David could no longer keep his books, Heer took many of them, but Massiczek also agreed to take care of some.

These visits and gifts were, as Amalie wrote later, not only of material benefit, but also an extremely valuable form of moral support. My grandfather, however, was able to give Massiczek something back, something that never left him. Their conversations were a turning point in Massiczek's intellectual life. He became fascinated with the Jewish way of looking at the world, not in a religious sense, but in the sense of the distinctive attitudes and emotions that he describes in the passage quoted above. After the war Massiczek's whole life began to revolve around his interest in things Jewish. He lived with a Jewish woman whose family had returned to Vienna and wrote a major study of Marx entitled *The Humane Man: the Jewish Humanism of Karl Marx*. The book interprets Marx positively by emphasizing his youthful, more humanistic writings, in which, Massiczek argues, the unconscious influence of a humane Jewish outlook is evident.

December 1998

I am in Eva Berger's apartment on Porzellangasse, where my mother used to come to spend time with her friend after school. Now ninety-one and a widow, but intellectually as sharp as ever, Eva is still living here, surrounded by the furniture and paintings handed down by her parents. From here she used to walk across the Danube canal to visit my grandparents. I asked her what their general mood was like, once their hopes of joining their children had dwindled to the vanishing point. It was, she recalled, one of patient endurance: "They believed that they would be able to keep living there, quietly, a restricted life, but physically unharmed." Then she tells me that on one occasion when she visited them she found David in a state of high anxiety. Sometime earlier the Nazis had decreed that Jews must give up all weapons. The time for handing in weapons had expired, but David had forgotten that he still had his saber from the time when he was an officer in the Imperial and Royal Army. Now, he realized, the house could be searched at any time, the weapon found, and David sent to a concentration camp. But for him to take it out into the street and throw it away was even more risky. What should he do? Eva left with the saber under her coat. Her route home took her over the Danube canal, and she thought of throwing it in, but it was too public a place, and she could be observed. Further on, she passed an army barracks, and there in a dark corner of the walls, the sword my grandfather had kept for more than twenty years was abandoned.

After seeing Eva, I visit Albert Massiczek. A remarkably sprightly and alert gentleman of eighty-two years comes to the door, grasps my hand firmly, and holds it for a long moment, a warm smile on his face and a single eye beaming at me. He no longer wears the black patch, and the hollow space where his right eye used to be gives his face a strikingly unsymmetrical, but not unpleasant, appearance. He is evidently delighted to see me, and takes me into the kitchen, where he has prepared a light vegetarian dinner. We speak of my grandparents and their influence on his life. He shows me a letter that David wrote to him in January 1942, congratulating him on the birth of his first child. My grandfather's characteristic mode of thought is instantly recognizable in the opening lines, in which he tells Massiczek that his daughter's name, Anna, means in its original language,

Hebrew, simply "mercy." Knowing his friend's mind, he thinks this meaning will please him. From the fact that the child is a girl, and will not have to take part in war, he sees a sign that "after all a peace will spring from this hellish war." David goes on to say that he and Amalie, "who are now the lowest of the low," can have no way of repaying what Massiczek and his wife have done and continue to do for them, other than by closely sharing in their lives. He concludes by looking forward to Massiczek's next visit "with an impatience that I would call joyful, if there were still any joy in my personal life." To avoid possible problems for Massiczek, the letter is signed only "Your faithful Ernst" — David's second, and non-Jewish, name.

Our conversation wanders over many topics, including those that Massiczek discussed with my grandfather. Before we part, he takes from his bookshelves a volume containing the writings of the earliest Greek philosophers, known as the "pre-Socratics" because they flourished before Socrates. It has the Greek texts on one side and a German translation on the facing pages. My grandfather gave it to him, not as part of his library to be safeguarded for better days, but as a gift. Now he presents it to me, so that the book that was once part of my grandfather's library will be part of mine.

31

Renunciation

As THE FATEFUL YEAR 1939 draws to an end, the topic of David and Amalie's emigration fades from the letters, though Amalie continues to report on other family and friends who try to leave. Just before Christmas David writes that he is working again at English, but "no longer spurred on by the definite prospect of having it put soon and decisively to the test." He has given away some of his books and is sorting out the rest of his library "so that I can quickly give it away in orderly sections, should this be necessary." This means that he is not without something to keep himself busy, but "it is no longer work that makes any progress. We will have to leave that up to you young people."

David and Amalie's life revolves ever more closely around their distant children. Here, at least, there is something new to look forward to: Kora is expecting a child, due in May. David greets the news of his first grandchild with great solemnity, telling Kora and Ernst that they are now creators of a "small world," because it did not come about by chance, "but rather you decided carefully and with all seriousness to create it from nothing." Amalie finds the joyful news a welcome sign that Kora and Ernst really feel at home in their new country. Yet her joy is mixed with concern about the complications that a child will bring to Kora, "a working mother," and she writes that both she and Philippine are very distressed that "we grandmothers cannot reduce these concerns by taking over the care of the little one." Whereas a week ago she had "calmly accepted the necessity of our being separated forever," now she finds it painful that "at least for the duration of this sad war" they cannot come to their children and be useful to them. That because of the war she "cannot even send an outfit for the grandchild, am not even allowed to send a little jacket, that really hurts."

In his first letter of 1940, David writes of the joy they had in getting a letter written from Australia a month earlier. Nevertheless, despite their repeated requests, Doris has not sent a photograph of herself, withholding one that Ernst took because it makes her look too fat. David scolds her for her vanity. He reports on his own health, which is reasonably good. The hardships they are enduring are lightened by the assistance of friends such as Margit, and this help is not only material, but also "a proof that we are not so abandoned as it appears." In general, he writes, "we continue to be in a position to keep ourselves quite well. It is just that the future looms so dark, and it is so difficult to have hope." Amalie agrees: "We are, God be praised, healthy and content and even happy, if we have good news from you."

During the first quarter of 1940 the letters flow more regularly again, through Budapest. Kora evokes her parents' admiration by continuing to work throughout her pregnancy. This gives her and Ernst a reliable income, which is important because the outbreak of war has brought with it import restrictions that threaten my father's newly established business. Doris receives some lighthearted banter about her frequent changes of career, as she moves from being a shop assistant to a customs-office clerk, then takes a position in my father's office, and then becomes a beautician. The last of these posts leads Amalie to send her a book about cosmetics, but by the time it arrives she has moved on to yet another new job. The letters from David and Amalie no longer refer to any specific plans to join their children. These have, as David writes on January 15, "melted away or retreated into the foggy gray distance." The Singers' "unfortunate affair" is still not settled. In January Amalie writes that Philippine "does not want to press it, and perhaps with good reason." At the beginning of March Amalie tells Ernst that his parents "are waiting patiently for their immediate and more distant future to be decided, *for there is nothing else one can do* and we hope that everything turns out well." David's and Amalie's accounts of their own lives are generally limited to statements that they live "quietly," "monotonously," and in a "withdrawn" manner. Amalie goes out only when she has something to do; David goes for a short daily walk. Not a day goes by without someone coming to visit. Although many members of their old circle of friends have already emigrated, "new friends emerge and the few old ones draw closer together." They see the Singers every Sunday afternoon. They talk of their children, and of their hopes of seeing them again, and David and Albert spend some of the time practicing English together. They all keep their minds on the fact that their children, at least, have won for themselves "a worthwhile existence," and these hours pass quickly and pleasantly. David tells his children that their letters, with their accounts of parties and holiday travels, "sound to us like reports from a better beyond." As for themselves, they can scarcely ask for any break in their everyday routine. They are highly satisfied if it "just keeps rolling along *its old track*," and "the less we concern ourselves with how long, or where it is going to, the better we feel."

Amalie is, as always, more positive. She "lives a lot in remembrance of times gone by," but is happy as long as David is well. Physically, she reports, he has completely recovered from his illness, but he is "spiritually quite dejected." As for her own mood: "I am once again, praise God, on top of things, and do not let my courage and confidence sink." The gifts they get from friends mean that they are well provided for, lacking only "Ernst's commodity"—by which she must mean coffee. Amalie even writes, in February:

> You know that I am always fundamentally satisfied with everything, if that is just somehow possible! Since father's recovery, that is how I am again. Time passes better that way than with moaning.

The winter of 1939–40 is an unusually cold one, with a lot of snow. Amalie writes: "Spring must come." David, on the other hand, says: "Spring is, no doubt, still far away." Both comments seem to refer to more than the weather.

By the end of February David has completed his work of reorganizing his library. Hearkening back to Ernst's remark, more than a year earlier, about his "torn books," he says that he wishes Ernst could see his library, for he would not find many torn books there now. Even with this pared-down collection, however, he says, "I'll hardly be able to keep it. But if that were the only obstacle to our trip, we would soon be with you." The remark is both an admission that there was a time when his reluctance to part with his books had been a deterrent to emigrating, and a statement that this time is past—David knows now that some things mean even more to him than his books. David's doubts about his ability to keep his books are most likely a reference to the continuing eviction of Jews from their homes, forcing them to share apartments with other families. The Oppenheims have so far been spared the need to leave their home, but in March they write in some alarm that it appears that they will have to move. In the next letter, written on March 19, David regrets the disquiet caused by the earlier letter, saying: "We can stay here for the time being, and we hope to be able to continue staying here, mainly because I am a disabled war veteran." This hope, Amalie writes, "gives us back the tranquillity and confidence we need for the immediate future."

From April 1940 the letters from David and Amalie are again written by hand. David explains that: "Mother has parted with her typewriter, because she was convinced that there was an incomparably more pressing need for it elsewhere." He continues:

Renunciation is the rule of the day, and we have already practiced it so often, even in far more difficult circumstances. We have even learned to bear loneliness; no typewriter, nothing that one could call an object of value, could help us get over that. The only thing that can help with that is the confidence that things are going well for you, my beloved ones, and will continue to go well.

Two weeks later David bemoans the fact that the regularity of their correspondence appears to be breaking down again. The usual weekly letter from Australia has not arrived, and so they themselves have not written for fourteen days, because "in the same way that our life is now only as much as you give us through the contents of your letters, so our writing is barely more than an echo and a response to what we hear from you." Amalie finds the lack of news difficult to bear: "Particularly during these weeks I would so like to be with you, so that I could stand by you, dear Kora, with advice and assistance. Please send us a telegram immediately that, may G. provide, mother and baby are well."

Passover comes around again, and Amalie writes:

I celebrated the Seder, as is the custom, thinking of the exodus of the children of Israel, and believe me, my thoughts were mostly with you, and my heart was so full that tears came to my eyes. But one must be strong, and I am, once again.

A letter from Kora and Ernst intended for David's birthday arrives late, but shows that letters are still getting through, if less regularly than before. My parents' birthday wish for David is that he should be reunited with them. He replies that this is also his "highest and only want," but the difficulty is to "move beyond the realm of pious hopes." Since all they can do is wait, they will do that, as they have so far, with "patient endurance." On the very next day, however, David and Amalie's hopes suffer another blow, for they receive news from my parents that the application for an extension of the entry visa to Australia has been rejected. There remains only a slim chance that this decision can be reversed. In the face of this setback, David says that it would be best to follow the example of the Stoics, abandoning both hope and fear, and willingly accepting the "irresistible course of fate." Unfortunately, David admits, despite his acquaintance with the ancient philosophers, he lacks the inner strength to take this course.

On May 7, 1940, David again has to write without having had a letter to which he can respond, and he repeats how difficult he finds this. The thought that exclusively occupies them, he says, is: "*What will become of us?*" But that is a thought that is "essentially formless" and so he cannot write a letter about it. But then he goes on to say that perhaps it is good that he has nothing new to report, because in the first days of May there was yet another series of housing restrictions, and many people, including Ernst's parents, had to move to even more limited space. Since nothing happened to him and Amalie, however, David says: "I can hope to remain undisturbed in my study for some time pursuing my language studies. I stay there from early in the morning until late at night." Amalie, on the other hand, is still thinking "the whole day and a large part of the night" about her children, especially Kora, and praying for everything to go well.

Since the defeat of Poland in September 1939, a state of war had prevailed between Germany, on the one side, and England and France on the other, but there had been no fighting between the belligerents. On May 10, 1940, this "phony war" phase came to an abrupt end with the German invasion of Belgium and the Netherlands, obviously a preliminary to the real objective, the invasion of France. On the same day, Chamberlain resigned, and Winston Churchill took over as prime minister of Great Britain, marking a more defiant attitude toward the Nazi threat. David now felt his own powerlessness even more acutely, and struggled to take a philosophical view of his situation. His prophetic words seem to be written in some agitation, for his handwriting is again so illegible that Amalie has rewritten it:

> Now world history is marching at the double . . . the scales on which the fate of peoples is weighed are tilting, and the will of the individual cannot change this by a hair's breadth. One can only observe it, and prepare oneself not to be totally at a loss whichever way the decision goes. In thus living, predictably, through the course of world history, one can feel oneself to be a small, yet self-sufficient world, a Mr. Microcosm, as Mephisto mockingly put it. It is possible to do so with a certain pride, and not be humiliated by that mockery. And if the macrocosm rolls on in heedless "lordship" over the poor "knave," he may still be consoled by the awareness that the turn of the wheel that makes an end of his own knavish existence will not be the last.

While these momentous events are occurring, something else very significant to David and Amalie is taking place on the other side of the globe. On May 18, David and Amalie receive a telegram from Margit that reads "SPLENDID DELIVERY OF DAUGHTER." David characteristically greets the occasion with a classical reference, this time to Medea, the Greek sorceress who defends the bravery of women by saying that she would rather face the enemy in battle three times than give birth just once. But he also has a wish for the child's future: "Under your protection may she grow and thrive . . . and may she know only from hearsay, as a gruesome fairy tale, the evil times that burden us." (That wish, fortunately, has been fulfilled.) Amalie simply expresses her great joy at the good news, and then immediately gets down to the details: she still does not know her granddaughter's name, how the baby looks, whether Kora is able to breast-feed her, and many other things. She wants photographs, as many and as soon as possible, because "we, who have few hopes of ever seeing our grandchild in person, will be happy with her pictures."

Amalie's impatience must have continued to mount, for mail from Australia suddenly stopped getting through to Budapest. While the German army routed the French, the British evacuated their forces at Dunkirk, the

Nazis occupied Paris, and Hitler received the French surrender in the same railroad carriage that the Germans had surrendered in twenty-two years earlier, David and Amalie were still waiting to hear more of their granddaughter. In August a letter from David's sister Hannchen, now in New York, tells them that her name is Joan Rose. Then again there is no news for a long time. Amalie continues to write, although she admits that it is difficult to sustain a "monologue." At last, in December, Amalie writes with some good news: "Mama's matter has, praise G., been settled satisfactorily, and we have all been freed from one pressing worry. There are enough other worries, but that was the most serious." "Mama" is Philippine Singer, and the news was that, somehow, the prosecution had been settled with a fine. Just how serious this worry over the "Singer matter" was can be gauged from the next sentence:

> There is no lack of work—we have in the last two weeks had a lot of troubles with the changes in our apartment, in connection with which Dadi's [David's] library gave us much to do that was disagreeable. We are never bored, for there are now, quite without warning, 12 persons in our residential community.

This was a consequence of further restrictions on where Jews could live. Twelve people in an apartment that had previously housed at most five (including the maid) would not have been an easy adjustment. Neither Amalie nor David say who the other ten are, nor where they all sleep. David writes:

> We can't really report much at all. Even the great increase in our household, of which dear Amalie has already written, is according to our views nothing special, and completely unsuited to a more detailed discussion. On this point I will add just one comment: once more I have already learned here what I thought I would only have to get used to in a foreign land. It is possible to live, even without rooms filled with books. The work involved in getting rid of them with the required speed was, granted, very demanding, in body and soul. Now, however, I sit once again at my desk and fanatically—in the truest sense of the word—pursue my language studies. If it achieves nothing else, it is at least a proven tranquilizer.

In Budapest, Margit adds to this letter a plea for a rapid answer, "so that your parents can enjoy this injection of life." How consciously chosen this phrase was, I do not know; but that it was quite literally close to the truth is apparent from the next letter that David writes, on December 30, 1940:

> If we after all pluck up the courage for the traditional wish: A Happy New Year!, then we mean above all, may it at least give us the happy knowledge that you are well, your child thrives, and your work is rewarded. Cruelly though the war may rage, *we both are no longer far from the peace that no earthly might is powerful enough to disturb.* You need not be shocked at such thoughts. If to be ready is everything, then it follows that one must be ready *for every eventuality.* Then, and only then, one can calmly await one's lot.

Nearly forty years earlier, when doubtful about his abilities to be a classical scholar, David had contemplated the Stoic teaching that when you can no longer fulfill your life's task, it is rational to commit suicide. Now, in very different circumstances, he was close to acting on it. But Amalie's letter of the same date shows that she has not quite given up all hope of a happier ending to their lives, because it contains a veiled inquiry about the possibility of going to Australia:

> Ernst's parents are also well, and would, like his parents-in-law, like to make the postponed visit; yet that may scarcely be possible, for the invitation is lacking. Philippine's health is restored, so that she could make the trip.

In other words, both the Singers and the Oppenheims are ready to go to Australia, if only a permit to enter the country can be obtained. There was no previous reference to Philippine's health being a problem, so it is more likely that this is intended to tell Ernst that his parents now have their passports back. But the "invitation" that is lacking is presumably the Australian entry visa. Two weeks later, Amalie writes again, mentioning that "Philippine has completely recovered from her recent ailment, so that she could endure the rigors of an overseas trip."

Coming directly after the news that the "Singer matter" had been settled, this sudden renewal of interest in emigration confirms that David and

Amalie's parents (and my great-grandparents), Marcus Pollak and Minna Pollak.

Amalie Pollak on the day of her graduation, March 1905.

David's parents (and my great-grandparents), Heinrich Joachim Oppenheim and Ernestine Oppenheim.

David (seated) with his older sister, Cornelia.

David as a young man. This photo was taken in Brünn, perhaps before he left to attend the University of Vienna in 1899.

David as an officer of the Austro-Hungarian army.

David, seated second from left with other officers at the outset of World War I.

Summer holidays, 1931, by the lake at Velden am Wörthersee. David is standing at the back, the third from the left. His sister, Hannchen, stands next to him. Amalie, wearing a dress, is seated in front of her, while Hannchen's husband, Sandor Kunstadt, is to the left of her. The children in front include my aunt, Doris Oppenheim, third from the left, with Gerti and Georg, the children of Sandor and Hannchen Kunstadt, on either side of her.

On an excursion to Kobenzl, in the Vienna Woods. Taken in the summer of 1938, this is the last photograph of the Oppenheim family together. Ernst Singer, the author's father, is standing at the back.

Amalie with my mother, Kora Oppenheim (later Kora Singer and, after coming to Australia, Cora Singer).

My father's family. Ernst Singer, my father, is seated in front with his father, Albert Singer. Behind them, from left to right, are Ernst's grandfather, Gustav Ernst; his mother, Philippine Singer; his grandmother, Rosa Ernst; and his younger brothers, Hans and Fritz.

Otto Soyka, taken in Vienna in 1934. David was greatly drawn to "the power of his personality."
Photograph courtesy of the Picture Archive, Austrian National Library, Vienna

Lise Tarlau, Amalie's friend, of whom David wrote to Amalie: "You can speak freely with Lise about your love . . . she finds it quite natural, she strives to be loved by you, and is surprised only when you give your love to a man."

The Akademisches Gymnasium, or Academic High School, in Vienna, where David taught for thirty years until he was summarily dismissed after the Nazi annexation of Austria. *Photograph courtesy of the Picture Archive, Austrian National Library, Vienna*

Freud's waiting room, where the Wednesday Group met. *Photograph by Gerald Zugmann. Copyright © Sigmund Freud-Gesellschaft*

The author with his mother and
grandmother in Melbourne,
Australia, 1946.

Dr. Eva Berger (née Hitschmann), my
mother's closest friend, in her Vienna
apartment. (1998)

Dr. Albert Massiczek, former
member of the SS, who during the
Nazi period became a friend of
the Oppenheims. (1998)

The author and his daughter, Marion, at the gravestone of David's parents, Joachim and Ernestine Oppenheim, in the Jewish cemetery in Brno. (1998)

The crematorium in Theresienstadt, where David was cremated. Some gravestones are nearby, but David's ashes would have been thrown, with those of thousands of others, into the nearby river. (1998)

Amalie were unwilling to leave without the Singers. The "Singer matter" first arose in June 1939, more than a month before David's prostate operation, and it was not finally settled until November or December 1940. David's health would have prevented him from traveling between August and November 1939, but that still left time for him and Amalie to get away. After their permits were canceled it would have been more difficult for them to go to Australia, but even then they might have been able to go somewhere, perhaps to their relatives in the United States. Amalie's sister-in-law, Recha Pollak, was still able to leave Vienna early in 1941. Other relatives went to Bolivia. But as time passed, getting away became increasingly difficult, and by the end of 1940 it was close to impossible. Thus Albert and Philippine's attempt to get some of their money and valuables out of Germany trapped them, as well as David and Amalie, under Nazi rule. That ill-fated attempt has to be seen in its context. The Nazis took Albert and Philippine's business and forced them to sell their house for a fraction of what it was worth. Then they levied a heavy tax on what assets they had left. Like many others in the same situation, Albert and Philippine tried to save a little from this naked robbery. We might think that they were unwise to risk their lives in order to have more money, but it is easy to be wise with the benefit of hindsight.

David might have survived if he and Amalie had been prepared to go without the Singers. The Singers were not their blood relatives, indeed, only two years earlier, had not been related to them at all. In English, there is not even a word for the relationship between the parents of a married couple. In Yiddish, there is: they are *machetunim*, and the relationship is more significant than in Anglo-Saxon circles. They had drawn even closer after their children left, meeting regularly to share news. Nevertheless, Philippine urged David and Amalie to go without them. They would not hear of it. So it was not, in the end, David's initial, misguided confidence that the Nazis would not harm a decorated, injured war veteran, but his and Amalie's refusal to abandon their *machetunim* that prevented them escaping the Nazis. How high a price they would have to pay for staying, they did not know; but they certainly knew that the price was going to be, at best, a bare existence as despised pariahs under Nazi rule and, what pained them even more, prolonged separation from the children they were longing to see. David and Amalie were much less well-off than the Singers, and never seemed interested in money, unless it was needed for something like

David's operation. I have no way of knowing their private thoughts about the Singers' attempt to get around the Nazi theft of their assets. But nowhere in David and Amalie's letters is there the slightest hint of criticism of what the Singers did.

My father must have felt an awful responsibility for the twist of fortune that sealed his parents' fate. It was his suggestion that his brothers should bring the camera that began the tragic chain of events. At one point Philippine told him so. Shortly after Ernst's brothers arrived in Australia, he wrote to his parents saying that Fritz and Hans had not taken seriously his advice about learning English, and other skills that would have been useful for earning a living in Australia. She wrote back defending her younger children, saying that they had done their best to take his advice, but had had little time or opportunity to do so because of all the excitement and worries they had. Then she added, in words that must have wounded my father more terribly, and for longer, than she could have realized at the time:

> And to be candid, you are also responsible for these things, for the advice that you gave was doubtless well meant, but badly carried out. The one thing that was done, that you asked them to do, has become our doom. I don't want to criticize you, dear child.

My father replied immediately that he didn't want to quarrel across a distance of many thousands of kilometers, but it was news to him that he was responsible for "the unfortunate matter," because "we had not thought at all of that possibility"—by which he might have meant the attempt to send the camera through a paid intermediary, rather than to ask his Yugoslav cousin to come to Vienna to pick it up himself. I am sure that that is true, but I am equally sure that he never forgot what his mother had written to him. When he was dying, in 1981, he told me that the greatest tragedy of his life was that he did not get his family out in time. His mother's letter was then in a cupboard in another room of our family home, in which we were, but he never mentioned it to me, and I read it for the first time in 1999. Now I can only guess at the extent to which the bitter regret he felt during those forty years was sharpened by a sense that he had himself contributed in some way to the tragedy.

AT LAST, after months in which Amalie and David are without news from Australia, the mail brings five separate letters, written in December 1940 and January 1941. In one of them, to Amalie and David's great delight, is the first photograph of their grandchild. This burst of communication elicits much livelier letters of response, particularly from David. Kora has gone back to work, and has a new position that David believes may draw her into medical psychology. If so, he says, this would be the satisfaction of a wish that he had for her when she was a medical student. But the thought that psychology is being widely practiced in Australia has a bittersweet edge, for David takes it as evidence that he too would have found suitable work there, if only he had been able to seek it.

In February 1941 a new fear swept over Vienna's remaining Jews. Until then fewer than a thousand Jews had been deported from Vienna. They were all men and were said to be going to work in Poland. But beginning on February 15, and for the next five weeks, one thousand Jews a week were sent from Vienna to ghettos in Poland. This context explains Amalie's repeated inquiry, though in even more disguised terms, about the possibility of obtaining permission to go to Australia:

> Have you told Hedi [a relative who was also living in Melbourne] that Ernst's parents and parents-in-law would like to visit her, if she could send an invitation to you? I spoke to them today, but told them that I thought it was unlikely. Many people are now going from here to Shanghai, but you need a lot of money (400 dollars) to get in, which the people do not have.

As Amalie states more explicitly the following month in a letter to her relatives in America, the increasingly desperate Albert and Philippine are now willing to go to Shanghai—one of the last places that would still accept Jewish refugees—in the hope that they will later be able to join their children in Australia. The fact that their plans are in jeopardy for want of four hundred dollars shows how thoroughly the Nazis have stripped them of their once-substantial assets. Ernst wrote to Hugo Ernst, a cousin of his mother's who had emigrated to America many years earlier and was now quite well-off. (My father addresses him as "Uncle Hugo," so he might have been the same "uncle" who refused to be a guarantor for my mother when my parents were seeking to go to America in 1938.) Hugo Ernst wrote back offering, not to provide the money himself, but to act as an intermediary in transferring the money from Australia to Vienna. This letter was opened by the Australian censor, who forwarded it to the government office responsible for enforcement of the exchange-control regulations. My father received an official warning that any attempt to circumvent currency restrictions on dealings with the enemy would lead to a long term of imprisonment, and the money would be confiscated.

The deportations that began in February 1941 stopped in March. Few believed that this would be more than a breathing space, but David might still have hoped that his war service would protect him. On March 22, David writes about the pleasure they have in looking at a newly arrived picture of Joan, sitting up in a big armchair with a "heartwarming smile." If only they could see her in real life, this might conjure back their own lost smiles, but he thinks this miracle is unlikely to be granted. A month later he sends to his sister in America, by registered letter, "the previously discussed description of my literary and scholarly work"—obviously, the few pages written in English headed "My Scientific Work." He asks Hannchen to send a copy to Alfred Adler's daughter, Dr. Alexandra Adler, who is living in New York and carrying on the work of her father, who died in 1937. Another copy should go to an acquaintance who he hopes will show it to professors in psychology, psychiatry, or philology. Perhaps he has heard that scholars who are sought by American universities are able to bypass the quota system. But he has no real hope for this, and says that he is in any case pleased to have done the work, if only because he found it so demanding "that it kept me a healthy distance from other thoughts."

Passover is again a sad time for Amalie:

> Today is the first Seder, and I can't get out of my head the memory of just how beautiful and emotionally moving those evenings and days were during my childhood and later in Brünn. To prepare something that in no way corresponds with the old customs and habits but is just a feeble compromise, is very difficult for me. Indeed, I am almost prepared to do without the remnants of the old customs altogether, so that I can shake off the burden of the upsetting memories. Will we ever again celebrate a real Pesach?

The same is true of David's sixtieth birthday, on April 20, 1941. "Under other circumstances," Amalie writes, "we would have celebrated it better.

But one has to be pleased if one can spend this day like all others, quietly and in good health." Albert and Philippine were there too, but now all hopes and plans have become impossible because the port of Lisbon, the only route to the United States, has been closed, and Shanghai, the only other place one could get permission to enter, is out of reach because Japan has ceased to grant transit visas.

The next surviving letter is dated June 13, 1941, and is written by Amalie to Hannchen. It was understood that it was to be passed on to Australia, but to protect her children from any possible charge of communicating with the enemy, she disguises their names. She tells Hannchen that she has heard from Margit that "Dorilde" is "keeping pleasant company," and she is eager to learn something more about the person in question. Dorilde is young, she says—Doris was then twenty-two—and while she, Amalie, has never thought much of early marriage, either for herself or for her daughters, since Dorilde lacks the protective and caring love of her parents, it would relieve their anxieties to know that she was being cared for by a good husband. Amalie mentions that some friends are trying to go to Cuba, if they can raise enough money for the "caution"—a substantial sum that the Cuban government required as a security against becoming a burden on the state. Amalie says that she is not going to yield to such "beautiful illusions. . . . I aspire only to the wish that we may live out the rest of our lives here in peace, and hear good news from you as often as possible." A week after this letter was written, whatever faint hopes the Singers or Oppenheims might still have had of traveling to Shanghai were finally ended by the German invasion of Russia, which put travel across that country out of the question.

One of the wishes that Amalie expressed in her letter was fulfilled with surprising rapidity. In July David and Amalie got news that Doris was engaged to be married. Mixed with their great pleasure at this news is a touch of vexation at how little they know about their future son-in-law. They know that he is Jewish, a refugee, several years older than Doris, and was able to bring his mother out to Australia. Kora has expressed her warm approval of the match, and this encourages them to believe that she has made the right choice. But they do not know the man's name, or where he comes from.

The part of the letter directed to Hannchen shows that the conditions of entry to America have been changed in a way that gives David and Amalie new hope of going there. Even now, though, with the risk of deportation to the East hanging over them, Amalie remains concerned about being a burden on her relatives:

> . . . the question of how we will provide for ourselves is an enduring concern for me, despite all your goodness and helpfulness! For in spite of the will to work and all our efforts to better our qualifications, professional work is out of the question at our age. We cannot do anything else but trust in G. and you!

One passage in David's part of the same letter shows that something of the old David, teacher and freethinker, has survived all his trials. Hannchen's son Georg, who went to Palestine in 1938, joined his parents in New York in April 1941. In Palestine he attended an agricultural school that was religiously Orthodox, and he continued to live an Orthodox lifestyle after arriving in America. Hannchen mentioned this in one of her letters to Vienna, and through her, David addressed some questions to Georg about this. Georg replied simply that he was not of David's opinion. Now David asks him to add something to this "self-evident comment," saying that it is for his, Georg's, sake that he poses these questions, for to fall back on "an inflexible standpoint" is not in keeping with his youth. But Georg declines David's invitation to discuss these matters further. (Sixty years later, now called George and living near Los Angeles, he continues to be a religious believer. After we got in touch, while I was writing this book, I had with him the debate that he was unwilling to have with my grandfather, and I could honestly defend the same standpoint with regard to religion that David would have defended. The discussion did not, however, lead to any shift in the convictions of either of us.)

On August 20, 1941, David wrote a letter that, apart from a brief telegram, has become his final words to his children and grandchildren. For that reason it deserves fuller quotation than others:

> That Doris, by learning to sew gloves, now stands firmly on her own two feet, is a credit to her, as is everything that puts our hands industriously to work. But he to whom the power has been given to make her heart beat faster, her "intended," as she calls him, we still don't even know his name, let alone "his type" and "from whence he comes," all of this is as mysterious to us as if he had really come "from a far-off land" drawn by a

swan through a "mighty flood" and has to "flee" if he is recognized. We dare, nevertheless, to ask this question, indeed we ask too whether her knight, since he is after all so "learned" that he reads "books," is himself willing to prepare an answer. He doesn't need to be able to tell us of the Castle of the Holy Grail, the Sepulchre and the Last Supper, but might modestly write about a cozy family home, the mysterious cup of the prophet Elijah and the festive Seder table. But if he is not so communicative, then Doris should start already now to play the part of his better half and write about him; the more, the better. For the lively interest that I take in every human character is naturally even more intense when it has been determined that such a character will be numbered among my dear ones. . . .

We are much better instructed about little Joan. What you have told us about her first birthday is really impressive. People bring gifts to her as if to a Queen. And no wonder. She now wears pants and is so big and strong that no Amazon would be ashamed to have such a baby. And how significant, that she pounds her birthday cake into crumbs! Perhaps one day she will play the same cruel game with hearts and spare only those which are freely given over to her, like ours, which belong completely and solely to her.

Otherwise we do not have much to say. This letter has already shown you the best of it: even in the fiery oven of the manifold trials that the Demiurge, the divine foreman, subjects us to, my "humores" have not dried up. Admittedly, that is least true of the precious secretion of the insulin apparatus. For that reason my diabetes gives me a lot to do. . . . Loving greetings and kisses to all of you, your faithful David.

Through all his "manifold trials," David remains recognizably the person he always was. His reiteration of his interest in human character links this letter to the very first words I have from him, from 1904. His perennial skepticism toward religion is evident in his ironic remarks about the divine origin of the trials to which he has been subjected. He mentions Jewish cultural icons—Elijah and the Seder table—but, despite all that Germans have done, and are doing, to him, his playful references to Wagner's *Lohengrin*, from which comes the image of the knight drawn through the flood by the white swan, show that he remains fully at home in German culture.

From September 1941, all Jews going out in public had to wear, sewn onto their clothing on the left side of their chest, a large yellow Star of David, with the word *Jew* written on it. On October 15 deportations from Vienna to Poland recommenced. My father received an urgent request from his parents for landing money so that they could go to Ecuador. He wrote again to Hugo Ernst:

> if people at their age who never in their life traveled far want to go to Ecuador, a rather uncivilized country, although their children are in Australia, their lives must be in real danger. Most probably they are threatened with deportation to Poland, where Jews cruelly die of hunger in overcrowded ghettos. The most unfortunate part about it is that I cannot do anything from here to help my own parents.

Two weeks later, the emigration of Jews from the Reich was prohibited. Then in December came the Japanese attack on Pearl Harbor, and the declaration of war, not only between the United States and Japan, but also between the United States and Germany. In January 1942 Hugo Ernst writes again to my father, saying that the outbreak of war between America and Germany has frustrated all his efforts to save his relatives. As for Albert and Philippine:

> On October 22nd I sent a registered letter to your Dad in Vienna by clipper. This letter arrived in Vienna on November 10th but could not be delivered because the party had departed without leaving any forward address. I am enclosing, herewith, the envelope and on the back of it you will see, with pencil "Adressat Polen Verzogen—November 9, 1941." That indicates that at the time the letter arrived in Vienna, your parents had already been sent to Poland.

Meanwhile, David and Amalie had sent a Red Cross message to Kora and Ernst on December 23, 1941. It reached its destination in May 1942, and from it my parents learned:

> Singer parents Litzmannsdorf-Getto, Reiter St. 13/32. All well. Request Red Cross answer about the health and welfare of you all, Joanny's growth and Doris's future plans. Heartfelt greetings and kisses.

"Litzmannsdorf" is a slip for "Litzmannstadt," the German name that the Nazis gave to the Polish city of Lodz. Albert and Philippine were in the second of five transports taking a total of 4,995 Jews from Vienna to Lodz in October and November 1941. Their transport left on October 19.

After this there was one more Red Cross message bearing news of Albert and Philippine:

> Parents in Litzmannstadt, hopefully well like you. Also Githa and her husband have departed, send heartfelt kisses.

This message was stamped "German Red Cross 24. Aug. 1942." It reached Australia in February 1943. It was the last my father heard of his parents. The records of the Lodz ghetto list them as being sent away on May 15, 1942. At that time older Jews from Lodz were taken to Chelmno, where they were locked into the backs of trucks and murdered by exhaust fumes redirected into the truck's rear compartment.

David and Amalie were able to send one more Red Cross message, on June 22, 1942. Their address is no longer Krafftgasse, but instead "Förstergasse 7, Door 20, Vienna, 2nd District." They had been forced to leave the apartment in which they had lived for more than twenty years, moving just a block or two away, to a building that was used as a kind of holding area for Jews awaiting deportation. At this point, according to what Amalie was later to tell Doris, their desire to continue the struggle for survival was at an end, and they resolved to carry out the joint act of suicide at which David had hinted in his letter eighteen months earlier. Just then they received a Red Cross message sent by Doris in March, telling her parents of her marriage. That message encouraged them not to put their plan into action yet. The Red Cross message that they sent reads:

> Well. Made happy by joyful tidings, send heartfelt blessings to the young couple, Joan and you all. Report on how you are all faring, Doris's new surname. Kisses!

Eleven months after David and Amalie had asked for details about the man Doris was to marry, they still did not know his name. David was never to learn it.

32

In My Grandparents' Flat

December 1998

KRAFFTGASSE 3, VIENNA II. An address I have read so often is now in front of me. Shallow bay windows relieve the otherwise flat lines of a gray stucco apartment block, three stories high, built right up to the street line. The street is the same on both sides, giving it a barren, uniform appearance. Definitely one of the less elegant streets of Vienna. I press the bell marked "Jakubowicz" and a woman answers. I give my name. She is expecting me, and a buzzer sounds. I push the door and pass through it—as David and Amalie must have done so often during the time they lived here. Inside is a wide stone staircase that circles around an elevator shaft. I imagine my mother as a ten-year-old girl, running down this staircase, eager to get out into the nearby park, perhaps followed by David, recovering from the wounds, mental and physical, received in the war. I think of Doris, twenty years later, breathlessly climbing the stairs in a state of shock after her encounter with the Nazi youths who forced her to scrub a building, ready to tell her parents that she was going to leave.

At the door of apartment 8 I am welcomed by Romana Jakubowicz, a friendly looking woman who lives there with her two daughters and a son called David. I find myself in my grandparents' entrance hall. Mrs. Jakubowicz takes my coat, hat, and scarf, and shows me around. First we go down the passage to the kitchen. It has been modernized, but it is easy to imagine Amalie, who liked to bake, standing here rolling out the paper-thin pastry for her apple strudel, or shaping her "Wurst-schokolat," a concoction of crushed sweet biscuits, chopped nuts, raisins, and melted chocolate that was rolled into a sausage shape before being cooled and sliced. (On arriving in Australia, my mother wrote home for the recipe, but the normally careful Amalie must have had other things on her mind, because in copying it out, she omitted the chocolate.)

Next to the kitchen is a small windowless room. It is now David Jakubowicz's bedroom, but as Romana points out, it can be aired only by leaving the door open and at the same time opening the door of the toilet, which is across the passage, and the toilet window. This was the maid's room, occupied for many years by the faithful Marie Spott. Back past the front door and up the passage in the other direction, we pass the bathroom, which like the kitchen has been refurbished since my grandparents lived there. At the end of the passage there is a large room with windows onto the street. This was the salon, in which visitors were received and the family ate. In the middle of the walls on both sides are the original wooden double doors that lead to adjacent rooms. The brass handle I hold to open it is the one that my grandparents used. I enter what used to be David's study. Here is the bay window I had seen from the street. Like all the rooms, except for the maid's room, it is of a generous size. It needed to be, for David used it to house his library, which filled it from floor to ceiling on all sides with books, and he needed space for a desk too. Here between 1938 and 1941 he wrote the letters, first hopeful, then forlorn, that I had been reading. Opposite the window another set of double doors leads to what was David and Amalie's bedroom. In one corner stands an upright tiled stove, certainly a legacy from my grandparents' time, but still in use to provide a gentle warmth to what is now Romana Jakubowicz's bedroom. It has room for chairs and a coffee table as well as a bed, and we drink a cup of coffee and eat a piece of cake there. I have brought her a copy of Adolf Gaisbauer's book, because I like the idea that the letters should return, in some form, to the place in which they were written. She thanks me for them, and tells me that the apartment is, after all, quite fittingly occupied. Her former husband, the father of her children, was Jewish.

Before I leave, I try to imagine what the apartment would have been like with twelve people living in it. Heinrich Fichtenau, one of David's students, recalled that when he first visited the Oppenheims there were others living with them, but they still had two rooms to themselves. Later they had only one, and at the end only half a room, which was divided by large sheets. Eva said: "You must not forget what difficulties in hygiene that entails, when 10 or 12 people are in a flat that normally houses 2 or 3. [David] suffered terribly. [Amalie] did too, but she bore it well. Outwardly, she maintained her manner of living." But the worst thing about the last year that my grandparents spent living in this apartment would not have been the loss of their privacy. It would have been the ever-present anxiety about something likely to be much worse: deportation to the East.

33

Theresienstadt

IN MAY 1942 David and Amalie were notified that they would be deported. This order was then withdrawn. It was evident, however, that the Nazis were "cleansing" Vienna of Jews and that this would be only a temporary reprieve. More important than exactly when they would be deported was where they would be sent. Some transports, such as that which took the Singers away, were going to Poland. Others were heading to Theresienstadt. David and Amalie would have known of this little Czech town, lying amid pleasant rural scenery only sixty kilometers from Prague. It dates back to 1780, when Emperor Joseph II ordered his military engineers to build a fortress in Bohemia. They chose a site inside a bend of the Elbe River, near where it is joined by a tributary, the Ohře. The fortress is in the shape of an eight-pointed star, with huge ramparts protected by deep moats. Joseph II named it after his mother, Empress Maria Theresa. It was never besieged, and remained largely intact over the next 150 years, becoming a garrison town with a mixture of large barracks for soldiers and modest houses for civilians. Inside the fortifications, broad streets form a rectangular grid. In one section, called the Small Fortress, Gavrilo Princep, the assassin of Archduke Franz Ferdinand, had been held until he died of tuberculosis in 1918. By 1930 about seven thousand people lived in the town that had become known by its Czech name, Terezin. When the Nazis made Bohemia and Moravia a German "protectorate," its official name reverted to Theresienstadt.

Theresienstadt was the least bad of all the possible destinations for Jewish deportees. To Viennese, Poland was "the East," a place of harsh winters and hostile, uncouth Poles. Moreover, if reports of Jews starving to death in the ghettos of Warsaw and Lodz had reached my father in Australia, they surely would have reached Vienna too—and perhaps also rumors, scarcely credible but disturbing nonetheless, of mass killings of Jews. Theresienstadt, on the other hand, is in a region that had for centuries been ruled from Vienna, near the familiar and—until the Nazi annexation—highly cultured city of Prague, similar in language, people, and climate to Moravia, where David and Amalie had grown up. Adolf Eichmann, the Nazi head of Jewish "resettlement," had told the Czechs that the Nazis were giving Theresienstadt to the Jews in order to allow them to develop a self-governing Jewish community, a small-scale Zionist experiment for a future Jewish state. There would be no SS troops within the walls of the town. It would be run by Jews for Jews, a ghetto with its own administration, and even its own currency, with a picture of Moses bearing the Ten Commandments on the notes. The Czech Jewish community, thinking they would be spared deportation to the East, greeted the news with relief and willingly organized squads of volunteers to prepare the town for its new occupants.

For once, David's belief that his war record would protect him seemed justified. He and Amalie were put on a train to Theresienstadt. The meticulous German records show that they were assigned the numbers IV/8-339 and IV/8-340. The "IV" shows that the transport was from Vienna, the "8" that it was the eighth transport from the city; my grandparents were the 339th and 340th people to be placed on that transport. At the station and during the journey, they had to wear the numbers on large pieces of cardboard hanging from strings around their necks, and the numbers remained their identity numbers in Theresienstadt. Transport number 8 left Vienna on August 20, 1942, and arrived at its destination on the following day. Each passenger was told to bring fifty kilos of personal belongings. Between June and October, 13,776 Jews were sent from Vienna to Theresienstadt. By the middle of October, the Nazis had achieved their initial objective: apart from a few hundred who had gone into hiding, there were no Jews left in Vienna.

What did the Nazis really have in mind when they set up Theresienstadt as a place to which Jews were to be taken? For a time they did treat Jewish war veterans, especially those wounded and decorated in the service of the fatherland, differently from other Jews. That privilege faded as the goal of the elimination of the entire Jewish population became more clearly defined. Theresienstadt may have been created to avoid alienating the older generation of military leaders, who might inquire about the fate of a "decent Jew" they had known during the 1914–18 war. To Theresienstadt, too, were sent internationally renowned musicians, artists, and spiritual leaders, among them Rabbi Leo Baeck, as well as the relatives of famous people, such as the sisters of Freud and Kafka.

IN A LETTER to my father written after her liberation, Amalie described their arrival:

> When we arrived in Theresienstadt on 21.VIII.42, we spent the first night in the "Sluice," a barracks in which one's luggage is examined, that is "sluiced," in that the most valuable things are taken from you.

The "Sluice" is mentioned in the memoirs of other survivors of Theresienstadt. Good clothing, shoes, feather quilts, even brushes and combs were taken for the use of Germans. Items of lesser quality, down to half-squeezed tubes of toothpaste, notebooks, and boxes of matches went to the ghetto's own warehouse, to be sent later to the ghetto "stores," where they could be purchased back by the prisoners with the currency that the Nazis had printed for them. Especially disastrous for David would have been the loss of whatever insulin he had managed to bring from Vienna—if he still had any at all. A Danish Jew witnessed just such an occurrence when he arrived: "Everything was taken away. The Professor's wife begged that her daughter might be allowed to keep the insulin so essential for her survival, but it was confiscated."

The location of the Sluice varied, but usually it was a large dank cellar in the fortifications. It was always crowded, and especially so in the summer of 1942, when transports were pouring into the ghetto at a previously unheard-of rate. People just sat or lay down wherever they could find space, clutching whatever luggage they had. Some new arrivals were in the Sluice for five days while their baggage was plundered, forms were filled out, and the community administration sorted out where they were to live. The newcomers slept on the wooden or stone floor, at best with some wood shavings to lie on. David and Amalie were lucky to have to spend only one night there. Norbert Troller, a Theresienstadt survivor, has described how people would enter the Sluice more or less properly dressed, despite all they had already been through, as apprehensive but respectable middle-class ladies and gentlemen. "Two days later they all looked alike, gray, decrepit, unwashed." All they had had to eat was some soup with potatoes and pieces of bread floating in it, served out of wooden tubs. That was their introduction to ghetto food.

In addition to the SS officials, the administration in the Sluice included members of the Jewish ghetto. They handed out the forms on which the details of every newcomer were recorded, to be kept in the central registry, and on the basis of which the newcomers were allocated rooms and work.

Amalie's letter continues:

On the next day we (1200 persons) went up to the previously uninhabited attic of the Dresden barracks, where we spent about 8–9 days on the bare tile floor, without blankets etc.—oppressive heat, lack of air and light, every step dangerous because of the posts and boards.

Just one week before David and Amalie reached Theresienstadt, Gonda Redlich, who was working in the ghetto's housing office, wrote in his diary:

There wasn't room for thirty-seven thousand. There wasn't room for forty thousand. There wasn't room for forty-five thousand. And tomorrow another thousand arrive from Vienna. . . . Where will we put them? Into the attics. A dangerous precedent. The houses and barracks are full beyond their capacity.

A week after my grandparents arrive, Redlich notes that the attics have been completely filled, although on summer afternoons they are "a true hell. . . . Suffocating air and a stench hover like a cloud above the people, trapping their souls."

The memoirs of the survivors demonstrate that in Theresienstadt, even more than in the world outside, whom you knew was more important than what you knew. Amalie's letter shows that the same was true for David and herself: "As a result of the protection of Rabbi Dill from Olmütz," they were able to go to a house where "naturally, we were separated, but nevertheless could lie on wooden floors in rooms." Olmütz was the town near

Brünn where David had got to know Victor, his first love. He might have been visiting it because his father's cousin was then the rabbi there, and he might have known Rabbi Dill from this time; or perhaps just the fact that he was a relative of Dill's predecessor was enough. "Protection" was the term used in Theresienstadt for the vital influence of someone who could help you, not only to get better living conditions, but if you were very lucky, to avoid selection for the transports to "the East." For many, it was the difference between life and death.

Amalie writes "naturally we were separated" because men and women had segregated sleeping quarters in Theresienstadt. But "naturally" is written with hindsight. It isn't clear what she and David had expected. Some German Jews had been told that they were coming to a "spa town" and had even been made to pay heavily for the privilege of a pleasant "retirement" there. On arriving they asked for "a room with a southern exposure" or "a view of the lake." I doubt that David and Amalie had such illusions, and there is nothing to suggest that they paid to go to Theresienstadt, but for people in their sixties who have been used to comfortable beds, to suddenly be forced to sleep apart, in crowded rooms on bare tiles or wooden floors, must still have been a shock.

> Since in the meantime we had got our "soft luggage," rucksack and bedding, we could make a camping place out of this. Space 65 cm. wide per person, one right next to the other, 22 women, e.g. in one room, not big, with 2 windows, without stove. Father was in a former workshop, of which one wall consisted entirely of windows, just as crowded . . . we never got the main pieces of luggage, the suitcases that we had brought along from Vienna.

The reason David and Amalie never got the fifty kilos of luggage that they had carefully put together in Vienna, apart from the personal effects they had carried with them, and their bedding, is that in July 1942 the Nazis had adopted a simple new policy for dealing with the deportees' luggage: they confiscated it.

> The worst thing about the living conditions was the toilets, if one can call them that. That, and what went with it, the common, in fact unavoidable, diarrhea, which especially at the beginning was a form of dysentery

and was very dangerous, is one of the most shocking memories. In the first months people literally lay and died in excrement, and there were so many dead that one could not remove the bodies, they often lay for 2 days in the room and then in the hall. Three women died in that manner in my room in September 1942.

In the summer of 1942 about 30 percent of the population of Theresienstadt was seriously ill, with diseases including scarlet fever, tuberculosis, typhoid, septicemia, gastroenteritis, and pneumonia. With scarcely any medicines or proper equipment, the ghetto doctors did their best, but by September more than one hundred people were dying every day.

The hygiene situation was miserable, the well water was contaminated, "danger of typhoid fever," the so-called plumbing was mostly turned off, and also this water was often very cloudy and suspect. I weaned myself almost entirely off drinking water, father drank a lot of "coffee," that was the concoction that one got in the morning and evening, a black water, but since it was, at least, boiled, harmless. I got so much of that, thanks to the generosity of a friend of my niece Fritzi, that we could drink coffee instead of water the entire day, also a good means of preventing hunger.

Officially, the inhabitants of the ghetto received three meals a day, but breakfast consisted only of the unsweetened "coffee," not really coffee at all, but made with some kind of coffee substitute. Lunch was a watery turnip soup, clear if your ladleful was taken from the top, but if the people serving knew and liked you, they dipped the ladle deep, and you got a few pieces of potato or turnip peel. Sometimes the soup was described as "lentil soup" but it was made from the dried ground pods of the lentils, not from the lentils themselves, "gray, tasteless, unappealing, stinking water without any nutritional value." Dinner was the same soup. There was a ration of bread, and once a week there was a dumpling, but how much you got and how often varied. Vera Schiff, who survived Theresienstadt, writes that the rations "seemed deliberately designed to shorten life. . . . Every fibre of our bodies seemed to scream for something to eat. It was the protracted starvation the Nazis inflicted upon us that reduced us to indescribable suffering before death mercifully released us from the bondage." As a young woman,

Schiff would have received more food than David and Amalie, because the Council of Elders at the time was dominated by Zionists, who believed that the young needed to be protected so that they could be the future founders of a Jewish state. Accordingly, their rations were increased, and the elderly got their bread ration, one-eighth of a loaf, only once every three days, instead of daily. Some tried to make it last for three days; others could not resist eating it immediately. Schiff describes the "pathetic, heart-breaking sight" of "the old German Jews," reduced to standing beside the long soup queues, begging: "This, then, was Europe's former intelligentsia: distinguished, illustrious university professors, physicians, lawyers, businessmen, now reduced to derelict beggars for a spoonful of so-called soup." Troller found the "enfeebled, demoralized, tired" elderly people "an unforgettable sight." They would cluster around the heaps of potato peelings in the kitchen, gnawing off any potato left in the peel. If David was saved from this humiliation, it was thanks to Amalie:

> I myself suffered less from feelings of hunger than poor father, who was already condemned to be hungry because of his diabetes. I gave him some of my food, I got a "supplement" through Fritzi and her friend, I bought bread at crazy prices—the hunger could not be overcome. Only in the last weeks father did not have so great a desire to eat, I even had sometimes to persuade him to eat more. Naturally I cooked in addition to the official mess, sometimes improving it, sometimes cooking something different, as far as it was possible, e.g. I couldn't touch the awful "bread soup" that father liked to eat so much, which a dear old roommate cooked him.

By December David was among the sick—given the food shortage and the absence of insulin, it is remarkable that it did not happen sooner. At least his illness meant that he was placed in a warmer room. On November 26 Gonda Redlich noted: "They put men, women, children in the attics, where temperatures go down to four degrees below zero." David's workshop with its wall of windows could not have been much warmer. In December he was admitted to the sickroom, where there were added comforts like a bed with a wooden frame and a mattress, and a stove close by. But early in February the pressure on hospital beds was so great that, over Amalie's strenuous resistance, he was discharged as "healthy." Amalie did manage to get him put in a room in the building in which she worked, the ghetto's registry office:

> Naturally I was with him as much and as often as possible—until suddenly on 18.II., when at 10 o'clock I brought him the morning soup, I found him already in the throes of death. His roommates thought that he was sleeping! At 7.30 in the morning he was already up and remarkably cheerful, while he had otherwise been very gloomy and pessimistic.

That is all Amalie says here about David's death, and she hadn't really set out to say even that, it just slipped into her description of their living conditions. In a letter to another relative she writes that David died "from his old disease and from the severe Theresienstadt illness, he was also tired of life and almost without hope." By "the severe Theresienstadt illness" Amalie means the chronic diarrhea, known in the ghetto as "Terezinka." David died, then, from a combination of this, his diabetes, and the lack of sufficient and suitable food, perhaps also from the lack of a will to live. In Theresienstadt, as Vera Schiff has written, anything less than "a persistent determination to fight, resist and nurture daily the resolve to survive . . . sent the inmate over the precipice in a short time."

Since the First World War, David had been given to depression. Now he had more cause than ever. Not only were his physical circumstances humiliating and barely compatible with satisfying his physical needs, but everything he stood for seemed to have been defeated. The highest values of the European Enlightenment—equality, liberty, and fraternity, as well as education, reason, and knowledge in the service of humankind—had been swept away by men who cared only for force and the triumph of the so-called Aryan race. David's greatest consolation was that his children had escaped, and were founding a new family in a new land. Perhaps he could also find comfort in the Stoic philosophies of Seneca and the other ancients he loved, or in the thought that, as he had suggested in 1940, the turn of the wheel that was making an end of him would not be the last one, and would eventually crush those who were crushing him. But none of that was enough to make him determined to fight on.

34

Terezin

December 10, 1998

I RECOGNIZE this street from photographs taken when it had long lines of weary people carrying or wheeling their possessions along it. It is the road from the railway station at Bohusovice to Theresienstadt, the road my grandparents must have traveled before arriving at the Sluice. We—Renata, I, and our daughters Ruth, Marion, and Esther, ranging in age from nineteen to twenty-five—are driving along it, warm and comfortable in a minibus. At first the buildings are the same as those in the photographs, but as we reach the outskirts of the old fortress town they give way to 1960s Communist-style multistory apartment blocks, ugly and out of place against the rural backdrop. In a few minutes we see the bastions of Theresienstadt. We swing around the corner, drive through a gap between them, and are inside the walls that for a time bounded my grandparents' world. I have seen these streets too in dozens of photographs and in the Nazi propaganda film *The Town That the Führer Gave to the Jews*. But the people have changed. Terezin, as the town is called once more, is not a museum, but a place in which people live, shop, and take their children to school. Many of the old barracks buildings have been returned to the use of the Czech army, and the private houses that were taken over by the Germans for the use of the ghetto in 1942 are now again being used for private purposes. This includes L416, which was David's address on the only document I have from his life in Theresienstadt, a slip of paper from the chief medical officer denying him the status of "war invalid." Looking at L416 now it is not easy to imagine the distress that David must have felt when he received this life-threatening verdict. Jewish soldiers who were classified as war invalids had a privileged status, and were, until 1944, exempt from deportation from Theresienstadt to the East. But L416 today suggests no such threats: it is a pleasantly aged two-story building, with a corner store on the ground floor, and a large sign in the window saying "Coca-Cola."

Though the town is not a museum, there is a museum of the ghetto. An introductory film juxtaposes footage from the Nazi propaganda film with drawings made by artists there. The commentary is largely a list of the transports from Theresienstadt, giving the numbers on them—always at least one thousand—and the number of survivors—sometimes none, never more than a handful. Upstairs a documentary display begins with Nazi racist propaganda, including extracts from the minutes of the "Wannsee Conference," the meeting near Berlin in 1942 at which Heydrich, Eichmann, and others planned the murder of all of Europe's eleven million Jews, including those in countries they had not yet conquered, such as England and Switzerland. The minutes allocate to Theresienstadt the role of an "Old Person's Home." The section of the museum that makes it hard not to cry, though, displays paintings and drawings done by children in Theresienstadt. The children who painted these brighter, more hopeful worlds died in Auschwitz.

The museum has staff to assist people seeking information about relatives. Ilona Smékalová looks up my grandfather in the *Theresienstadt Book of the Dead*, and confirms the dates of his arrival and his death. The list of deaths shows that eighty-one people died in Theresienstadt on that day. The museum has a chart comparing the death rate for Theresienstadt with that for Prague in the same period: it is ninety times higher.

From the museum we walk to an intersection from where we can see the walls of the town in all four directions. It is just a few blocks each way, a tiny space to confine fifty-eight thousand people. To Jana Renee Friesova, who arrived as a fifteen-year-old girl in December 1942, the streets were "narrow" and "unbelievably overcrowded." On her first day, she was horrified to see a two-wheeled cart being pushed through the streets, heaped up with "bodies, stiff and unreal, thrown here and there, legs and arms dangling from the cart." Every now and again the cart puller stopped to adjust his load. She had never seen a corpse before, and could not imagine that human bodies could be treated with so little respect. I try to imagine the crowds, the dirt, the vermin, the smells, the hunger, the fear that I have read about, but this quiet provincial town has come too far from its past to allow me to make the necessary imaginative leap.

We walk a few blocks to the Magdeburg barracks, where one attic has been refurnished with bunks, and fitted out with suitcases and clothes donated by survivors. Sixty people would have lived in this space. A bucket stood in a corner, to be used as a toilet in the night. A small stove provided some heat and made it possible to boil water, but coal was very limited. Still, our guide says, among Nazi concentration camps it was the most luxurious. People even had their own bed.

The Nazis allowed the prisoners in Theresienstadt to run their own cultural life, and part of the Magdeburg barracks shows what an extraordinary cultural life it was, under those conditions. One room shows the musical life of the camp, including the famed performance of the children's operetta *Brundibar*. There are portraits of the well-known composers and musicians who were there. Another room displays paintings and drawings by artists who had been sent to Theresienstadt. The SS set up an official art section, to draw the kind of paintings they wanted of the ghetto, for propaganda purposes, and to design posters encouraging good hygiene. But there was a much larger quantity of illegal work, some showing the real conditions of the camp, others just drawings of subjects that the artists found interesting. I wonder if I will chance upon a drawing of David or Amalie, but I find no one resembling either of them.

From the Magdeburg barracks we walk back across the town to the Dresden barracks, and along one wall of that immense building, taking up an entire block, three stories high, with massive walls along the streets, and a large inner courtyard. Here Amalie worked and David was living when he died. Now it is again being used by the Czech army, and is not open to the public.

By the time we come to the cemetery and crematorium it is 3:00 P.M. The light is soft and misty, the sun low in the sky. During the first months of the ghetto's existence, the dead were buried in mass graves in the cemetery, but by the time David died, the number of dead had outgrown the cemetery, and a crematorium had been built. That is where David's body was taken. Before one of the Red Cross visits, the ashes of about eighteen thousand dead were dumped into the river. Among them were those of my grandfather.

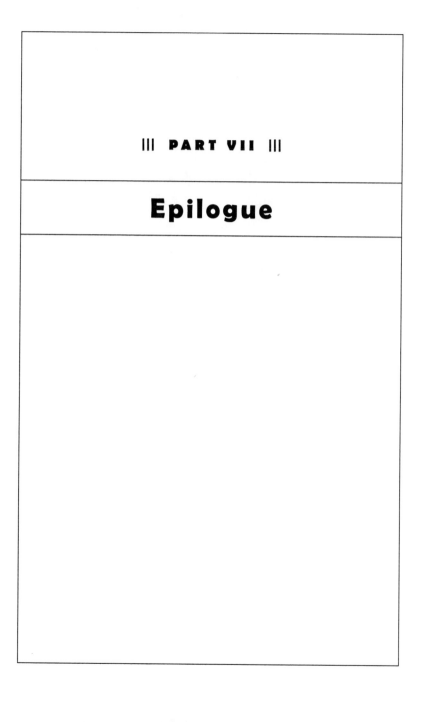

||| PART VII |||

Epilogue

35

Survival

It is hard, frightfully hard, to write to you after such a long, sad time. I must tell you first the hardest and saddest—your beloved father is no more. On 18.2.1943 he died, after long suffering and yet with unexpected suddenness.

About other aspects of life, I cannot and do not want to say any more today.

AMALIE WROTE this short, painful letter to her children on June 12, 1945, just over a month after her liberation. When she returned to Vienna those of her friends and relatives who had not left were nearly all dead. Hilde Koplenig, a cousin of David's, had left but was already back. Hilde was the wife of the leader of the Austrian Communist Party, and with her husband had fled to the Soviet Union in 1938. They were asked to go back to Vienna very soon after the Soviet army entered it so that Hilde's husband could help to found a new Republic of Austria. Returning to her apartment one evening, Hilde found Amalie sitting by her door. She recalled only one element of their conversation. "I asked her where she got her food—because she had kept the Jewish dietary laws, and there was no kosher food to be had in Vienna then. She said to me: "If God allows such a good man as my husband to die, I don't have to follow his laws."

In the letter in which Amalie described life in Theresienstadt, she mentions that the roommate who cooked David the bread soup is dead, and adds, all the other good friends are dead, some died, some were deported in transports to Auschwitz. But about that, another time. The transports and the anxiety about them is one of the saddest chapters of Theresienstadt. Please, Ernst, write to me if you want to have this report, or would rather not.

I found no letter about the transports. Perhaps the subject was too painful for my father to ask about. But I could not help wondering: Did Amalie know, at the time, of the fate of the people being transported? And how did she herself avoid transportation?

One clue comes from a letter that Amalie wrote after liberation, to her nephew Max Rudolfer. Max and his wife, Ilke, had managed to reach Palestine as illegal immigrants. It would have been impossible to take their son, Tomas, who was only three or four years old, on such a journey, so they left him with a relative, hoping to send for him later. Instead the relative died, and Tommy went to an orphanage in Prague, from where, at the age of eight, he came to Theresienstadt. Amalie's letter explains the rest:

> About half a year after [David's death] Tommy came from the Prague orphanage to Theresienstadt. . . . With him sunshine again came into my gloomy, sad life. Everyone, young and old, loved the splendid lad, who was as beautiful as he was good. He came to me about every second day, and we enjoyed being together. I was happy to have someone for whom I could care, for it gave some purpose to my life, that otherwise seemed already completely senseless and purposeless. Yet I do not want to agitate either you or myself: in October 1944 he left Theresienstadt with the entire children's home—he parted almost cheerfully, for he anticipated pleasure in the change of place. I watched with tears as he merrily went away. Since then I have heard nothing more from him—I can only fear that like most who went to Auschwitz, he will not come back anymore.

The Nazis said that the people being transported would be "resettled." Some postcards came back to Theresienstadt saying how nice everything was in Auschwitz. The people who wrote them were threatened with death if they did not write them; then they were sent to the gas chambers anyway, and the postcards sent later. But the Nazi deception was not entirely successful. During 1943 rumors began circulating in Theresienstadt that no one wanted to believe, but that, once heard, could not be entirely disregarded. Some of those going on transports prearranged coded indications that would convey the truth to the recipients. A few messages came back, confirming the worst fears.

By October 1944, when the transports took Tommy with all the children and most of the young adults, there were some in Theresienstadt who knew what their fate was going to be. An escapee from Auschwitz had managed to sneak back into Theresienstadt, where he told Rabbi Leo Baeck and members of the Council of Elders that the Jews transported from Theresienstadt were being murdered in gas chambers. The revelation put Baeck and the other Jewish leaders in an unimaginable moral dilemma. Should they tell the helpless prisoners in the ghetto what their fate was going to be if they were selected for transportation? Didn't people have a right to know? But what good would be achieved by telling them? What would be the consequences of the resulting panic and despair? The Jews in Theresienstadt were powerless to avert their fate, lacking weapons of any kind, and if they attempted an uprising they would all be killed on the spot. As things were, at least some might survive. Or so it seemed to Baeck. He advised keeping the revelations secret, and that is what the council did. But those with close contacts to the council learned of them all the same. Amalie, who worked in the central filing office of the ghetto, might have been one of those who knew—in which case her despair, in seeing thousands of people going to their deaths, would have been indescribable.

For Amalie to escape selection in any of the transports that left during the three years she was in the camp, she had to be either extraordinarily fortunate, or very skillful, or both. In another letter written after liberation, she writes, "What helped me to get through life was unremitting and inexhaustible work in the service of the community." This suggests that her work gave her something to occupy herself with, to distract her from her sorrows, and make her feel useful and ready to go on. But it could also be true that her work helped her to survive in a more direct sense. People were exempted from selection for a transport if their work was deemed indispensable to the running of the ghetto, and Amalie, who had previously worked for many years in a senior administrative post, might have avoided selection on those grounds.

I have to face up to another, more disquieting, possibility. Heinrich Fichtenau, who met Amalie after the war, has said that she told him that she was in a position to know in advance the criteria used to determine who would be selected for each transport, and this made it possible for her to re-arrange her own file card into a safer category. Since the Germans simply told the Council of Elders how many people they needed for the next trans-port, and perhaps what kind of people—old, young, male, female—but not the specific individuals themselves, anyone who succeeded in avoiding se-lection knew that someone else would have to be selected in his or her place. Did my grandmother, under these circumstances, become ruthless about looking after herself and her own survival? Norbert Troller, who tried his utmost, for a long time successfully, to use his "protection" for the same goal, discusses the way in which he thought about this:

> Self-doubts arise in all of us, doubts about our ethics, our humanity, fairness, justice, and decency. It was the time when we were forced by unforeseen, desperate, critical, life-threatening circumstances to relinquish hesitantly, slowly, unhappily, all rules, laws, and principles of decency, etc. We had to rationalize our own behavior to the point where we accepted the fact of our own demoralization and corruption. Who can say today whether all of this was inexcusable? . . . Whoever has not lived for a few weeks, months, or even years in such a situation can hardly comprehend the indescribably immense power, the insuperable force of self-preservation.

If Amalie did use her office to save herself, she might have had the same thoughts as Troller. But she might have survived simply because she did her job so well that her superiors genuinely thought her irreplaceable and did not want to lose her. The truth cannot now be known.

What I do know is that my grandmother somehow lived through the en-tire incredible story of the Theresienstadt ghetto. She was there on a cold and rainy morning—November 11, 1943—when the commandant decided that there must be an accurate count, to the last person, of all forty-five thousand or so prisoners. Surrounded by guards with machine guns at the ready, the entire group was marched outside the walls to a nearby craterlike valley. Many thought they were going to be executed. Instead they were or-dered to stand still while they were counted by three independent groups. When the numbers did not tally, the Germans became angry and shouted that the count would be taken again until agreement had been reached. Darkness fell and everyone was still standing there. Already weak from the limited rations, they had had nothing to eat or drink all day, nor any possibility of going to the toilet. Dysentery was rife, and many people simply had to soil themselves. Others fainted onto the wet grass. More than two hundred died. Not until midnight did the Germans call the operation off, and the sick and the dead were carried home by those who still had the strength to do so.

Amalie would also have seen the farce of the inspection of Theresienstadt by the International Red Cross, in June 1944. For months beforehand the Nazis frantically organized labor gangs to beautify the central square, installing shops, a bank, and a coffeehouse, so that there appeared to be something on which the inhabitants could spend the money that the Nazis had printed for them. In fact there was nothing to buy. Rations were increased before the Red Cross came so the inhabitants looked, and were, a little healthier. A more cynical method of achieving that effect was the transportation to Auschwitz, a month before the inspection, of 7,500 of the most frail and sickly inmates. The inspection day itself was meticulously planned. The SS commandant, Karl Rahm, led the inspection team through the town. Like a king for a day, the Elder of the Jews was given a suit, a car, and a uniformed SS driver who bowed to him politely as he opened the door for him. The inspection team's route took them past a sports area where a soccer match was in progress—and a goal was scored on cue, to well-rehearsed applause. The inspectors saw workers unloading carts full of green vegetables. A group of children approached Rahm and spoke a well-rehearsed line: "Uncle Rahm, are we going to have sardines for lunch *again?*" "Uncle Rahm" assured them that they would have something better today. They had, of course, never seen sardines in Theresienstadt. As soon as the inspection team left, the green vegetables were taken away. Within four months, the Elder of the Jews had been shot by the SS, and the children who recited their lines so well had all been sent to Auschwitz.

Amalie must also have experienced the violent swings between fear and hope in the last few months of the war, when it was obvious that the Germans were losing, but not at all clear what they would do with the Jews of Theresienstadt. In February 1945 the Nazis announced that three transports of prisoners would leave for Switzerland, as part of an exchange organized by the Red Cross. Just another Nazi ruse, many thought, but the joyful postcards that came later were, this time, quite genuine. Around the same time a labor gang was ordered to make alterations to some of the underground passages in Theresienstadt. The work included sealing up all ventilation holes and fitting an airtight door. With Poland falling into Russian hands, rumors spread that the Germans would gas the remaining Jews where they were. The rumors were well founded, but what people in Theresienstadt did not know was that a power struggle was going on in the SS between the truly fanatical anti-Semites, who wanted to complete the Final Solution at all costs, and the pragmatists, who were thinking that living Jews might be more useful, as hostages or as witnesses to their own decency and restraint. Himmler, realizing that the war was lost, swung behind the pragmatists. He deluded himself into the belief that he could rehabilitate his own reputation by showing that he had saved the Jews of Theresienstadt. The gas chamber there was never put into operation.

In April Jewish prisoners from concentration camps closer to the front began arriving in Theresienstadt, by train and on foot, remnants of much larger groups, most of whom had died on the way. Their condition caused deep shock in the ghetto. These people were barely recognizable as human beings, just skeletons covered in skin, some clinging to life, others lying dead in the cattle trucks. If anyone in the ghetto still had illusions about the fate of their friends and relatives transported to the East, now they could see the reality before their eyes. The desperate efforts of those in Theresienstadt to care for these emaciated people were often in vain. With German forces collapsing on all fronts, Theresienstadt was put under the control of the Red Cross on May 1, and liberated by the Russian army on May 7. The next day the war in Europe was over. Of 141,000 people who had been sent to Theresienstadt, only about 17,000 lived to see this day.

AFTER LIBERATION Amalie's overriding desire was to be with her children and grandchild in Australia. But as in 1938 there were obstacles to overcome before this goal could be realized. Amalie had to spend another winter in Vienna, sustained by her American relatives, who were able to send her food and warm clothing. She arrived in Australia on August 19, 1946. There she met not only the six-year-old granddaughter who had occupied her thoughts during the dark years of Hitler's rule, but also her six-week-old grandson, myself. To both of us, for the nine years that she was still to live, she gave all the pent-up love that had been frustrated during so many years of sadness.

A Good Life?

CROESUS, the fabulously wealthy king of Lydia, is said to have asked Solon, the lawgiver of Athens, to tell him who was the happiest of all. Croesus expected to hear that he was the happiest of all, for in wealth and power he was unsurpassed. Solon dashed his expectations by naming an Athenian called Tellus. Taken aback, Croesus demanded to know the reason for this choice, and Solon replied that Tellus lived in a prosperous city, had children and grandchildren, sufficient wealth, died bravely in a victorious battle against his city's foes, and was honored with a public funeral on the spot where he fell.

In an unpublished essay, "Views of Life from Early Greece," David uses this story to contrast Croesus's view of a good life—one that is essentially competitive, seeing success as consisting in having more than others—with Solon's more self-sufficient view. From Solon's conception of a good life, David distills ten key elements, and in so doing provides a measuring stick by which we can assess his own life:

1. A period of peaceful prosperity for one's country

2. A life long enough to see one's children and grandchildren

3. Death before one loses the complete vigor of a valiant man

4. A comfortable income

5. Well-brought-up children

6. Assurance of the continuation of one's line through numerous thriving grandchildren

7. A quick death

8. Victorious confirmation of one's own strength

9. The highest funeral honors

10. The preservation of one's own name through glorious commemoration by the citizens

If David were compiling his own list, rather than endorsing Solon's, he would surely add at least two more points:

11. Close personal relationships, in particular living in loving companionship with someone who understands you and with whom you can enjoy an intellectual as well as an emotional and physical relationship

12. Understanding, defending, and passing on to others the highest and most humane ideals of wisdom, goodness, and beauty that can be gathered from thousands of years of human literature, philosophy, and art

On these last two points, David's life can be counted a success. His relationship with Amalie was an unqualified blessing, and the impact he made on such students as Heer, Ringel, and even, right at the end, Massiczek was a significant passing on of a cultural and intellectual tradition in which he strongly believed. In terms of the ten points David draws from Solon's answer to Croesus, he did not do so well. Since he had no interest in being rich, he had sufficient income to live as he wished, until the Nazis made that impossible. He had two independent-minded daughters in whom he could rightly take pride. Moreover, for the first half of his life, his country was peaceful and prosperous. Then, however, came the war that consumed Austria-Hungary, in which he too suffered dreadfully, and after which he never again lived in a country with that same sense of security that he had known beforehand. He lived long enough to know that he had a grandchild, but not long enough to see her except in a photograph. The conditions he was forced to endure in the last years of his life destroyed what vigor he had left at sixty years of age. His death was not quick, he had no victories, no funeral honors, and his ashes were thrown into a river with those of thousands of others.

Solon's last point, the preservation and commemoration of one's name, is different from the others, for it raises a deep philosophical issue about what can make someone's life go well. It implies that what happens to you after you die can make a difference to how well your life has gone. The ancient Greeks took that for granted. To us it seems odd—how can what happens after you die make any difference to you? This peculiar philosophical divide lies at the heart of the project that is this book. In writing it, I have felt that it is something I can do *for my grandfather*, some way of mitigating, however slightly, the wrong that the Nazis did to him. Is that a defensible thought? I don't believe in an afterlife any more than he did, so I have no illusions about him looking down from above on what I am writing. It can make no difference to him *now* if he and all his writings are left in the obscurity that has enveloped them for the past sixty years, or if I read them and bring them to a wider audience. So shouldn't I simply dismiss as nonsense the feeling that I am writing this book for him? Perhaps I should; yet I cannot entirely dismiss the feeling that by allowing David's writings to reach across the years to me, I am doing something for him.

Like Stefan Zweig, David could have said, near the end of his life, that the values for which he had stood throughout his life had suffered the most terrible defeat, the greatest fall, from lofty heights to abysmal depths, that history had ever known. In fascism, my grandfather saw the victory of force and brutality over reason, education, and learning, and the triumph of those who preferred to burn books rather than refute the arguments in them. It is easy to imagine how sad this must have been for a man who cared so much for books that my parents feared that his reluctance to part with them was delaying his departure. When he lay ill, hungry, and dying in Theresienstadt, he was at the center of a Nazi empire that, with its fascist allies, ruled from the Atlantic coast to the gates of Leningrad, and from Norway's North Cape to North Africa. Add to that the Stalinist regime in the Soviet Union, and democracies were hard to find anywhere across the entire Eurasian landmass, from the Atlantic to the Pacific and on to Japan. Hitler had proclaimed that his empire would last for a thousand years, and even to more sober minds it might have seemed that democracy had suffered a blow from which it would take a century or more to recover.

David foresaw, however, that the turn of the wheel that put an end to his own existence would not be the last one. So it has proved. Liberal democracies are more firmly established in Europe today than they have ever been, and more widespread than before in Asia, Africa, and Latin America. Racism, which first made David an inferior being and then sent him to his death, was emphatically rejected by the Universal Declaration of Human Rights, and is no longer openly embraced by any regime. Justice has been done to many of the Nazi leaders who planned the murder of that vast multitude of which David was one. Steps are being taken to make it more difficult for such atrocities to recur. The precedent of the Nuremburg War Crimes Tribunal, impotent during the cold war period, has finally led to a permanent International Criminal Court with wide jurisdiction to prosecute those guilty of genocide or crimes against humanity. Though the world will remain divided into nation-states for the foreseeable future, the development of a global community, at many different levels, is beginning to make it possible to think in terms of universal human values and the more open, cosmopolitan world that David always favored. His belief in the possibility of such a world, a world in which we can once again appreciate the humane, nonsectarian, universal values embodied in the greatest writers of both ancient and modern times, is something that time has not pushed away.

Notes on Sources

GENERAL

The principal sources for this book are:

- Letters from David Oppenheim to Amalie Pollak, 1904–6.

- Letters from David and Amalie to my parents and aunt, 1938–41.

- Letters from my father's parents, Albert and Philippine Singer, and from other family members in Europe and America to my parents, 1938–41.

- Letters from my parents to their parents and to other family members, 1938–41.

- David's writings, published and unpublished.

- Interviews with those who knew my grandparents, conducted by me, by Dr. Adolf Gaisbauer, by my niece Tessa Dwyer (with my mother), and for the documentary *Einer der uns fehlte: David Oppenheim, 1881–1943*, by Johanna Peltner-Rambeck and Hans Rambeck for Südwind-Film, Munich, 1991.

- Documents from Austrian state archives relating to David's war service and teaching, provided to me by Dr. Gaisbauer.

- Minutes of the Vienna Psychoanalytic Society and of the Society for Individual Psychology.

- Doris Liffman, *David Ernst Oppenheim, 1881–1943: The Man, His Time, His Work*, a thesis submitted to the Department of German, Monash University, for the degree of Master of Arts, 1988.

- Adolf Gaisbauer's "*. . . von Eurem treuen Vater David*": *David Oppenheim in seinen Briefen 1938–1942* (Vienna: Böhlau, 1996).

  I have not cited the unpublished family-held sources in the text, for that would have cluttered it with notes of little use to the reader. Scholars interested in further details of these sources may contact me at the University Center for Human Values, Princeton University. The translation from the German originals is my own. Published sources for specific points in the text are listed below.

1. VIENNA, NOW AND THEN

For Hitler's life in Vienna, see Frederic Morton, *Thunder at Twilight* (New York: Macmillan, 1989), pp. 11–14; J. Sydney Jones, *Hitler in Vienna* (New York: Stein and Day, 1982), p. 144 ff.; Brigitte Hamann, *Hitlers Wien: Lehrjahre eines Diktators* (Munich; 1996). The quotation from Stefan Zweig is from *The World of Yesterday* (London: Cassell, 1944), p.vi.

3. "A RELATIONSHIP OF THE HEART"

On Oscar Wilde's trial, see H. Montgomery Hyde, ed., *The Three Trials of Oscar Wilde* (New York, 1956), p. 236; and more generally on this topic, see Jens Rieckmann, "Knowing the Other: Leopold von Andrian's *Der Garten der Erkenntnis* and the Homoerotic Discourse of the Fin de Siècle," in *Gender and Politics in Austrian Fiction*, eds. Ritchie Robertson and Edward Timms (Edinburgh: Edinburgh University Press, 1996), and Linda Dowling, *Hellenism and Homosexuality in Victorian Oxford* (Ithaca, N.Y.: Cornell University Press, 1994). Details on the discussion of homosexuality in Germany are drawn from James D. Steakley, *The Homosexual Emancipation Movement in Germany* (New York: Arno Press, 1975), especially pp. 23–25, 35. Stefan Zweig's account of the sheltered life of unmarried young women is in *The World of Yesterday*, p. 53.

4. "LET THERE BE TRUTH BETWEEN US"

Freud's comment on "restriction of sexual aim" in homosexuals is made in his *Three Essays on the Theory of Sexuality*, trans. and ed. James Strachey (London: Hogarth Press, 1962), p. 12.

5. THE ENGAGEMENT

Plato's account of Socrates' view of love may be found in *Phaedrus*, beginning at 249a, and see also 265a. I have drawn on both the translation by Benjamin Jowett, available on the Web at *http://plato.evansville.edu/texts/jowett/phaedrus12.htm*, and that by James Nichols Jr., *Gorgias and Phaedrus* (Ithaca, N.Y.: Cornell University Press, 1998). Information on Joachim Oppenheim's salary comes from Hugo Gold, ed., *Die Juden und Judengemeinden Mährens in Vergangenheit und Gegenwart* (Brünn: Jüdischer Buch- und Kunstverlag, 1929), p. 169. On Amalie's appearance, see Gaisbauer, " . . . *von Eurem treuen Vater David*," p. 27.

6. Brno

The Zweig quotation is from p. 1 of *The World of Yesterday*.

7. The Religious Problem

The essay by Lisa Tarlau (who also spelled her name "Lise") is "Der Jargondichter Morris Rosenfeld," pt. 1, *Dr Bloch's Österreichische Wochenschrift*, vol. 23, no. 6, February 9, 1906, p. 94. My sources on anti-Semitism in Austria and the reaction of leading Viennese Jews to Zionism are George F. Berkley, *Vienna and Its Jews: The Tragedy of Success, 1880s–1980s* (Cambridge, Mass.: Abt Books/Madison Books, 1988), especially pp. 38–39, 81, 117–24; and Erwin A. Schmidl, *Jews in the Habsburg Armed Forces*, vol. 11 of *Studia Judaica Austriaca* (Eisenstadt: Österreiches Jüdisches Museum, 1989), pp. 124–27, 135–36. Hans Tietze's comment was made in *Die Juden Wiens* (Vienna, 1933) and is quoted in Berkley, p. 41. Rothschild's remark is taken from Hellmut Andics, *Der Untergang der Donaumonarchie* (Vienna: Molden Taschenbuch Verlag, 1976), p. 26. Ernst Schneider's anti-Semitic proposal is cited in David Kertzer, *The Popes Against the Jews* (New York: Knopf, 2001), p. 202; and the comment about Zola was made in the *Arbeiter-Zeitung* (Vienna), January 25, 1898, and is cited in Sigurd Paul Schiechl, "The Contexts and Nuances of Anti-Jewish Language: Were All the 'Anti-Semites' Anti-Semites?" in *Jews, Anti-Semitism and Culture in Vienna*, eds. Ivar Oxaal, Michael Pollak, and Gerhard Botz. (London: Routledge and Kegan Paul, 1987), pp. 89–90. Zweig describes his apparently charmed life in this respect on p. 17 of *The World of Yesterday*. The more significant discussions of anti-Semitism in Arthur Schnitzler's *The Road to the Open*, trans. Horace Samuel (Evanston, Ill.: Northwestern University Press, 1991), are on pp. 113, 142, and 155.

8. The Erotic Factor

Lise emigrated to America, where she published short stories and a novel in English under the names Lisa Tarleau and Lisa Isaye. Biographical details were provided by her granddaughters, Liz Tarlau Weingarten and Jill Tarlau. On Joseph Bloch, see Robert Wistrich, chap. 9 in *The Jews of Vienna in the Age of Franz Joseph* (Oxford: Littman Library/Oxford University Press, 1990). Weininger's impact on Wittgenstein is described by Ray Monk in *Ludwig Wittgenstein: Duty of Genius* (London: Cape, 1990), pp. 19–25, 498.

9. That New, Troublesome Highway

Psychopathia Sexualis was first published in German in 1886. An English edition appeared in 1892. The article on pedophilia in Afghanistan is Craig A. Smith, "Shh, It's an Open Secret: Warlords and Pedophilia," *New York Times*, February 21, 2002. On the terms used in ancient Greece, see Mark Golden, *Children and Childhood in Classical Athens* (Baltimore: Johns Hopkins University Press, 1990), pp. 12–13. The quotation from *Phaedrus* is on 255b. Sappho's *Poems* are widely available on the Web. The fragment referred to is no. 94. Diotima's account of love is in Plato, *The Dialogues of Plato, II: The Symposium,* ed. R. E. Allen (New Haven, Conn.: Yale University Press, 1991), especially pp. 144, 153, 156, 201d, 209b, 211d. The reports of the controversy over the award of the Imperial Ring to Amalie are in *Die Zeit* (Vienna), February 23 and February 28, 1905. For Lise Meitner, see Ruth Lewin Sime, *Lise Meitner: A Life in Physics* (Berkeley: University of California Press, 1996).

11. VENETIAN REFLECTIONS

The epigram is quoted from Johann Wolfgang von Goethe, *Roman Elegies and Venetian Epigrams,* trans. L. R. Lind (Lawrence, Kans.: University of Kansas, 1974) no. 8, p. 87. I have slightly modified the translation. The advice given to Richard Tull is in Martin Amis, *The Information* (London: Flamingo, 1995), p. 88, while Ischomachus' view of marriage is in Xenophon's *Oeconomicus,* VII.10–11. Hilde Koplenig's view of my grandparents' marriage is taken from her interview with Gaisbauer in ". . . *von Eurem treuen Vater David,*" p. 27; Eva Berger, Doris, and others have said the same.

12. AN INVITATION FROM FREUD

Ernest Jones writes of the odium that greeted *Three Essays on the Theory of Sexuality* in *Sigmund Freud: His Life and Work* (Penguin: Harmondsworth, pp. 315–16. On the slow sales of Freud's earlier book, see Hellmut Andics, *Der Untergang der Donaumonarchie* (Vienna: Molden Taschenbuch Verlag 1976), p. 26. Hanns Sachs's account of Freud's lectures is in his *Freud, Master and Friend* (London: Imago, 1945), pp. 37–43. Sachs gives the year as 1904, but this must be a mistake because Paul Klemperer states that both Sachs and Oppenheim were part of the group in the year he attended the lectures, 1906. Klemperer's accuracy is supported by the fact that 1906–7 is the only year in which my grandfather could have participated, for he would surely have mentioned Freud in his letters to Amalie if he had gone to his lectures in 1904–5, and in the winter of 1905–6 he was doing his military service in Brünn. See Paul Klemperer, interview with Dr. K. R. Eissler, March 4, 1952, Manuscript Division, Library of Congress; see also Ernest Jones, *Sigmund Freud: His Life and Work* (London: Hogarth Press, 1967), vol 2, p. 16. My grandfather's essay on Tibullus was published as D. Ernst Oppenheim, "Apai (zu Tibul I.5)," *Wiener Studien. Zeitschrift für klassische Philologie,* vol. 30 (1908), pp. 146–64. On the standing of the Akademisches Gymnasium, see Steven Beller, *Vienna and the Jews, 1867–1938* (Cambridge, England: Cambridge University Press, 1989), pp. 50, 53. Freud's handwritten letter to my grandfather is reproduced in facsimile, as well as in printed versions, in both German and English, in Sigmund Freud and D. E. Oppenheim, *Dreams in Folklore* (New York: International Universities Press, 1958). The translation here is my own. Freud's letter to Jung in which he first mentions David is reprinted in Sigmund Freud and C. G. Jung, *Briefwechsel,* ed. William McGuire and Wolfgang Sauerländer. (Frankfurt: S. Fischer, 1974), pp. 286–87, my translation; for an English version, see *The Freud/Jung Letters: The Correspondence between Sigmund Freud and C. G. Jung,* ed. William McGuire, trans. Ralph Mannheim and R. F. C. Hull, Bollingen Series 94, (Princeton, N.J.: Princeton University Press, 1974), p. 260. The German professor's reaction to Freud is taken from Ernest Jones's biography, cited above, p. 381. The membership of the Wednesday Group is discussed in Ronald Clark, *Freud: The Man and the Cause* (New York: Random House, 1980), p. 214. The minutes of the early years of the society have been published in English in Herman Nunberg and Ernst Federen, eds., *Minutes of the Vienna Psychoanalytic Society*, trans. M. Nunberg (New York: 1962–75), vols. 1–4. The collection of essays on suicide in students was published as *Diskussionen des Wiener* psychoanalytischen Vereins, I Heft, *Über den Selbstmord insbesondere den Schüler-Selbstmord* (Wiesbaden: Verlag von J. F. Bergmann, 1910). The quotation from Horace is from *The Satires*, Book 1, Satire 9, as translated in Kenneth Haynes and Donald Carne-Ross, eds., *Horace in English* (London: Penguin, 1996).

13. David's Choice: Freud or Adler?

For accounts of the split between Freud and Adler, see Bernhard Handlbauer, *The Freud-Adler Controversy*, trans. Laurie Cohen (Oxford: Oneworld Publications, 1998); Jones, *Freud*; Wilhelm Stekel, *Autobiography: The Life Story of a Pioneer Psychoanalyst* (New York: Liveright, 1950); and Fritz Wittels, *Freud and His Time*, trans. Louise Brink (New York: Liveright, 1931). The letters from Freud to Jung quoted in this chapter are dated March 12, 1910, March 30, 1911, and June 15, 1911; that from Freud to Ferenczi, February 5, 1911. Freud's footnote reference to the forthcoming work with my grandfather can be found in *The Standard Edition of the Complete Psychological Works of Sigmund Freud*, ed. James Strachey (London: Hogarth Press, 1953–74), vol. 5, p. 621n. Jones's suggestion that socialist ideology lay behind the departure of the Adlerians is made in his *Freud*, vol. II, p. 151. Alexandra Adler's comment on David's politics is quoted, from a personal communication, in Heinz Ansbacher and Rowena Ansbacher, eds., *Alfred Adler: Superiority and Social Interest* (Evanston, Ill.: Northwestern University Press, 1964), p. 345n. The declaration by Adler's followers is quoted by Handlbauer, *The Freud-Adler Controversy*, p. 140. The Furtmüller quote is from his essay on Adler in *Alfred Adler: Superiority and Social Interest*, p. 353. Klemperer's comments, and the story of Freud later ignoring him, are from his interview with Eisler, cited above, pp. 13–14. On Freud's treatment of the former members of his circle, see also Paul Roazen, *Freud and His Followers* (New York: Knopf, 1975), p. 207. On the sole exception, see Lou Andreas-Salomé, *The Freud Journal of Lou Andreas-Salomé*, trans. Stanley Leavy (New York: Basic Books, 1964), pp. 40–41.

14. "Dreams in Folklore"

Quotations in this chapter are from *Dreams in Folklore*, with minor changes in translation. In addition to the edition cited above, the work is now included in James Strachey, ed., *Standard Edition*, vol. 12, pp. 177–203.

15. PSYCHOLOGY, FREE AND INDIVIDUAL

The account of the early days of Adler's group is based on Carl Furtmüller, "Alfred Adler: A Biographical Essay," in *Alfred Adler, Superiority and Social Interest*, pp. 353–54. Lou Andreas-Salomé's comment on David's lecture is in *The Freud Journal of Lou Andreas-Salomé*, pp. 42–43; the editor's annotation suggesting that this refers to "H. Oppenheim" is incorrect.

16. THE EASTERN FRONT

For a popular view of Franz Ferdinand, see Josef Redlich, *Schicksalsjahre Österreichs, 1908–1919: Das politische Tagebuch Josef Redlichs* (Graz: Böhlau, 1953), vol. 1, p. 235. The Zweig quotation is from *The World of Yesterday*, p. 151. My account of the war draws on Holger H. Herwig, *The First World War: Germany and Austria-Hungary, 1914–1918* (London: Arnold, 1997), pp. 94–95, 105, 108, 113, 136–39, 204, 274. Information on David's war record from the Austrian archives was provided to me by Adolf Gaisbauer. The line David uses to express his reluctance to speak of his war experiences is from Virgil, *Aeneid*, II, 3. Thomas Mann's view of the war is from "Gedanken im Kriege" (1915), in *Gesammelte Werke*, vol. 12 (Frankfurt: Fischer, 1974); quoted by George Clare, *Last Waltz in Vienna* (London: Macmillan, 1981), p. 56. Wittgenstein's remark is from Monk, *Ludwig Wittgenstein: Duty of Genius*, p. 112. David's essay on Horace appeared in *Zeitschrift für die Österreichischen Gymnasien*, vol. 66 (1915), pp. 825–29, and was briefly reported on in *Wiener Zeitung*, no. 27, February 4, 1916.

17. THE BATTLES OF THE ISONZO

For an account of Austrian military life on the Isonzo front, see Adolf Schärf, *Erinnerungen aus meinem Leben* (Vienna: Verlag der Wiener Volksbuchhandlung, 1963), pp. 46–47; and for other details of the battles, see Herwig, *The First World War: Germany and Austria-Hungary, 1914–1918*, p. 336. David's references to his wartime experiences when he was teaching are recalled by Fritz Schopf in an unpublished memoir quoted by Gaisbauer, ". . . von Eurem treuen Vater David," pp. 45–46. On the role of the Austrian censors, and the opinions revealed in the letters they read, see Herwig, *The First World War: Germany and Austria-Hungary, 1914–1918*, pp. 362–63. Doris referred to David as uncontrolled in an interview with Adolf Gaisbauer, quoted in ". . . von Eurem treuen Vater David," pp. 46, n78. The "more and more red" comment is recalled by Dr. Peter Schramke in his interview for the film *Einer der uns fehlte*. That he marched on May 1 is mentioned by Doris in her thesis, p. 43.

18. THE NEW REPUBLIC

On the postwar Austrian famine, see David F. Strong, *Austria, October 1918–March 1919* (New York: Octagon Books, 1974), pp. 183–84, 197; for the evacuation of children my source is *Reichspost*, February 18, 1919, and February 23, 1920, quoted in

Christine Klusacek and Kurt Stimmer, eds., *Dokumentation zur Österreichischen Zeitgeschichte, 1918–1928* (Vienna: Jugend und Volk, 1984), pp. 155–56. On the inflation, see F. L. Carsten, *The First Austrian Republic, 1918–1938* (Aldershot, England: Gower, 1986), p. 47. Marie Jahoda is the social democrat who speaks of the enriching illusion of Red Vienna; from Helmut Gruber, *Red Vienna: Experiment in Working-Class Culture, 1919–1934* (New York: Oxford University Press, 1991), p. 6. Furtmüller's comment on the role of the Adlerians in the culture of this period is from his essay in *Alfred Adler: Superiority and Social Interest*, p. 387. The essential source for the early history of the Society for Individual Psychology, which includes a partial list of lectures presented to the society, is Bernhard Handlbauer, *Die Entstehungsgeschichte der Individualpsychologie Alfred Adlers* (Wien-Salzburg: Geyer, 1984). David's talk on Schiller's *Tell* is described in *International Zeitschrift für Individualpsychologie* (henceforth *IZI*), 1924, p. 30.

19. "The Secret of the Human Soul"

David wrote of the way in which we can understand our fellow human beings in the preface to his book *Dichtung und Menschenkenntnis* (Munich: Bergmann, 1926); and also in "Shakespeare's *Menschenkenntnis*," presented to the First International Congress for Individual Psychology, Munich, December 1922; *IZI*, September 23, p. 37; and in "Links between Art and Psychology," an unpublished lecture given on February 9, 1920.

20. My Grandfather's Book

A. C. Bradley's *Shakespearean Tragedy* was first published in 1904. F. R. Leavis still misses the significance of racism in *Othello* in *The Common Pursuit*, which appeared in 1952. On the appreciation of the significance of racism in *Othello* in the 1970s, see Michael Mangan, *A Preface to Shakespeare's Tragedies* (London: Longman, 1991), p. 151. Phyllis Bottome's *Alfred Adler: Apostle of Freedom* was published by Faber, London, in 1939, and the passage quoted is on p. 152. Pick-Seewart's review of David's book appeared in *IZI*, vol. 5 (1927), p. 156.

21. Independence

David's essay on Seneca appeared in L. Seif and L. Zilahi, eds., *Selbsterziehung des Charakters: Alfred Adler zum 60. Geburtstage Gewidmet* (Leipzig: Hirzel, 1930), pp. 62–70.

22. The Teacher of Humanity

Ringel's comments on David as a teacher are included in *Einer der uns fehlte*. He mentions the students in his class who were arrested by the Gestapo in *Die Österreichische Seele* (Vienna: Böhlau, 1984), p. 124. Heer's essay "Austrian Genius and Judaism" appeared in *Kontinente*, vol. 8, no. 8 (April 1955), p. 10, and his reference to David's grading is in his *Jugend Zwischen Hass und Hoffnung* (Munich: Bechtle, 1971), p. 47.

23. THE SECULAR JEW

David's review of Felix Stähelin, *Der Anti-Semitismus des Altertums in seiner Entstehung und Entwicklung*, appeared in *Zeitschrift für die Österreichischen Gymnasien*, vol. 59 (1908), pp. 668–69. His reply to Dr. Heymann is in his unpublished papers, but the exchange was also published, though without Dr. Heymann's name, in *IZI*, 1925, pp. 335–37.

24. SEXUAL EQUALITY

The first talk on Schönherr's play was published in *IZI*, vol. 2 (September 1923), pp. 26–30, and subsequently in *Dichtung und Menschenkenntnis*; the second is mentioned in the society's list of lectures, but I found no trace of it among my grandfather's papers. The essay on Dido appeared in *IZI*, vol. 3 (December 1924), and also in *Dichtung und Menschenkenntnis*. David's paper on woman's struggle for position appeared in *IZI*, vol. 3, pp. 287–90.

26. THE END OF AUSTRIA

George Clare's *Last Waltz in Vienna* (London: Macmillan, 1981) gives a personal account of a Viennese Jewish family's feelings before and during the Nazi takeover of Austria. Friedrich Heer tells the story of the storm troopers' visit to my grandparents' apartment in *Jugend zwischen Hass und Hoffnung*, p. 47, cited by Gaisbauer, ". . . *von Eurem treuen Vater David*," p. 60. Doris's story of these days is from the same source and page. On the referendum and the support of the Catholic Church for a pro-Nazi vote, see Bruce F. Pauley, *From Prejudice to Persecution: A History of Austrian Anti-Semitism* (Chapel Hill, N.C.: University of North Carolina Press, 1992), p. 291. David's immediate exclusion from his school is mentioned by Erwin Ringel in ". . . *von Eurem treuen Vater David*," pp. 14–15, where Ringel also states his view of the reasons behind David's reluctance to leave.

27. NEW LIFE AND OLD

For the steadily increasing restrictions on Jews, see Pauley, *From Prejudice to Persecution*, pp. 282–84. David's quotation from *Faust* is from Part I, "Vor dem Tor."

29. "BEST TO STAY"

For the new round of restrictions on Jews at the outset of the war, see Pauley, *From Prejudice to Persecution*, p. 291. This book, at p. 294, is also the source of the figures on emigration.

30. GOOD AUSTRIANS

Albert Massiczek's account of what he gained from his visits to my grandparents is from "As an Austrian I Only Did My Duty: From Nazism to Resistance and Jewish

Wisdom," unpublished typescript of a lecture given at the Hebrew University in Jerusalem, undated, probably 1990, English original, p. 8; see also Albert Massiczek, *Ich habe nur meine Pflicht erfüllt* (Vienna; Junius, 1989), pp. 44–46. Massiczek showed me the letter he received from Amalie, dated September 11, 1945, thanking him for his help during the dark days. His book on Marx is *Der Menschliche Mensch—Karl Marxs jüdischer Humanismus* (Vienna; Europa Verlag, 1968).

31. Renunciation

On the deportation of Jews from Vienna, see Martin Gilbert, *The Holocaust* (New York: Holt, Rinehart and Winston, 1985), pp. 143, 146.

33. Theresienstadt

On the origins of the Theresienstadt ghetto, see Nora Levin, Foreword in Saul S. Freidman, ed., *The Terezin Diary of Gonda Redlich* (Lexington, Ky.: University of Kentucky Press, 1992), p. viii; and Chaim Potok, Foreword in Hana Volavková, ed., *I Never Saw Another Butterfly*, 2nd ed. (New York: Schocken Books, 1993), p. xiv. On the "Sluice," ghetto food, and "protection," see Norbert Troller, *Theresienstadt: Hitler's Gift to the Jews*, trans. Susan E. Cernyak-Spatz (Chapel Hill, N.C.: University of North Carolina Press, 1991). The confiscation of insulin is described by Ralph Oppenhejm in *An der Grenze des Lebens* (Hamburg, 1961), p. 79, cited by Gaisbauer, ". . . von Eurem treuen Vater David," p. 163n. Gonda Redlich's diary has been published as *The Terezin Diary of Gonda Redlich*, and the passages quoted in this chapter are on pp. 64, 67, and 86. The confiscation of luggage from July 1942 is mentioned by Gaisbauer, ". . . von Eurem treuen Vater David," p. 163, citing H. G. Adler, *Theresienstadt 1941–45* (Tübingen, 1955), pp. 266f. On the death rate in the ghetto, see Zdanek Lederer, *Ghetto Theresienstadt* (New York: Fertig, 1983), pp. 143–44; Adler, *Theresienstadt 1941–45*, p. 527. For Schiff's memoir, see Vera Schiff, *Theresienstadt: The Town the Nazis Gave to the Jews* (Toronto; Lugus, 1996); the passages quoted are on pp. 54–56, 84–85.

34. Terezin

Jana Renee Friesova's memoirs are entitled *Fortress of My Youth*, trans. Eleanor Morrisby and Ladislav Rosendorf (Hobart, Tasmania: Telador Publishing, 1996). The passage referred to is on pp. 75–76.

35. Survival

The story of the letters from Auschwitz is documented in Troller, *Theresienstadt: Hitler's Gift to the Jews*, pp. 49–50, and Schiff, *Theresienstadt: The Town the Nazis Gave to the Jews*, pp. 38, 49, 82, 122. Fichtenau's recollection of what Amalie told him is from Gaisbauer, ". . . von Eurem treuen Vater David," p. 167n. Troller's reflections on the morality of strategies for surviving in Theresienstadt are in *There-*

sienstadt: Hitler's Gift to the Jews, pp. 33–34, 36. The description of the November 11 count is from the same work—see p. xxv—and of the Red Cross inspection, from Schiff, *Theresienstadt: The Town the Nazis Gave to the Jews*, p. 101. The story of the Theresienstadt gas chamber is drawn from Schiff's book, p. 124, and from Miroslav Karny, "Die Theriesienstädter Herbsttransporte 1944," in Miroslav Karny, Raimund Kemper, and Margita Kárná, eds., *Theresienstädter Studien und Dokumente 1995* (Prague: Academia, 1995), pp. 23–24.

36. A GOOD LIFE?

The story of Solon's conversation with Croesus is taken from Herodotus, *The Histories*, Book 1, 28–33.